AQA

For AQA

AQA GCSE physics

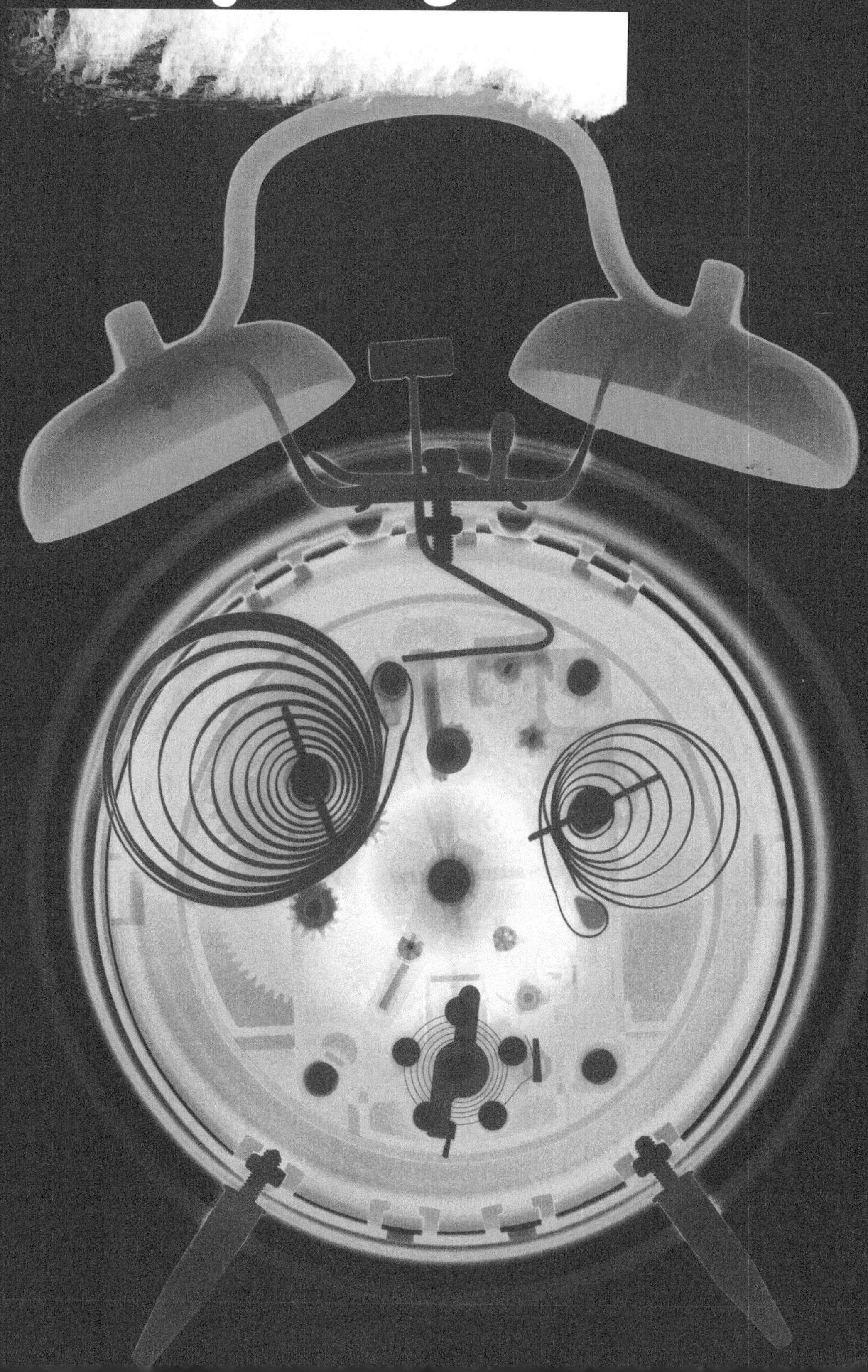

Authors

Graham Bone

Michael Brimicombe

Contents

How to use this book

Welcome to your AQA GCSE Physics revision guide. This book has been specially written by experienced teachers and examiners to match the 2011 specification.

On this page you can see the types of feature you will find in this book. Everything in the book is designed to provide you with the support you need to help you prepare for your examinations and achieve your best.

Specification and student book reference: These show how the pages in the unit match to the exam specification and to your textbook so you can track your progress through the unit as you learn.

Key words: These are the terms you need to understand for your exams.

Exam tip: These hints will help you to think about what may come up in the exam.

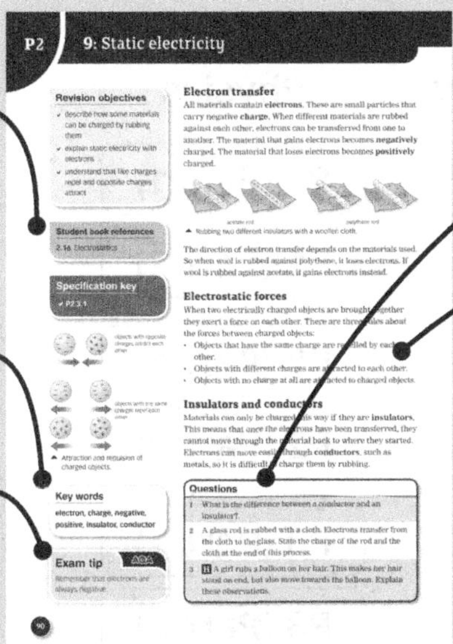

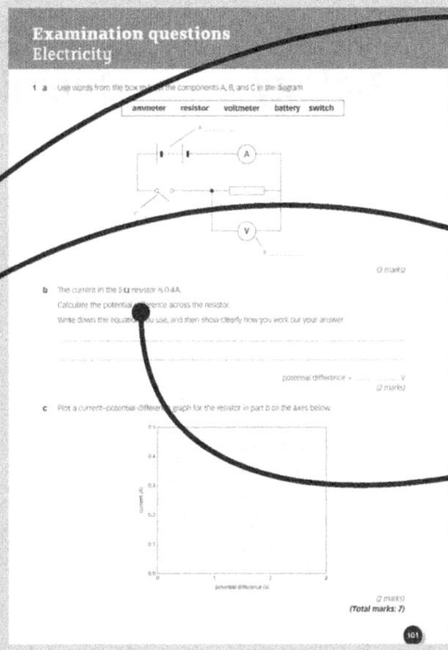

Questions: Use the questions on each page and at the end of the section to test yourself on what you've just read.

Higher-Tier content: Anything marked with a H is only for students taking the Higher-Tier paper.

Examination questions: Using these questions you can practise your exam skills, and make sure you're ready for the real thing.

Upgrade: Upgrade takes you through an exam question in a step-by-step way, showing you why different answers get different grades. Using the tips on the page you can make sure you achieve your best by understanding what each question needs and what an examiner is looking for in your answer.

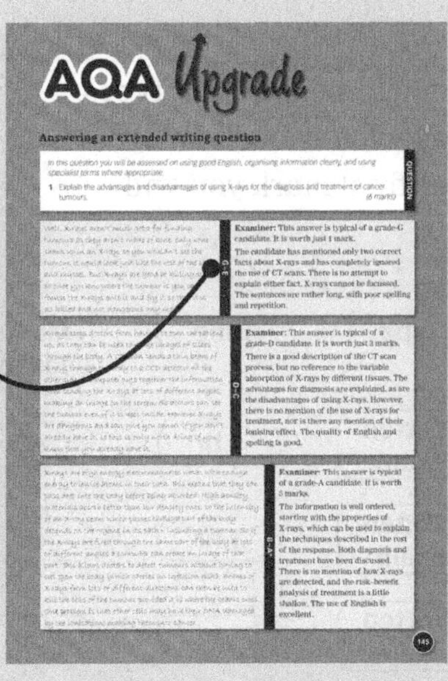

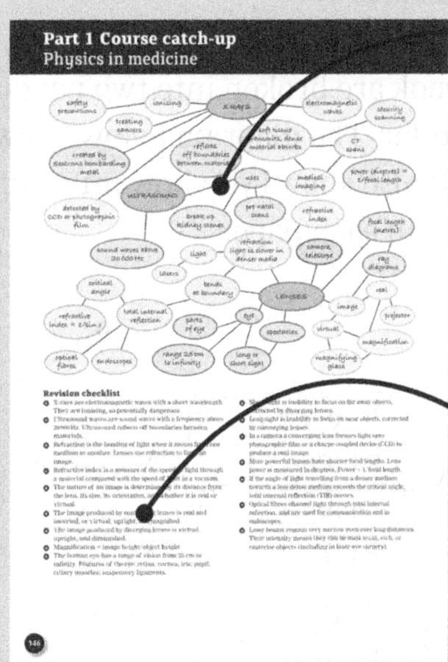

Visual summary: Another useful revision tool is a visual summary, linking ideas together in groups so you can see how one topic relates to another. You can use this page as a start for your own summary.

Revision checklist: This is a summary of the main ideas in the unit. You can use it to check that you know and have understood the big ideas covered in the unit.

Routes and assessment

Matching your course

The units in this book have been written to match the specification for **AQA GCSE Physics**.

In the diagram below you can see that the units and part units can be used to study either for **GCSE Physics** or as part of **GCSE Science** and **GCSE AQA Additional Science** courses.

	GCSE Biology	GCSE Chemistry	GCSE Physics
GCSE Science	B1 (Part 1)	C1 (Part 1)	P1 (Part 1)
	B1 (Part 2)	C1 (Part 2)	P1 (Part 2)
GCSE Additional Science	B2 (Part 1)	C2 (Part 1)	P2 (Part 1)
	B2 (Part 2)	C2 (Part 2)	P2 (Part 2)
	B3 (Part 1)	C3 (Part 1)	P3 (Part 1)
	B3 (Part 2)	C3 (Part 2)	P3 (Part 2)

GCSE Physics assessment

The units in this book are broken into two parts to match the different types of exam paper on offer. The diagram below shows you what is included in each exam paper. It also shows you how much of your final mark you will be working towards in each paper.

Unit		%	Type	Time	Marks available
Unit 1	P1 (Part 1) P1 (Part 2)	25%	Written exam	1 hr	60
Unit 2	P2 (Part 1) P2 (Part 2)	25%	Written exam	1 hr	60
Unit 3	P3 (Part 1) P3 (Part 2)	25%	Written exam	1 hr	60
Unit 4	Controlled Assessment	25%		1 hr 30 mins + practical	50

Understanding exam questions

When you read the questions in your exam papers you should make sure you know what kind of answer you are being asked for. The list below explains some of the common words you will see used in exam questions. Make sure you know what each word means. Always read the question thoroughly, even if you recognise the word used.

Calculate
Work out your answer by using a calculation. You can use your calculator to help you. You may need to use an equation; check whether one has been provided for you in the paper. The question will say if your working must be shown.

Describe
Write a detailed answer that covers what happens, when it happens, and where it happens. The question will let you know how much of the topic to cover. Talk about facts and characteristics. (Hint: don't confuse with 'Explain')

Explain
You will be asked how or why something happens. Write a detailed answer that covers how and why a thing happens. Talk about mechanisms and reasons. (Hint: don't confuse with 'Describe')

Evaluate
You will be given some facts, data or other information. Write about the data or facts and provide your own conclusion or opinion on them.

Outline
Give only the key facts of the topic. You may need to set out the steps of a procedure or process – make sure you write down the steps in the correct order.

Show
Write down the details, steps or calculations needed to prove an answer that you have been given.

Suggest
Think about what you've learnt in your science lessons and apply it to a new situation or a context. You may not know the answer. Use what you have learnt to suggest sensible answers to the question.

Write down
Give a short answer, without a supporting argument.

Top tips

Always read exam questions carefully, even if you recognise the word used. Look at the information in the question and the number of answer lines to see how much detail the examiner is looking for.

You can use bullet points or a diagram if it helps your answer.

If a number needs units you should include them, unless the units are already given on the answer line.

1: Infrared radiation

Revision objectives

- know that all objects emit and absorb infrared radiation and that the hotter the object the more infrared radiation it emits
- describe whether a surface is a good or poor emitter, absorber or reflector of infrared radiation

Student book references

1.1 Infrared radiation and surfaces

Specification key

✔ P1.1.1

Emitting and absorbing infrared radiation

Energy may be transferred by **infrared radiation** (IR). This is a type of **electromagnetic wave**. It can travel through a vacuum such as space, without the need for any particles.

- All objects emit and absorb infrared radiation.

How much is emitted and absorbed depends on the *temperature* of the material and the *colour of the surface*.

Emission

- Hotter objects emit more infrared radiation than cooler ones.

This is why people show up as bright colours on infrared cameras compared to the darker, cooler surroundings.

- Dark, matt surfaces are *good* **emitters** of infrared radiation.
- Light, shiny surfaces are *poor* emitters of infrared radiation.

Whenever an object emits infrared radiation it gradually cools down. The faster the rate of emission the quicker the object cools. An object designed to reduce the transfer of energy to the surroundings via infrared is often shiny. This reduces the emission of infrared radiation.

Absorption

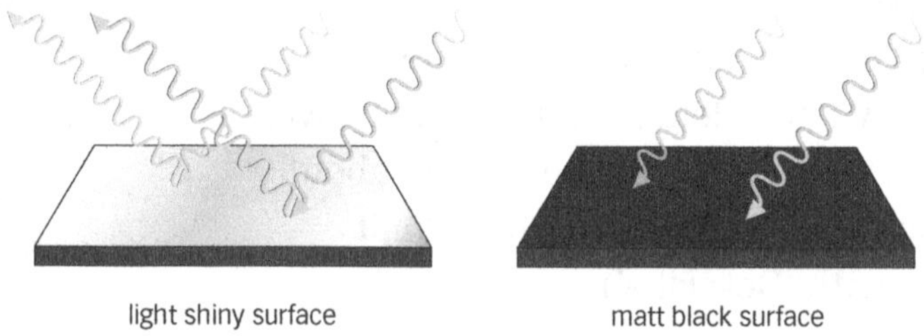

▲ How infrared radiation is absorbed by different surfaces.

- Dark, matt surfaces are *good* **absorbers** of infrared radiation.
- Light, shiny surfaces are *poor* absorbers of infrared radiation.

A matt black surface is a good absorber of infrared, so heats up quickly. Instead of absorbing infrared radiation, shiny surfaces are good **reflectors**. This means they don't heat up as fast.

Exam tip — AQA

Make sure you can explain why an object might be painted a matt black or shiny silver (either to increase or reduce the rate of energy transfer to its surroundings).

Key words

infrared radiation, electromagnetic wave, emitter, absorber, reflector

Questions

1 Describe how the colour of a surface affects the emission of infrared radiation.

2 Explain why pipes inside solar panels are painted matt black.

Kinetic theory

Everything you see around you is made up of particles.

The particles in **solids**, **liquids**, and **gases** are arranged differently.

Kinetic theory can be used to explain different **states of matter** in terms of particles.

Solids	Liquids	Gases
Particles are regularly arranged, close together, and they are not able to move around, only vibrate.	Particles are a little bit further apart; they are able to move around.	Particles are very far apart and are moving very fast.
solid 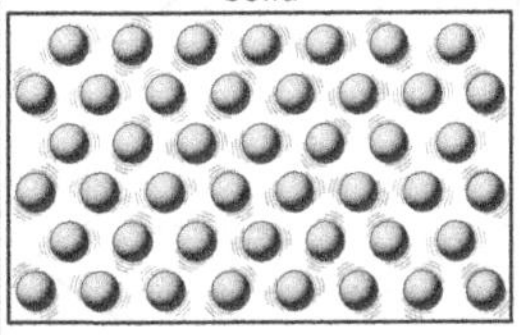	liquid 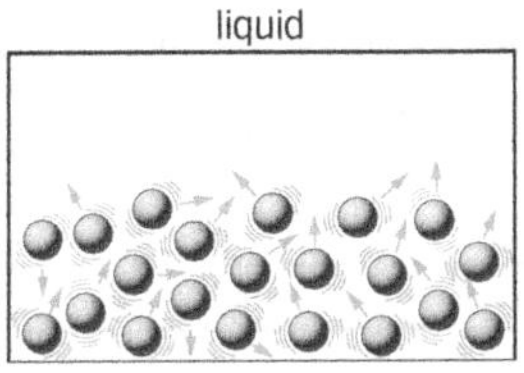	gas 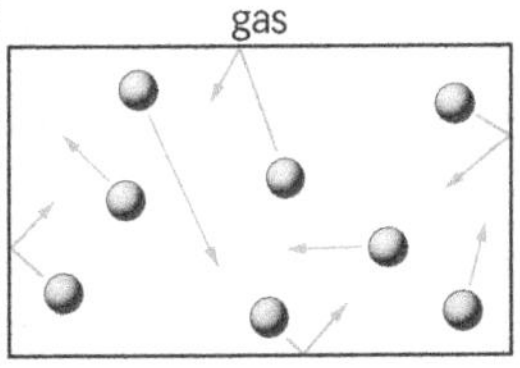

Particle energy

The particles in solids and liquids and gases have different amounts of energy.

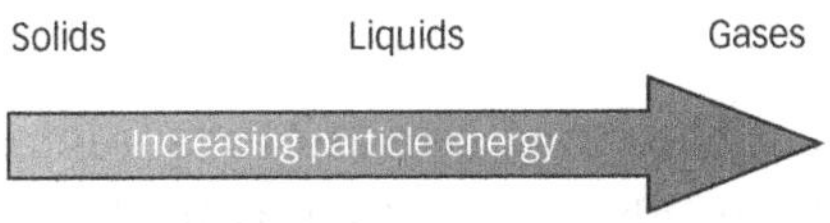

The particles in gases have the most energy as they are moving the fastest. The particles in solids have the lowest energy.

If you increase the **temperature** of a substance, the particles gain energy and move faster. This causes solids to turn to liquids and then eventually into gases.

Revision objectives

- ✔ use kinetic theory to describe the three states of matter
- ✔ describe differences between the energy of particles found in solids, liquids and gasses

Student book references

1.2 Solids, liquids, and gases

Specification key

✔ P1.1.2

Exam tip AQA

Practise drawing simple diagrams showing how particles are arranged in solids, liquids, and gases.

Questions

1. Draw three diagrams to show how the particles are arranged in solids, liquids, and gases.
2. Explain, in terms of particles, why heating a block of ice causes it to melt and eventually turn into a gas.

Key words

solid, liquid, gas, kinetic theory, states of matter, temperature

3: Energy transfer by heating

Revision objectives

- describe how conduction (including conduction in metals), convection, evaporation, and condensation transfer energy
- know the factors that affect the rate of evaporation and condensation

Specification key

- P1.1.3 a – b

Transferring energy

Energy may be transferred from hotter objects to cooler surroundings by **conduction**, **convection**, **evaporation**, and **condensation**. This cools the hotter object, and at the same time warms up the surroundings.

All of these processes involve **particles** and so they cannot take place in a vacuum (like space).

Conduction

Conduction takes place in **solids**. When one end of a solid object is heated the particles in the solid gain energy and vibrate more.

These vibrations are passed on to neighbouring particles and energy is transferred through the solid.

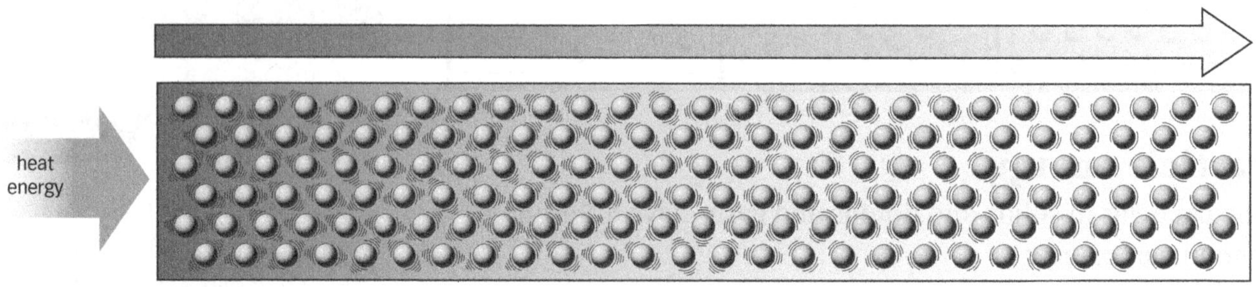

▲ Energy can be transferred through a solid via conduction.

Metals are the best **thermal conductors**. Metals contain **free electrons**, which are able to move within the metal. These transfer energy even faster through the metal.

Particles in liquids and gases are too far apart to be good thermal conductors. Liquids and gases are **thermal insulators**.

Convection

Convection can only take place in **fluids** (liquids and gases). In convection particles must be free to move. In a solid the particles are fixed, so convection cannot take place.

Convection occurs when part of the fluid is heated:

- The particles in that region gain kinetic energy and speed up.
- The region expands as the particles move further apart.
- This makes this part of the fluid less dense and it rises.

In convection, hotter regions of fluid rise through colder ones. This transfers energy from hotter regions to cooler ones.

Convection currents can be created. When the hotter fluid has risen, cooler fluid is drawn in to replace it. This is then heated and rises as part of a cycle.

Student book references

Exam tip AQA

When describing conduction, don't forget to say that when the particles gain energy they vibrate *more* – not just vibrate (they are always vibrating).
In convection, don't say 'heat rises', instead say 'hotter fluids rise'.

▲ Convection currents are used to heat a room.

Convection currents have many uses. For example, the heating element is always placed at the bottom of a kettle. When heated, the hotter water rises – it transfers energy to the rest of the water. The convection current means all the water inside the kettle gets heated.

Evaporation and condensation

Evaporation

Evaporation has a cooling effect on liquid. As a liquid starts to evaporate, the particles with the most energy (those on the surface) leave the liquid and turn into a gas. This transfers energy away from the liquid and so it gets cooler.

This is why we sweat. It helps cool us down by transferring energy from the surface of our skin to the surroundings.

There are three main ways to increase the rate of evaporation from a liquid:

- increase the surface area of the liquid
- pass an air current over the surface (for example, blowing on a hot drink)
- increase the temperature of the liquid.

Condensation

In condensation the reverse happens. When a warm gas strikes a cooler surface the gas turns into a liquid. The temperature of the surface increases as some of the energy from the gas particles is transferred to it.

Key words

conduction, convection, evaporation, condensation, particle, solid, thermal conductor, free electrons, thermal insulator, fluid, convection current

Questions

1 Explain why metals are the best thermal conductors.

2 Describe how a convection current may form inside a kettle.

3 List the ways to increase the rate of evaporation of a liquid.

4: Comparing energy transfers

Revision objectives

- describe how different factors affect the rate of energy transfer by heating, including
- understand how to vary the rate of energy transfer by heating

Student book references

1.6 Energy transfer by heating
1.7 Comparing energy transfers

Specification key

✔ P1.1.3 c – d

Exam tip

AQA

Practise explaining energy transfers with a graph showing how the temperature of a hot drink changes over time.

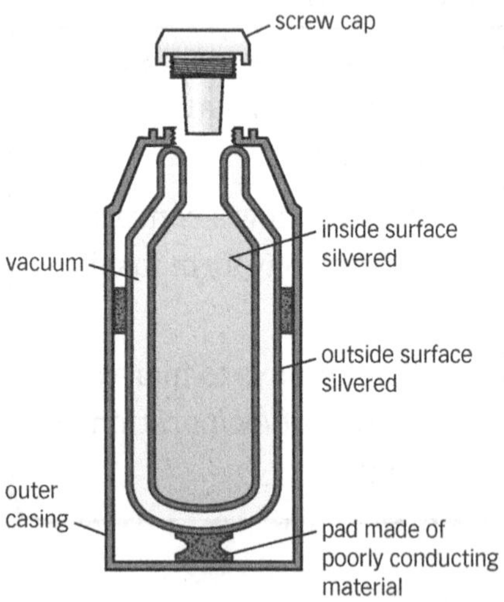

▲ Cross-section of vacuum flask.

Key words

energy transfer

Rate of energy transfer

The faster energy is transferred away from an object, the faster it cools.

The bigger the temperature difference between the object and its surroundings, the greater the rate of **energy transfer** by heating. This is why a hot cup of tea cools rapidly at the start, then cools more gradually as it approaches room temperature.

The rate of energy transfer from the object also depends on a number of other factors:

- the object's surface area and volume
- the material from which the object is made
- the nature of the surface that is in contact with the object.

Applications and examples

Cooling fins found in engines are usually metal and painted black. This has three advantages:

- Black: good emitter of infrared radiation – cooling the engine
- Metal: conducts heat away from the engine
- Fins: large surface area, increasing energy transfer through convection and infrared radiation.

Animals in warmer environments have evolved to have larger ears. They have a larger surface area to radiate heat to the surroundings and keep them cool. Animals in cooler environments have small ears. This reduces the transfer of energy to their surroundings, keeping the animal warm.

The vacuum flask is designed to minimise energy transfer. This keeps hot drinks hot and cold drinks cold. It has a number of key features, as listed below.

vacuum layer inside the glass vessel	prevents conduction and convection
shiny silver on both the inside and outside of the glass vessel	poor emitter of IR and good reflector
tight screw cap	reduces convection and evaporation

Questions

1. Produce a summary table showing all the factors that affect the rate of energy transfer away from a hot object. Include a description of the effect each factor has on the rate of energy transfer.
2. Explain how a vacuum flask is able to keep a cold drink cold on a very hot day.

Insulating your home

There are several techniques for insulating homes to reduce energy transferred to the surroundings through conduction, convection, and radiation.

- Cavity-wall **insulation**: a material in between the walls (usually foam) traps air in pockets, reducing conduction and preventing convection.
- Loft insulation: works in the same way as cavity-wall insulation – a material in the loft (usually fibre glass) traps air, reducing conduction and preventing convection.
- Double glazing: conduction is reduced by a layer of air or gas trapped between two panes of glass.
- Draft excluders: energy loss through convection is reduced by making it more difficult to set up convection currents.
- Curtains: reduces energy loss through radiation and conduction, by reducing the energy transfer to the windows.

Each technique reduces the amount of energy needed to heat your home (as less is transferred to the surroundings). This saves money as you do not have to have your heating on for as long or have it set so high (saving on fuel and electricity bills).

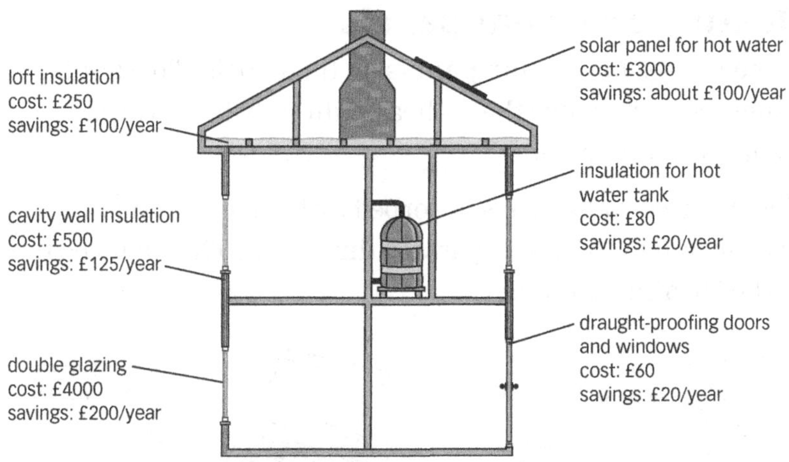

▲ Different ways of reducing your energy consumption.

Exam tip AQA

- Make sure you can explain how a particular method for insulating homes reduces energy transfer (most *trap air* – reducing conduction and convection).
- Remember, solar panels still work on cloudy days, but the water does not get as hot.

Revision objectives

- ✔ know how different techniques are used to insulate homes
- ✔ use payback time and U-values to compare different methods of insulating homes
- ✔ describe how solar panels are used to provide some homes with hot water

Student book references

1.8 Heating and insulating buildings

1.9 Solar panels and payback time

Specification key

✔ P1.1.4 a – c

Key words

insulation, U-value, payback, solar panel

U-values

U-values measure how effective a material is as an insulator.

- The lower the U-value the better an insulator.

For example:

Insulator	U-value (relative units)
single glazing	5.0
double glazing	2.9
50-mm loft insulation	0.6
100-mm loft insulation	0.3

Payback time

Each technique has a different **payback** time.

This is the time taken before the savings you get each year equal the cost of the materials and installation.

Payback time = cost/savings per year

For example, installing loft insulation may cost £250 but save you £100 per year in heating bills. It has a payback time of 2.5 years.

Heating and solar panels

Some houses have **solar panels** on their roofs. These solar panels contain water that is heated directly by infrared radiation from the Sun.

The infrared radiation is absorbed by the panel and is transferred to the water passing through it. This reduces the cost of heating the water.

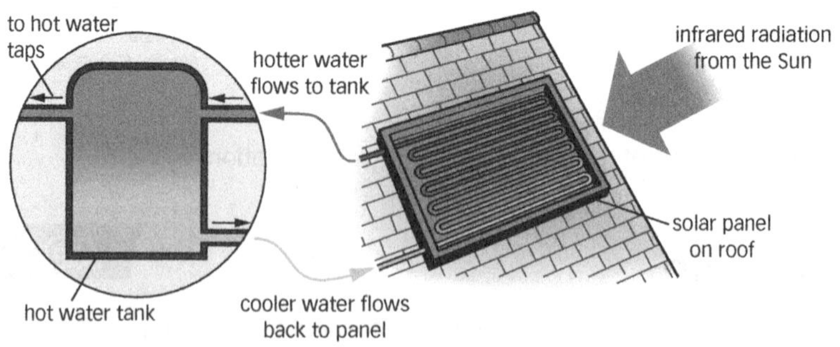

▲ How a solar panel works.

Questions

1 Produce a table to summarise the ways to minimise the energy transfer from a typical home. Explain how each method reduces the energy transfer.

2 Explain how the U-values of different loft insulations may help a home owner purchase the most effective one.

3 Purchasing and installing double glazing costs £1200. After it is installed it saves the home owner £60 per year. Calculate the payback time.

What is specific heat capacity?

The **specific heat capacity** of a substance is the amount of energy required to change the temperature of 1 kg of the substance by 1 °C.

Different materials have different specific heat capacities.

An object with low specific heat capacity does not take much energy to increase its temperature. An object with a high specific heat capacity requires more energy to increase the same mass of substance by the same temperature.

Water has a particularly high specific heat capacity, 4200 J/kg°C.

The specific heat capacity equation

E	=	m	×	c	×	θ
energy transferred (joules, J)	=	mass (kilograms, kg)	×	specific heat capacity (J/kg°C)	×	change in temperature (degrees Celsius, °C)

Applications of specific heat capacities

Water has a high specific heat capacity and this makes it particularly useful as a coolant in engines. It can absorb a lot of energy before it gets too hot and changes into a gas.

Electrical storage heaters contain large blocks of concrete. These have a high specific heat capacity (although not as high as water). They slowly absorb energy at night (when electricity is cheaper), transferring it to their surroundings during the day.

Oil-filled radiators use the same principle. Rather than heat the air directly, oil inside the radiator is heated. This stores lots of energy in the oil which is slowly transferred to the surroundings.

Revision objectives

- Understand the meaning of the term 'specific heat capacity'
- Compare the specific heat capacities of different materials
- Use the equation $E = m \times c \times \theta$

Student book references

1.10 Specific heat capacity

1.11 Uses of specific heat capacity

Specification key

✔ P1.1.4 d

Exam tip

AQA

- When using the specific heat capacity equation, make sure mass is in kilograms, not grams.
- You may need to rearrange the equation to find the specific heat capacity of a material. Practise doing this before the exam.

Questions

1 Explain what is meant by the specific heat capacity of a material.

2 Calculate the energy needed to increase the temperature of 2200 g of water from 20 °C to 90 °C. The specific heat capacity of water is 4200 J/kg°C.

Key words

specific heat capacity

Questions
Energy transfer by heating

Working to Grade E

1 Highlight the statements below that are **true**. If a statement is **false**, write a corrected version of that statement.
  a All objects emit and absorb infrared radiation.
  b Dark objects are good emitters of infrared radiation.
  c Dark objects are poor emitters of infrared radiation.
  d The particles in a solid are very far apart and move very fast.
  e Conduction takes place in solids. Metals are the best thermal conductors as they contain free electrons.
  f The higher the U-value the better the material is as an insulator.
  g The cost of loft insulation is referred to as payback time.

2 In each sentence below, highlight the correct **bold** word.
  a Shiny surfaces are good **absorbers/reflectors** of infrared radiation.
  b The particles in **liquids/gases** have the most energy.
  c When a liquid evaporates from a surface, the temperature of the surface **increases/decreases.**
  d Water has an unusually **high/low** specific heat capacity.
  e The **bigger/smaller** the temperature difference between an object and its surrounding, the higher the rate of energy transfer.

3 Match the feature of a vacuum flask to the energy transfer it is designed to reduce.

Feature
vacuum
silvered surface
tightly fitting lid

Reduces energy transfer by...
radiation
conduction and convection
convection and evaporation

4 List three techniques to reduce energy transfer from a house.

5 Give two ways to increase the rate of evaporation from a liquid.

Working to Grade C

6 Draw a diagram to show how energy is transferred through a solid bar by conduction.

7 Complete the sentences below:
  a The rate of energy transfer from warmer objects to _______ objects depends on a number of factors. These include the _______ and _______ _______ of the object, the _______ from which it is made, and the nature of the _______ that is in contact with it.
  b Some animals in warmer climates have _______ ears. This increases the _______ _______ and more energy can be radiated to the _______, keeping the animal cool.

8 The table shows the installation costs and savings made per year for several different home insulation techniques (A, B, and C). For each technique, calculate the payback time.

Technique	Installation cost/£	Savings per year/£	Payback time/year
A	300	50	
B	2000	40	
C	150	15	

9 Explain why the high specific heat capacity of oil makes it useful in oil-filled radiators.

10 An engineering student is designing a component that forms part of a jet engine. She wishes to find out how much energy it would take to heat up the component by 300 °C. The component has a mass of 2.0 kg.
Complete the table below to find how much energy would be needed for several different materials (A, B, C, and D).

$$E = m \times c \times \theta$$

Material	Specific heat capacity/J/kg°C	Energy required to heat it by 300°C/J
A	900	
B	450	
C	3000	
D	70	

Examination questions
Energy transfer

1 This question is about the different techniques used to insulate a typical family home.

a Complete this table to show which energy transfers are reduced by each of the techniques. The first one has been done for you.

Technique	Conduction	Convection	Radiation
Loft insulation	✓	✓	
Cavity-wall insulation			
Double glazing			
Installing curtains			

(3 marks)

b Explain how a home owner might use U-values to determine which type of loft insulation to buy.

....

....

....

(2 marks)

c This table gives information about the costs and savings from some methods of conserving energy in a house.

Technique	Installation cost/£	Savings per year/£
Cavity-wall insulation	200	25
Double glazing	1500	150
100-mm loft insulation	150	10
350-mm loft insulation	300	25

i With a suitable calculation explain which technique should be installed first.

....

....

....

....

(3 marks)

ii Describe what happens to the energy that is 'wasted' from a typical home.

....

....

(2 marks)

d Solar panels could be installed to provide hot water for the house. Explain why the pipes inside most solar panels are painted matt black.

....

....

(2 marks)

(Total marks: 12)

2 Some saucepans have copper bases. Copper is a very good thermal conductor.

a Explain in terms of particles how energy is transferred through the base of the saucepan to its contents when placed on a hot cooking hob.

....

....

....

(2 marks)

b A convection current may form in the water inside the pan. Use the words in the box below to complete the sentences that follow.

You may use each word once, more than once, or not at all.

faster	**energy**	**rises**	**less**	**more**	**sinks**	**slower**

When the water is heated the particles gain .... and move .... The particles move further apart making the water .... dense. The warm water .... and cooler water is drawn into to replace it.

(4 marks)

c Before the water boils, some of the particles escape from the surface of the liquid and turn into a gas. What is the name given to this process?

....

(1 mark)

d As the water is heated it transfers energy to its surroundings. Describe what happens to the rate at which this energy is transferred as the water gets hotter.

....

(1 mark)

(Total marks: 8)

3 a Explain what is meant by the term 'specific heat capacity'.

....

....

....

(2 marks)

b A kettle is used to heat 1.4 kg of water from 20 °C to 100 °C. Calculate the energy supplied to the kettle and give the unit.

$$E = m \times c \times \theta$$

The specific heat capacity of water is 4200 J/kg °C.

....

....

....

Energy transferred ....

(3 marks)

(Total marks: 5)

Revision objectives

- describe the law of conservation of energy
- know the meaning of the term 'wasted energy' and describe its effect on an object's surroundings
- be able to use Sankey diagrams to show energy transfers

Student book references

1.12 Understanding energy

1.13 Useful energy and energy efficiency

Specification key

- P1.2.1 a – c

Law of conservation of energy

The **law of conservation of energy** is one of the most important rules in all of physics. It states:

- Energy can be *transferred* usefully, stored, or **dissipated** but cannot be *created* or *destroyed*.

There are many different forms of energy:

- **kinetic**
- sound
- light
- heat/thermal
- electrical
- **gravitational potential**
- **elastic potential**
- **chemical**
- **nuclear**

The law of conservation of energy states that energy can be transferred from one form into another. For example, a light bulb transfers electrical energy into heat energy and light energy. But energy can never be created or destroyed.

'Wasting' energy

Energy is often described as being '**wasted**'.

Energy cannot be destroyed; the term 'wasted' refers to energy that has been transferred into a form or forms we no longer require. For example, the heat energy from a light bulb is not usually needed; it can be described as wasted or waste energy.

Waste energy is often transferred to the surroundings as heat. The surroundings become warmer and the energy is slowly dissipated (spread out). As the energy becomes more spread out, it becomes less useful.

Whenever energy is transferred there is always some energy that is wasted.

Exam tip

AQA

Make sure you can identify which are the **useful** and which are the wasted forms of energy from common devices.

Sankey diagrams

Energy transfers can be represented as special arrowed diagrams called **Sankey diagrams**.

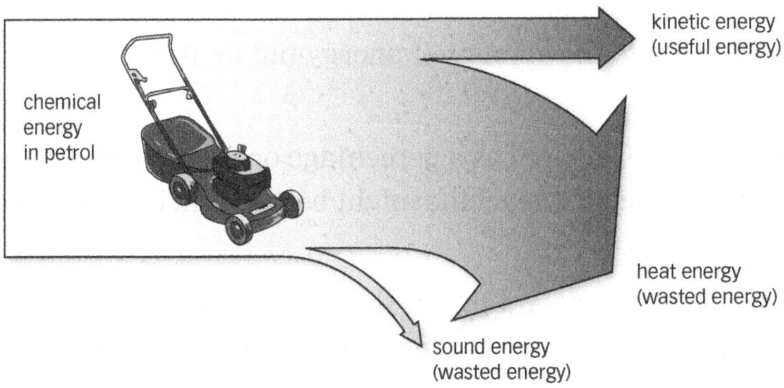

▲ Sankey diagram for energy transfers in a petrol mower.

These not only show the energy transfers but how much energy is transferred into each type. The thicker the arrow the greater the proportion of energy transferred into this form.

Remember, energy cannot be created or destroyed so the arrows must not get thinner or thicker. The total energy must stay the same.

Key words

law of conservation of energy, dissipated, kinetic energy, gravitational potential energy, elastic potential energy, nuclear energy, chemical energy, wasted energy, useful energy, Sankey diagram

Questions

1 Describe the energy changes inside a clockwork radio.

2 Sketch a Sankey diagram for an electric motor.

3 Explain why wasted energy tends to become less useful.

8: Energy efficiency

Revision objectives

- use Sankey diagrams to compare the efficiency of devices
- calculate the efficiency of various devices

Student book references

1.13 Useful energy and energy efficiency

Specification key

- P1.2.1 d

Efficiency

Whenever energy is transferred some of the energy is wasted: not all of the energy can be transferred into useful forms.

- The amount of energy transferred into useful forms, compared to the amount of energy put in, is called the **efficiency**.

Efficiency is measured as a percentage or decimal. For example, a washing machine might be 40% efficient or have an efficiency of 0.4.

This means it transfers 40% of the energy going into it into useful forms. Therefore it wastes 60% of the energy, 60 J for every 100 J supplied.

A more efficient machine transfers a greater proportion of the energy into useful forms. A more efficient washing machine may have an efficiency of 55%.

Appliances and devices can be sorted by their efficiency. A more efficient device wastes a lower proportion of the energy supplied. A device with an efficiency of 80% wastes a lower proportion, and so is more efficient, than a device with an efficiency of 65%. However, no machine can ever be 100% efficient.

Calculating efficiency

The key equation for working out efficiency is

$$\text{efficiency} = \frac{\text{useful energy transferred}}{\text{total energy supplied}}$$

You need to multiply the answer by 100 to get the answer as a percentage.

For example, a light bulb supplied with 300 J of energy transfers 60 J into light and wastes 240 J as heat. Its efficiency is given by:

$$\text{efficiency} = \frac{\text{useful energy transferred (60 J)}}{\text{total energy supplied (300 J)}}$$

efficiency = 0.2 (or 20%)

Exam tip

AQA

- When calculating efficiency, be careful to work out which energy is useful and which energy is wasted.
- Remember, the efficiency can never be more than 100% or, if you write it as a ratio, never greater than 1.

Sankey diagram and efficiency

You can compare the efficiency of devices using the information in a Sankey diagram.

The greater the size of the useful arrow, the more efficient the device.

▲ Sankey diagram for a filament lightbulb.

A more efficient light source (like an LED or compact fluorescent tube) will transfer a greater proportional of the electrical energy into light – the arrow showing the useful light output will be wider.

Key words

efficiency

Questions

1 Calculate the efficiency of:

a an electric heater that transfers 1300 J into heat and 700 J into light for every 2000 J supplied

b a petrol engine that wastes 900 J of heat energy for every 1500 J supplied.

2 Calculate the efficiency of the lightbulb shown in the Sankey diagram above.

3 Sketch a Sankey diagram to show the energy transfer by a more efficient light bulb.

Questions
Energy conservation and efficiency

Working to Grade E

1 Highlight which of the following are **forms of energy**:

friction vacuum chemical convection elastic potential heat/thermal lift nuclear gravitational potential gravity light sound kinetic generator electrical

2 Complete the sentences below:

a The law of conservation of energy states that _______ cannot be _______ or _______ but it can be _______ usefully, stored, or _______

b Energy that has been transferred into a form we no longer need is called .... energy. This energy is usually transferred to the surroundings as .... It becomes more and more spread out, making it less useful.

3 Match the device or situation to the main energy transfers that take place.

Device
kettle
lightbulb
wind-up radio
ball dropped from a height

Main energy transfers
electrical → heat
electrical → heat and light
gravitational potential → kinetic
elastic potential → electrical → sound

4 Highlight the statements below that are **true**. Then write corrected versions of the statements that are **false**.

a Energy cannot be created or destroyed.

b Energy is measured in watts.

c When wasted energy is transferred to the surroundings, the surroundings get cooler.

d The more efficient a device is, the lower the proportion of energy it wastes.

e In a Sankey diagram, the greater the size of the useful arrow, the more efficient the device.

Working to Grade C

5 Draw a Sankey diagram to show the energy transfers that take place inside a petrol engine.

6 The table shows the energy transfers for each 200 J supplied to five different light bulbs.

Bulb	Energy transferred into light/J	Energy transferred into heat/J
A	50	150
B	180	
C	120	
D		100
E		60

a Complete the table (the first row has been done for you).

b Draw Sankey diagrams for each of the bulbs.

c Calculate the efficiency of bulb C.

d Without calculation explain how you can tell which bulb is the most efficient.

7 a Describe the energy changes when a ball is dropped from 1 m above the ground and bounces back up to a height of 70 cm.

b Explain why the ball does not bounce back up to its original height.

8 An electrical lift is supplied with 5000 J of energy. As it lifts a concrete block it wastes 3500 J as heat and sound.

a How much energy is transferred usefully by the lift?

b Describe what happens to the wasted energy.

c Calculate the efficiency of the lift.

9 A company claims its new kettles are 120% efficient.

a Explain why this is not possible.

b Explain why the claims from any company about one of their products should always be supported with evidence collected by independent scientists.

Examination questions
Energy conservation and efficiency

1 a State the law of conservation of energy.

....

....

....

(2 marks)

b Describe the useful energy transfers that take place in the following devices. There may be more than one form of useful energy in each case. This first one has been done for you.

Electric kettle: *Electrical to heat*

Petrol engine: ....

TV: ....

Car battery: ....

(3 marks)

c i Draw a Sankey diagram to show the energy transfers for a typical electric filament lamp. You should consider the relative sizes of the arrows on your diagram.

(2 marks)

ii Explain how your diagram would be different for an energy-efficient lamp.

....

....

....

(2 marks)

(Total marks: 9)

2 a i Explain what is meant by the term 'wasted energy'.

....

....

(2 marks)

ii When wasted energy is transferred to the surroundings it becomes less useful. Explain why.

....

(1 mark)

b i A radio is supplied with 300 kJ of electrical energy. It transfers 50 kJ into sound. Assuming there are no other energy transfers, how much energy is wasted as heat?

....

Wasted energy .... kJ

(1 mark)

ii Calculate the percentage efficiency of the radio.

$$\text{efficiency} = \frac{\text{useful energy out}}{\text{total energy in}} (\times 100)$$

....

....

Efficiency .... %

(2 marks)

(Total marks: 6)

Electrical devices

Electrical devices are incredibly useful. Electricity can be transferred into most other forms of energy. Some examples are given in the table below:

Device	Energy in	Main forms of energy out
Kettle	electrical	heat, kinetic
Toaster	electrical	heat, light
Electric motor	electrical	heat, sound, kinetic
Speaker	electrical	sound, kinetic
Computer	electrical	heat, light, sound, kinetic

Different electrical devices have advantages and disadvantages. For example, a battery-powered radio will run for a long time but eventually the batteries will need to be replaced. A mains-electricity-powered radio will run for even longer, but cannot be used on the move.

Electrical energy transfers

The amount of electrical energy transferred by an electrical device depends on two factors:

- how long the device is used for
- the **power** of the device.

A more powerful device may be used for a shorter time and so may use less energy than a less powerful device, which has to be used for longer.

You can calculate the power of an device using the equation below:

$$E = P \times t$$

electrical energy transferred (**joules**, J) = power of device (**watts**, W) × time used for (**seconds**, s)

Revision objectives

- ✔ give examples of energy transfers from common electrical devices
- ✔ compare the advantages and disadvantages of different electrical devices
- ✔ calculate the energy transferred by electrical devices

Student book references

1.14 Using electricity

Specification key

✔ P1.3.1 a – c

Exam tip

AQA

Power can be expressed in **kilowatts**. Remember to convert this into watts (1 kW = 1000 W).

Key words

kilowatt, power, joule, watt

Reducing energy consumption

It is important to try to reduce our energy consumption. This not only saves us money, but it also conserves our natural resources and means less electricity needs to be generated.

There are several different methods to do this:

- Replace inefficient filament lightbulbs with low-energy lighting (compact fluorescent bulbs or LEDs).
- Consider replacing older electrical devices with more modern, energy-efficient ones (for example, replacing an old oven with a new one).

Different electric ovens may have different efficiencies. In general, cheaper ovens are less efficient: they waste a greater proportion of the energy supplied to them. However, it is important to consider payback time when purchasing new electrical devices.

Device	Cost	Savings per year	Payback time to the nearest full year
Oven A	£1000	£75	13
Oven B	£800	£45	18
Oven C	£650	£40	16
Oven D	£500	£25	20

Questions

1 List three different electrical devices and describe the energy transfers that take place when they are being used.

2 Which of the following uses more energy? (Include a calculation.)

a 20 W light bulb used for 10 hours.

b 2.2 kW kettle used for 250 seconds.

3 Explain why it might be a good idea to replace filament lightbulbs with more modern, energy-efficient alternatives.

The kilowatt-hour

Energy is usually measured in joules. However, one joule is quite a small amount of energy. So an alternative **unit** of energy is the **kilowatt-hour** (kWh).

- The kilowatt-hour is a unit of energy.

One kWh is the same as 3.6 million joules!

Calculating energy in kilowatt-hours

It is useful to calculate the energy transferred by an device in kilowatt-hours. This is sometimes referred to as the number of *units*.

We use the same equation $E = P \times t$, but there are two key differences.

To calculate energy in kilowatt-hours

- P (power) must be measured in kilowatts
- t (time) must be measured in hours.

E	$=$	P	$\times$	t
electrical energy transferred (kilowatt-hours, kWh)		power of device (kilowatts, kW)		time used for (hours, h)

1 kilowatt is 1000 watts, 500 watts is 0.5 kilowatts, 300 watts is 0.3 kilowatts, and so on.

Exam tip

AQA

- You need to be able to calculate energy in kilowatt-hours (kWh). Take care when converting power to kilowatts and time into hours.
- Practise using readings from electricity meters to find the cost of the electricity used.

Revision objectives

- know that kilowatt-hours (kWh) is a unit of energy
- calculate the energy transferred by electrical devices in kWh
- calculate the cost of running common electrical devices

Student book references

1.15 Paying for electricity

Specification key

✔ P1.3.1 d

Key words

unit, kilowatt-hour

Paying for electricity

We calculate the cost of electrical devices in pence using the energy transferred in kWh.

Cost	= Cost per kWh	× Energy transferred
(pence, p)	*(pence per kilowatt-hour, p/kWh)*	*(kilowatt-hour, kWh)*

The electricity meter

Every house in the UK has an electricity meter. This is a device that records the number of units used (this is energy transferred by all the devices inside the house, measured in kilowatt-hours).

This is used by electricity companies to calculate your electricity bill.

Month	Meter reading
January	40 568
March	41 589

The number of units used between January and March is:

Energy transferred = 41 589 kWh – 40 568 kWh
Energy transferred = 1021 kWh

If each unit costs 12p then the cost for this quarter would be

Cost = cost per kWh × energy transferred
Cost = 12p × 1021 kWh
Cost = 12 252p or £122.52

Questions

1 Calculate the energy used in kilowatt-hours by the following:

a 3 kW heater used for 6 hours

b 9.2 kW shower used for 30 minutes

c 2000 W electric pump used for 4 hours

2 If each unit of electricity costs 11p, calculate how much it costs to run a 4000 W boiler for 90 minutes.

Questions
The use and cost of electricity

Working to Grade E

1 Complete the table below to show the main forms of energy from each electrical device.

Device	Energy in	Main forms of energy out
kettle	electrical	
TV	electrical	
radio	electrical	
escalator	electrical	

2 Use either the word **increases** or **decreases** to complete each sentence below:

a The amount of energy transferred by an electrical device ______ the longer you use it for.

b If you use a more powerful electrical device for the same period of time, the total amount of electrical energy transferred ______ .

c In general, when comparing electrical devices, as the cost of the device decreases the efficiency ______ .

d The cost of electrical energy ______ as the number of units you use increases.

3 In each sentence below, highlight the **one bold** word that is correct.

a Power is usually measured in **joules/watts.**

b The kilowatt-hour is a unit of **power/energy**.

c Compact fluorescent tubes used in lighting are usually **more/less** efficient than filament lightbulbs.

d Replacing older electrical devices with more modern ones normally **reduces/increases** our energy consumptions as more modern devices tend to be more efficient.

4 Complete the table below to give the power of several different devices in both W and kW.

Power of device/W	Power of device/kW
1000	
5500	
800	
	1.2
	0.5
20	

Working to Grade C

5 Give two reasons why it is important to reduce our energy consumption.

6 An office block uses 1200 compact fluorescent tubes for lighting. Each tube has a power output of 15 W and is used for 10 hours each day. Use the equation below to calculate the electrical energy transferred in joules:

$$E = P \times t$$

a by each tube

b in total.

7 A heater has a power output of 3000 W. It is used for 30 minutes. Use the equation below to calculate the energy transferred:

$$E = P \times t$$

a in J

b in kWh.

8 An electricity company takes meter readings from three different houses. The first reading was taken in March, with a second reading taken in June.

House	March reading (units of electricity)	June reading (units of electricity)
1	88451	89326
2	45321	51630
3	98015	102576

a Which house used the most units between March and June?

b If each unit costs 12p calculate the electricity bill for each house.

9 A 12 kW power shower is used for 15 minutes a day for 28 days. Calculate:

a The length of time, in hours, the shower is in use over this period.

b The number of 'units' used in this time.

c The cost of running the shower over that period if each unit costs 11p.

10 Compare the advantages and disadvantages of using a battery-powered radio with a mains-powered one.

Examination questions
The use and cost of electricity

1 a An electric kettle has a power rating of 2.2 kW. It takes 2 minutes to boil. Calculate the energy transferred in joules.

energy transferred = power × time

....

....

....

Energy transferred ....

(3 marks)

b If a more powerful kettle was used for the same time, what effect would this have on the amount of energy transferred?

....

(1 mark)

(Total marks: 4)

2 An electricity company takes a reading from an electricity meter in January and again in March. The meter readings can be seen below:

January reading: 35 658   March reading: 35 978

a Calculate the number of units consumed between the two readings.

....

(1 mark)

b Each unit costs 12p. Calculate the cost of the units consumed and give the unit.

....

....

Cost ....

(3 marks)

(Total marks: 4)

How Science Works
Energy and efficiency

Factors affecting the rate of energy transfer by heating

There are a number of factors that affect how fast an object transfers energy to its surroundings (the rate of energy transfer by heating).These include:

- the temperature difference between the object and its surroundings
- the surface area and volume of the object
- the material from which the object is made
- the nature of the surface that is in contact with the object (this includes whether or not the object is insulated)

There are several different investigations you might be asked to carry out that look into these different factors. For each investigation you should consider the variables carefully. A variable is a quantity in an experiment that can be measured (for example, the temperature of the object, the volume of the object, the type of insulation used). Different variables are given special names:

- **Independent variable:** this is the variable you change as part of your investigation.
- **Dependent variable:** this is the variable you measure after changing the independent variable. The dependent variable *depends on* the independent variable.
- **Control variable:** a control variable is another quantity that would affect the dependent variable if not kept the same for the experiment. In order to be a **fair test**, control variables must be kept constant.

A class conducts two different investigations into the rate of energy transfer by heating. The greater the rate of energy transfer to the surroundings the faster a hot object will cool down.

Investigation One

Hypothesis: different insulating materials affect how fast an object transfers energy to its surroundings.

For this investigation a pupil put 300 cm^3 of water at 70 °C into four identical beakers wrapped in different types of insulating material (A, B, C, and D). She left them for 10 minutes and then recorded how much the temperature had fallen.

Material	Start temperature/ °C	End temperature/ °C	Change in temperature/ °C
A	70	62	
B	70	50	
C	70	34	
D	70	64	

Investigation Two

Hypothesis: different volumes of water transfer energy to their surroundings at different rates: the greater the volume the lower the rate.

For this investigation a pupil put different volumes of water at 70 °C into five identical containers. He left them for five minutes and then recorded how much the temperature had fallen.

Volume/ cm^3	Start temperature/ °C	End temperature/ °C	Change in temperature/ °C
100	70	38	
200	70	50	
300	70	55	
400	70	62	
500	70	65	

1 For each experiment:
- a Complete the table by calculating the change in temperature.
- b Name the independent variable.
- c Name three control variables.
- d Explain why the control variables must be kept constant.

Depending on the nature of the variable it can be described as either categoric or as continuous.

Categoric: this type of variable has values that are labels. If either the independent or dependent variable is a category, results must be presented in a bar graph.

Continuous: this type of variable can have any value (a number). When both the independent and the dependent variables are continuous they should be plotted on a line graph, normally with a line of best fit (this can be straight or curved).

2 For each experiment:
- a Identify whether the independent and dependent variables are categoric or continuous.
- b Plot an appropriate graph for each investigation.
- c Discuss your findings and whether or not the experiment supports the hypothesis.

AQA Upgrade

Answering a question with data response

QUESTION

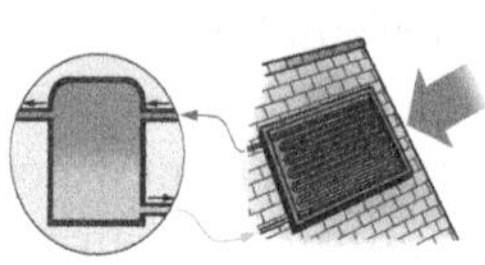

Solar panels are a frequent sight in Mediterranean countries and are increasingly common in some parts of the UK. They provide homes with hot water. However, they can be expensive to install and have a payback time of between 15 and 20 years.

1 Explain the meaning of the term 'payback time' in terms of solar panels. *(1 mark)*

2 Describe how solar panels are used to produce hot water and why this reduces the energy bills of home owners with solar panels on their roof.

In this question you will be assessed on using good English, organising information clearly, and using specialist terms where appropriate. *(6 marks)*

G–E

1 It is the time they are working. They don't work at night.

2 They absorb heat from the Sun and heat water in pipes. On sunny days the water gets very hot, but it does not work at night or when it is cloudy outside. They also generate electricity and you don't have to buy any as it is all free.

Examiner: The candidate has given an incorrect answer. They have not understood the term 'payback time'.

The answer is very vague and lacks key terms like *infra-red radiation* and *absorbed*. They have also confused solar panels with solar cells which are used to generate electricity. A maximum of one mark would have been awarded for a simplistic explanation of water in the pipes being heated from the Sun.

D–C

1 It the amount of money you save each year from installing the solar panel.

2 Money is saved as you don't need to pay to heat up water. The solar panels heat up the water by absorbing heat and light from the Sun. They are black as this is the best colour for absorbing heat. Water is stored in a tank and heated all the time.

Examiner: The candidate has made the link between installing solar panels and saving money, but they have not answered the question by explaining the meaning of 'payback time'.

A rather disjointed answer, but with some good use of key terms and a sound description of how the solar panel works. They should have mentioned infrared radiation rather than just heat and light from the Sun. They have outlined how the home owner is able to save money on their energy bills, but in a simplistic way. Some energy will still be needed to heat water; solar panels reduce the energy needed to warm the water and so savings can be made.

B–A*

1 Payback time is the time taken for the savings made by installing solar panels to cover the cost of purchasing and installing them.

2 During the day infrared radiation from the Sun is absorbed by the pipes inside the solar panel. The pipes are painted black as black is the best absorber of infrared radiation and so they get very hot. This energy is conducted through the pipes to the water inside. This increases the temperature of the water. The water is then stored in a hot water tank. Home owners with solar panels installed use less energy to heat up water, as their water has already been warmed by the Sun. This reduces the amount of energy they use and so they don't pay as much.

Examiner: Clear and correct.

An excellent answer that answers both parts of the question, using all of the correct technical terms. They have explained in detail how solar panels work and how a home owner saves money by having them installed on their roof.

Part 1 Course catch-up
Energy and efficiency

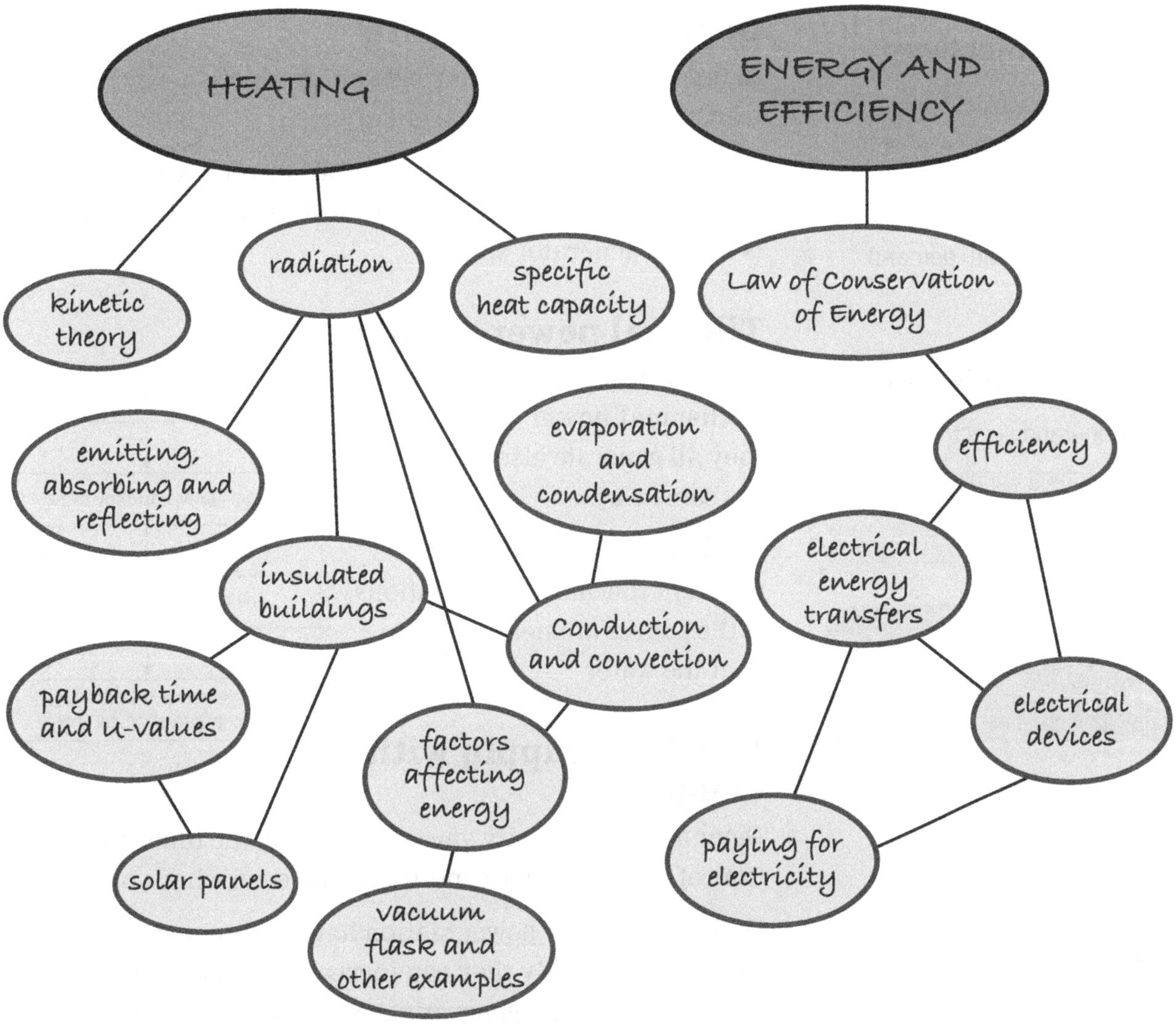

Revision checklist

- All objects emit infrared radiation (IR). Hotter objects emit more IR than cooler ones.
- Black, matt objects are the best emitters and absorbers of IR. Shiny, white surfaces reflect IR and are poor emitters and absorbers.
- Particles are arranged differently in solids, liquids, and gases.
- Particles in solids have less energy than those in liquids, which have less energy than those in gases.
- Energy can be transferred by heating through conduction, convection, evaporation, and condensation.
- Conduction happens in solids; energy is passed from one vibrating particle to the next. Metals are the best conductors because they also contain free electrons.
- Convection happens in fluids (liquids and gases). In convection a region of fluid is heated. The particles gain energy, move faster, and so the region expands. This makes it less dense and it rises.
- Convection currents form when cooler fluid is drawn in to replace the warmer fluid. It is then heated and rises in a cycle.
- Evaporation (when a liquid turns into a gas) has a cooling effect as the particles leaving the liquid transfer energy away with them. Condensation (when a gas turns into a liquid) is the reverse of evaporation.
- The rate of energy transfer from hotter objects to cooler ones depends on: surface area and volume, construction material, and surface in contact.
- The bigger the temperature difference, the greater the rate of energy transfer.
- When comparing techniques to insulate your home, you should consider payback time and U-value (lower U-values mean a better insulator).
- Specific heat capacity is the energy required to raise the temperature of 1 kg of a substance by 1 °C.
- Energy cannot be created or destroyed, just stored or transferred from one form into another.
- Sankey diagrams can be used to represent energy transfers.
- Efficiency is a measure of the amount of useful energy transferred compared with the total energy supplied.
- Electrical devices vary in their efficiency and the amount of energy they use.
- The kilowatt-hour is a unit of electrical energy. The cost of electricity depends on the number of kWh used.

P1

11: Generating electricity and matching supply with demand

Revision objectives

- describe how electricity is generated in thermal power stations
- describe techniques used to match supply with demand

Student book references

1.16 Generating electricity

1.23 Matching supply and demand

Specification key

- **P1.4.1 a**

Generating electricity

In order to generate electricity, one form of energy has to be transferred into electrical energy.

A **generator** is a special device that converts kinetic energy into electrical energy. To generate electricity all you need to do is make a generator spin.

Thermal power stations

There are many different kinds of **thermal power station** but they all generate electricity in the same way.

The only difference between different thermal power stations is the source of energy used to heat the water.

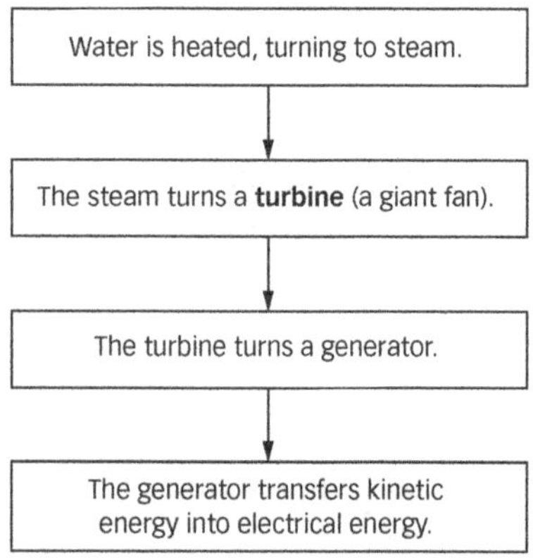

Matching supply with demand

Demand for electricity varies depending the time of day, the time of year, weather conditions, and even what's on the TV.

Different types of power station have different **start-up times**. This is how quickly they can increase or reduce the amount of electricity they are generating. Nuclear and coal have very slow start-up times but natural gas and hydroelectric power are much quicker.

Electricity cannot be stored in large quantities so when there is a sudden surge in demand a **pumped storage** station is used. This is a special type of hydroelectric power only used for changes in demand. At peak demand it starts generating very quickly and at times of low demand it can be used to store energy for later use, by using electricity to pump water back uphill.

Questions

1 Describe how electricity is generated in a thermal power station (include details of the energy transfers that take place).

2 Explain what is meant by the start-up time of a power station.

3 Describe how a pumped storage power station might be used to meet sudden increases in demand.

Exam tip (AQA)

You need to be able to describe the energy changes for thermal power stations. Try drawing a flow chart during your revision to help you remember.

Key words

generator, thermal power station, turbine, start-up time, pumped storage

The National Grid

The electricity generated at power stations needs to be distributed to homes and business all around the country.

In the UK we have a **National Grid**. This is a huge network of underground cables and overhead power lines linking houses to power stations, which are sometimes hundreds of miles away.

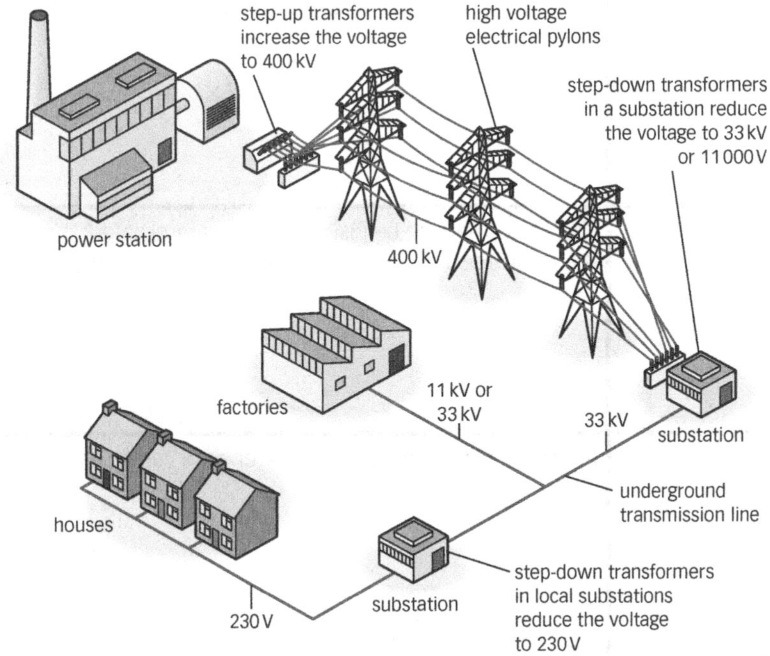

▲ The National Grid.

Transmitting at high voltages

The electricity is transmitted at very high voltages. When you increase the voltage (keeping the power the same), the current drops. A lower current means the wires don't get as hot. This means less energy is wasted in transmission.

Transformers are special devices that can increase or reduce the **voltage**. **Step-up transformers** are used to increase the voltage before it is distributed through the grid (up to 400 000 V). **Step-down transformers** are then used in **substations** to reduce the voltage to a safer level to be used in the home (230 V).

Revision objectives

- know how electricity is distributed through the National Grid and the role transformers play in this process
- compare the advantages and disadvantage of overhead pylons and underground cables

Student book references

1.22 The National Grid

Specification key

✔ P1.4.2

Exam tip AQA

Make sure you can explain *why* transformers are used.

Key words

National Grid, transformer, voltage, step-up transformer, step-down transformer, substation

Pylons versus underground cables

Some power lines are buried in the ground; others are suspended high in the air on pylons. Burying cables has a number of advantages and disadvantages when compared to using pylons.

Advantages of underground cables	Disadvantages of underground cables
The cables are not an eyesore, unlike large pylons. They can be used in areas of outstanding natural beauty and in national parks.	It is much more expensive to bury cables.
The cables are protected from severe weather and storms.	The cables have to be insulated and waterproofed; this means the cables get warmer, wasting more energy.
	It is very costly and disruptive to repair or renew damaged cables.
	The voltage used cannot be as high as in pylon lines, so more energy is wasted as heat.

Questions

1. Describe how electricity is distributed through the National Grid from power stations to homes. Include a description of each of the key parts.
2. Explain why it is more efficient to transmit electricity at high voltages.
3. Give two advantages and disadvantages of using pylons rather than burying cables underground.

Using fossil fuels

Fossil fuels include coal, oil, and natural gas. They were all formed from the remains of living plants or animals that died millions of years ago. They are a **non-renewable** energy resource as they will eventually be used up.

Fossil fuels are burnt in large quantities in order to generate electricity. Burning fossil fuels can produce huge amounts of electricity. The fuels are relatively cheap and the technology is well established. However, there are a number of disadvantages:

- Burning fossil fuel releases carbon dioxide (CO_2) into the atmosphere (in varying amounts). This increases global warming and leads to climate change.
- The fuels have to be mined/extracted and then transported. This damages wildlife habitats and there is the added risk of spills or leaks.
- The power stations and the mines/rigs are often very ugly and noisy.

Different fossil fuels are used in slightly different ways. In some natural gas power stations the exhaust gases from the burning gas are used to spin the turbine. This gives this type of power station a short start-up time, allowing it to increase rapidly the amount of electricity it generates if there is a surge in demand.

Fossil fuel	Substance heated	CO_2 production	Start-up time
coal	water	very high	long
oil	water	high	long
natural gas	exhaust gas	medium	short

Carbon capture

Carbon capture is a rapidly evolving technology, which in the future may dramatically reduce the amount of CO_2 that enters the atmosphere from the burning of fossil fuels.

Instead of travelling into the air, the CO_2 is trapped and stored underground (perhaps in old oil or gas fields). One day this may reduce the CO_2 released by a typical plant by as much as 80%.

Exam tip

AQA

You need to be able to describe the differences between how the three fossil fuels are used during energy production.

Revision objectives

- describe how fossil fuels are used to generate electricity
- outline the advantages and disadvantages of using fossil fuels to generate electricity
- know how the process of carbon capture may be used to prevent carbon dioxide building up in the atmosphere

Student book references

1.17 Fossil fuels and carbon capture

Specification key

✔ P1.4.1 a and f

Key words

non-renewable, carbon capture

Questions

1 Give two advantages and two disadvantages of using fossil fuels to generate electricity.

2 Outline the differences between the use of coal, oil, and natural gas to generate electricity.

3 Describe what is meant by carbon capture and explain why it might be beneficial to develop this technology.

14: Nuclear power

Revision objectives

- describe how nuclear power is used to generate electricity
- outline the advantages and disadvantages of using nuclear power to generate electricity

Student book references

1.18 Nuclear power

Specification key

- P1.4.1 a and f

Exam tip

AQA

Remember to stress that an advantage of nuclear power is that it can generate more electricity *per kilogram* of fuel than alternative sources.

Key words

nuclear reactor, nuclear fission, radioactive waste, decommission

Generating electricity from nuclear power

Electricity may be generated from **nuclear reactors**. Inside this reactor the nuclear fuel undergoes a nuclear reaction called **nuclear fission**. This reaction releases heat.

The heat released is then used to turn water to steam, which turns a turbine then a generator (in the same way as other thermal power stations).

The fuel used is either uranium or plutonium. We have plenty of this kind of fuel; however, it will eventually run out, so nuclear power is another non-renewable resource (like fossil fuels).

Advantages and disadvantages of nuclear power

Using nuclear power offers a number of advantages and disadvantages.

Advantages	Disadvantages
Huge amounts of electricity can be generated per kilogram of fuel.	Nuclear reactors produce highly **radioactive waste**. This is very dangerous and harmful. It needs to be stored carefully.
The fuel is not burnt, so there is no carbon dioxide released. Nuclear power does not contribute to global warming.	There is the risk of a nuclear accident releasing radioactive waste into the environment.
The fuel is relatively cheap and easily available – it will not run out for many years.	Nuclear reactors have a very slow start-up time. They can't react to sudden changes in demand.
	The power stations contribute to both noise and visual pollution.
	Nuclear power stations can be very expensive to build and even more expensive to **decommission** (dismantle) at the end of their useful life.

Questions

1 Describe how electricity is produced using a nuclear reactor.

2 Explain why nuclear power stations do not contribute to manmade global warming.

3 What is meant by decommission? Explain why this is often a costly process.

Renewable energy sources

Along with fossil fuels and nuclear power there are a number of other energy resources we can use to generate electricity.

Each resource is used in a slightly different way but most turn turbines, which turn generators in order to generate electricity.

All of these sources are classified as **renewable**. They don't use a fuel that will run out and so can be used over and over again.

Questions

1 Describe how geothermal power is used to generate electricity and outline one advantage and one disadvantage of this method.

2 Which two renewable energy resources are most useful for the production of small-scale local electricity in remote areas?

3 Explain why, despite releasing CO_2 when biofuels are burnt, biomass is a carbon-neutral energy resource.

Revision objectives

- describe how different renewable energy resources may be used to generate electricity
- outline the advantages and disadvantages of using different renewable technologies to generate electricity

Student book references

1.16 Generating electricity
1.19 Biomass and biofuels
1.20 Solar and wind power
1.21 Energy from water

Specification key

- P1.4.1

Key words

wind turbine, tidal barrage, hydroelectric power, solar cells, solar thermal tower, geothermal, thermal power station, biomass, biofuel, renewable, carbon neutral

Advantages and disadvantages of renewables

<table>
<tr><th></th><th>How electricity is generated</th><th colspan="3">Advantages</th><th>Disadvantages</th></tr>
<tr><td>Wind</td><td>The wind turns large wind turbines directly.</td><td rowspan="6">No atmospheric pollution (including no carbon dioxide). They don't contribute to global warming.</td><td rowspan="6">There are no fuel costs (only maintenance and construction costs).</td><td>Can be built offshore.</td><td>Visual and noise pollution.
Only generates electricity when it is windy.</td></tr>
<tr><td>Wave</td><td>There are several different kinds of wave generator. They all use the up and down motion of the waves to turn turbines.</td><td></td><td>Visual and noise pollution (can also be a danger to shipping).
Unreliable/untested technology.</td></tr>
<tr><td>Tidal</td><td>As the tides move in and out they turn turbines directly. There are different types of tidal power, including large tidal barrages (dams) across estuaries, or smaller tidal lagoons.</td><td>Reliable and predictable electricity generation.</td><td>Affects marine habitats.
Can be very expensive to build.
Limited number of suitable sites.
Can only generate power for a short period of 6–8 hours per day.</td></tr>
<tr><td>Hydroelectric power (HEP)</td><td>A large dam is built across a valley. The water builds up behind the dam. As it falls through pipes large turbines are turned by the falling water.</td><td>Large quantities of electricity can be generated.
Short start-up time and can be used as pumped storage.
Can be used (in small scale) in remote areas.</td><td>Building dams can be very expensive.
The dam floods valleys upstream and can have other environmental effects.
Only a few suitable locations.</td></tr>
<tr><td>Solar (cells)</td><td>Energy from the sun is directly transferred into electrical energy using special solar cells. No turbines or generators are needed. Alternatively, sunlight is reflected off hundreds of mirrors and focused on a solar thermal tower. Inside the tower, water is heated and turns to steam (this is used to turn turbines).</td><td>Very useful in remote locations (away from National Grid), such as roadsigns.
Works very well on the small scale.</td><td>Solar cells are very expensive to produce.
Output depends on the light level.</td></tr>
<tr><td>Geothermal</td><td>In some volcanic regions of the world there are hot rocks near the surface. Water and steam rises to the surface. This steam is collected and piped to a thermal power station to turn turbines directly.</td><td>Relatively cheap to build.</td><td>Only a few suitable locations around the world.</td></tr>
<tr><td>Biomass</td><td>Biofuels (specially grown crops or organic waste products) are burnt. The heat released turns water to steam – this turns turbines.</td><td></td><td></td><td>Uses waste products (fuel costs are low).
Carbon neutral (no overall increase in CO_2 as the amount released by burning is absorbed by growing the biofuel).</td><td>Visual and noise pollution.
In some countries land need for food is used to grow biofuels instead.</td></tr>
</table>

Questions
Generating power

Working to Grade E

1 Read the statements below. Highlight the ones that are **true** and re-write corrected versions of the statements that are **false**.

- **a** Nuclear power is a form of renewable energy.
- **b** In thermal power stations heat is used to turn water to steam; this steam turns turbines, which turn generators to generate electricity.
- **c** Non-renewable energy resources use fuels that will never run out.
- **d** Solar power is very useful in remote locations.
- **e** A hydroelectric power station has a long start-up time.
- **f** Natural gas produces more carbon dioxide than other fossil fuels.

2 Draw lines to match each renewable energy resource to its description.

Energy resource	Brief description
wind	The up-and-down motion of the sea is transferred into electrical energy.
wave	Biofuels are burnt; the heat is used to turn water to steam.
tidal	Large dams are built across river valleys.
hydroelectric power	Wind is used to turn large turbines.
geothermal	Hot rocks turn water to steam – this is used to turn turbines.
biomass	This may include tidal lagoons or larger tidal barrages.
solar (cells)	Energy from the Sun is transferred into electrical energy.

3 Give two ways in which electricity may be distributed through the National Grid.

4 List three examples of non-renewable energy resources.

Working to Grade C

5 Using the word **increases** or **decreases**, complete the sentences on transformers below:

- **a** A step-up transformer ________ the voltage. This ________ the current.
- **b** Transmitting electrical energy at high voltages ________ the amount of energy wasted, as the current is lower so the wires do not get as hot.
- **c** A step-down transformer ________ the voltage, making it safer for use in the home.
- **d** A step-down transformer ________ the current.

6 Sort the following methods of generating electricity in order of start-up time (from the longest start-up time to the shortest).

coal	natural gas	HEP	nuclear

7 Describe how electricity is generated in a nuclear power station.

8 Outline the advantages and disadvantages of using wave power and tidal power to generate electricity.

9 Draw a labelled diagram to show how carbon-capture technology may be used in the future.

10 The chart below shows how demand for electrical energy varies over the course of a typical day.

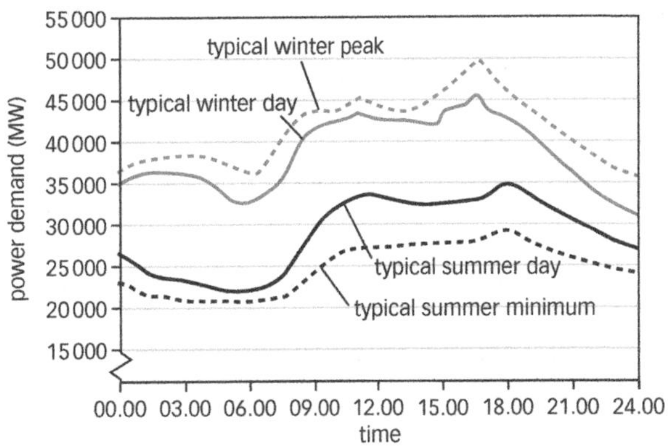

- **a** Explain the differences in demand between a typical summer day and a typical winter day.
- **b** Suggest why there is an increase in demand at around:
  - **i** 08.30
  - **ii** 17.00

Examination questions
Generating power

1 There are many different types of thermal power station. They all generate electricity in a similar way.

a The following statements outline the process of electricity generation in thermal power plants. Sort them into order from first to last.

A	The steam turns a turbine.
B	The turbine turns a generator.
C	Water is heated, turning to steam.
D	The generator transfers kinetic energy into electrical energy.

First .... Last

(2 marks)

b **i** Explain the meaning of the term 'start-up time'.

....

(1 mark)

ii Along with coal-fired and oil-fired power stations, which other non-renewable energy resource has a long start-up time?

....

(1 mark)

c Explain how pumped storage stations are used to ensure the supply of electricity always matches demand.

....

....

....

....

....

(3 marks)

(Total marks: 7)

2 The National Grid is used to transmit electricity energy from power stations to homes and businesses all over the country.

a Use words from the box below to complete the sentences that follow.

Each word may be used once, more than once, or not at all.

step-up	**energy**	**step-down**	**voltage**	**current**

Electricity is transmitted through the National Grid at very high voltages. A .... transformer increases the .... and reduces the .... The lower .... means less .... is lost in transmission as the wires do not get as hot.

(5 marks)

b The National Grid is made from wires that are either suspended by pylons or buried underground. Give **two** disadvantages of burying cables underground to transmit electrical energy.

1 ....

2 ....

(2 marks)

(Total marks: 7)

3 In this question you will be assessed on using good English, organising information clearly, and using specialist terms where appropriate.

Describe the advantages and disadvantages of using wind power to generate electricity.

....

....

....

....

....

....

....

....

(Total marks: 6)

16: Introduction to waves

Revision objectives

- know that waves transfer energy but not matter
- describe the two different types of wave and give examples of each
- explain the meaning of the terms 'wavelength', 'frequency', and 'amplitude'

Student book references

1.24 Waves all around us
1.25 Transverse and longitudinal waves

Specification key

✔ P1.5.1 a, b, c, f and j

What are waves?

Waves are a series of **vibrations** or **oscillations**. They are around us all the time.

There are many different types of wave but all *transfer energy* from one place to another.

Types of wave

There are two main types of wave:

- **transverse**
- **longitudinal.**

They both transfer energy but the oscillations that make up the waves are different.

Transverse waves

In transverse waves the oscillations are at right angles to the direction of energy transfer.

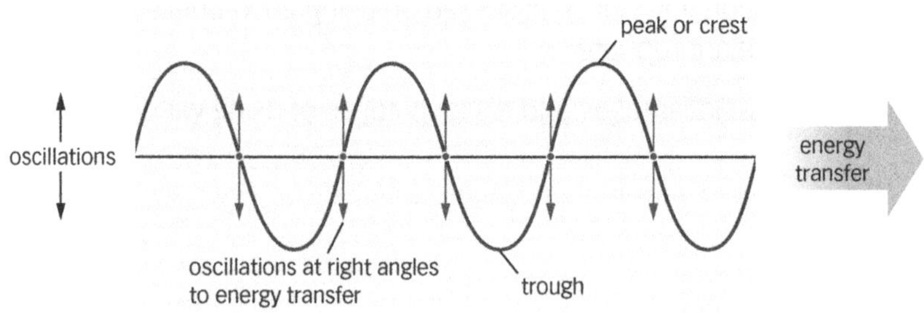

▲ A transverse wave.

Transverse waves look like ripples on water. They are made up of a number of *peaks* and *troughs*.

Examples of transverse waves include:

- light (all electromagnetic waves: radio, microwaves, infrared radiation, ultraviolet radiation, X-rays, gamma rays)
- some mechanical waves on springs or strings.

Exam tip

AQA

Remember, the amplitude of a wave is always measured to the middle of the wave (not from the peak to the trough).

Longitudinal waves

In longitudinal waves the oscillations are parallel to the direction of energy transfer.

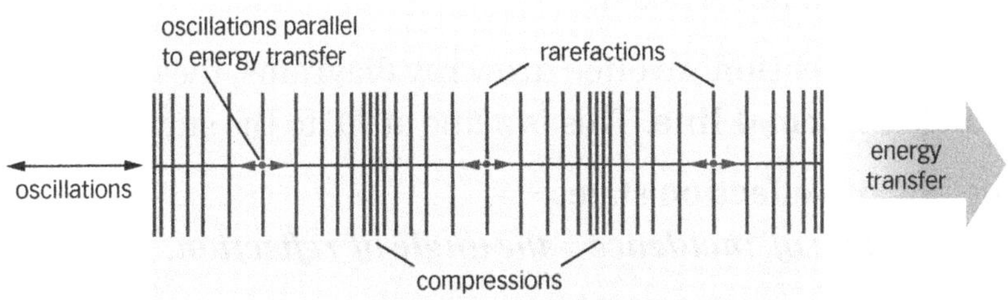

▲ A longitudinal wave.

A longitudinal wave is made up of **compressions** (where the particles are bunched up, closer together) and **rarefactions** (where the particles are further apart).

Examples of longitudinal waves include:

- sound
- some mechanical waves on springs.

Wave properties

Amplitude (in metres, m)	maximum height of the wave, measured from the middle of the wave
Wavelength (in metres, m)	the distance from one peak to the next
Frequency (in hertz, Hz)	the number of peaks passing a point per second

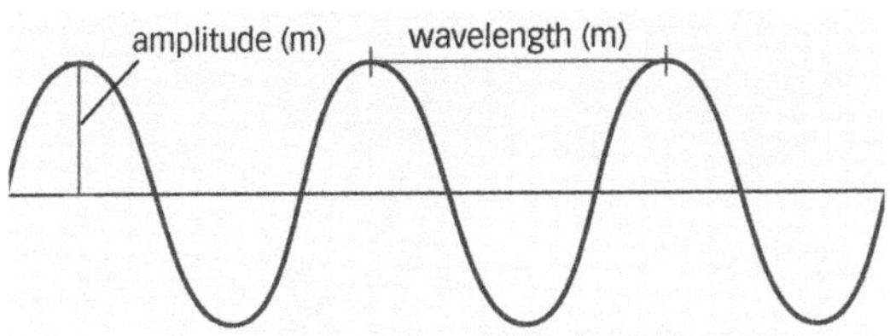

▲ Key features of a wave.

Questions

1 Describe the differences between transverse and longitudinal waves and give an example of each.

2 Draw a labelled diagram to show the wavelength and amplitude of a water wave.

3 If 30 wave peaks pass a point in 1 minute, what is the frequency of the wave?

Key words

vibration, oscillation, transverse, longitudinal, compression, rarefaction, amplitude, wavelength, frequency

17: Wave experiments

Revision objectives

- describe how waves can be reflected, refracted and diffracted
- know the law of reflection

Student book references

1.26 Experiments with waves

Specification key

- ✔ P1.5.1 g and h
- ✔ P1.5.2

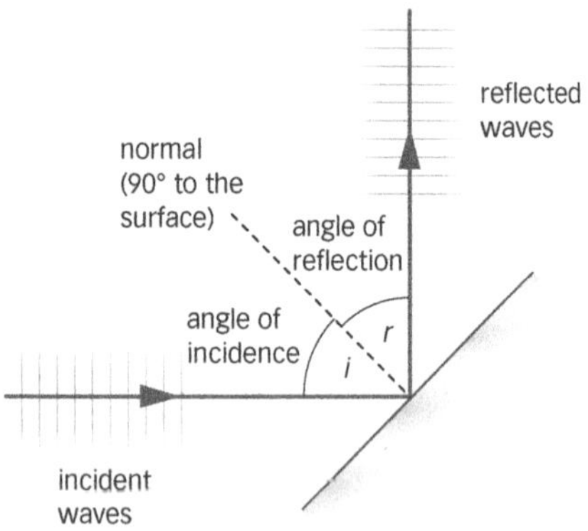

▲ Reflection of a wave.

Exam tip

AQA

Practise drawing diagrams for reflection, refraction, and diffraction. Make sure you can label the key features.

Reflection

When waves bounce off a surface they are said to be reflected. All waves can be reflected.

To draw **reflection** we often draw ray diagrams, these always include a **normal line**. This is a line at 90° to the surface.

The **law of reflection** states:

- *The **angle of incidence** = the **angle of reflection**.*

Refraction

When waves travel from one **medium** to another they can be refracted.

If the speed of the wave changes, the wave changes direction. This is called **refraction**.

Light can be refracted when it passes from air into a glass block. Light travels slower in the glass so the ray bends towards the normal.

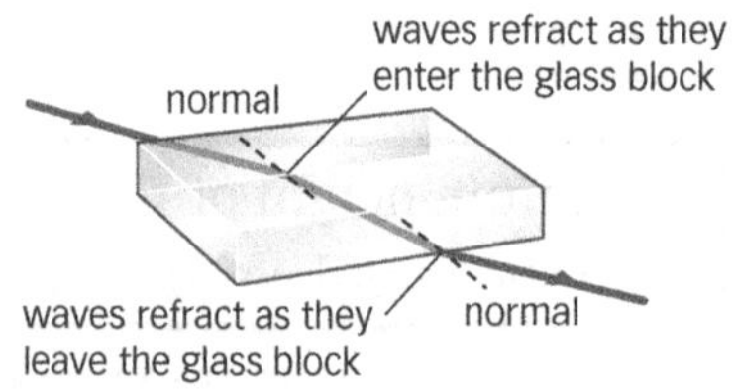

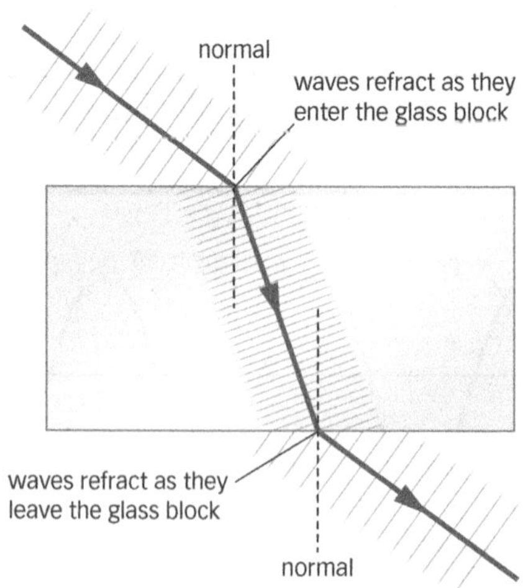

▲ Waves can be refracted.

If the wave travels along the normal then no refraction takes place.

All waves can be refracted, including sound.

Diffraction

When waves pass through a gap or around an obstacle they spread out. This is called **diffraction**.

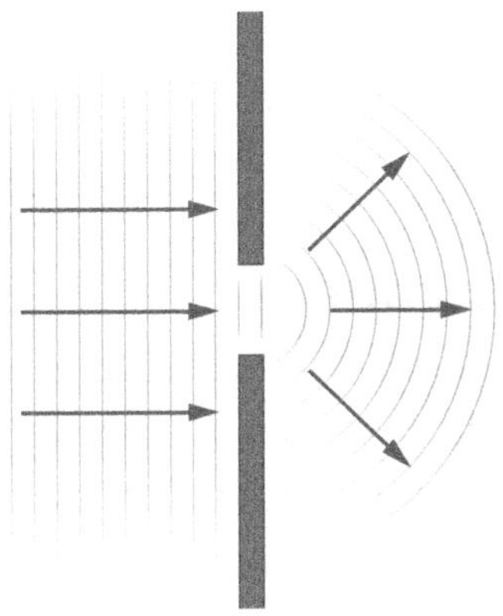

As the wave goes through the gap it spreads out.

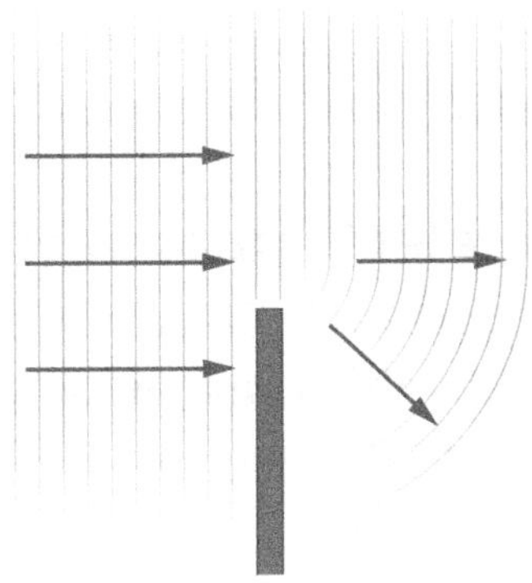

The same thing happens if it goes around an obstacle.

▲ Waves are diffracted when they pass through gaps and around obstacles.

Key words

reflection, normal line, law of reflection, angle of incidence, angle of reflection, medium, refraction, diffraction

There is a significant amount of diffraction when the wavelength of the wave is the same size as the gap.

To diffract light a tiny gap is needed (its wavelength is very small). Sound diffracts well through open doors because it has a wavelength that is bigger than the doorway. This allows you to hear what's going on outside without necessarily seeing it.

Questions

1 What is meant by the law of reflection?

2 a Draw a diagram to show light being refracted through a glass block.

b Describe what happens if the light enters the glass block along the normal line.

3 Describe what is meant by diffraction and state the conditions required for significant diffraction to take place.

18: The electromagnetic spectrum

Revision objectives

- list the order of the electromagnetic spectrum in terms of frequency, energy or wavelength
- describe the properties of electromagnetic waves
- give examples of how some electromagnetic waves are used in communications

Student book references

1.27 The electromagnetic spectrum

1.28 Communications and optics

Specification key

- P1.5.1 d and e

Exam tip

AQA

- Make sure you can list all seven electromagnetic waves in order of frequency, energy, and wavelength.
- Remember, despite having different frequencies, energies, and wavelengths, all electromagnetic waves travel at the *same speed* through a vacuum.

Electromagnetic waves

Electromagnetic (EM) waves are a special kind of transverse wave. Unlike other waves they don't need particles; they can travel through a **vacuum** like space.

Light is an example of an electromagnetic wave. It travels through space from the Sun to the Earth.

The electromagnetic spectrum

There are seven different electromagnetic waves that together form the **electromagnetic spectrum**. They can all travel through a vacuum but they have different frequencies and wavelengths.

Radio waves are the EM waves with the longest wavelength (lowest frequency). They can have wavelengths over 10 km.

Gamma waves are at the other end of the spectrum. They have the highest frequency and the shortest wavelength (down to 10^{-15} m).

Electromagnetic waves form a continuous (there are no gaps) spectrum. Radio waves are at one end and gamma waves are at the other.

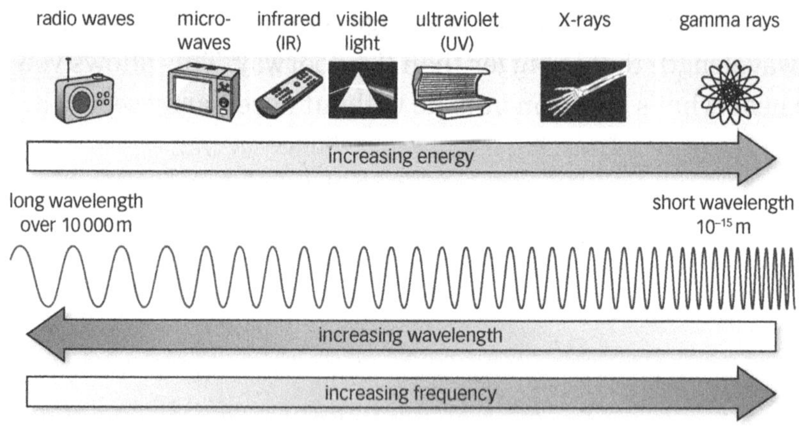

▲ The electromagnetic spectrum.

The higher the frequency, the higher the energy, so radio waves have the lowest energy and gamma rays the most.

Our eyes can only detect visible light, but other sensors can detect the other parts of the spectrum.

All electromagnetic waves travel at the same speed through a vacuum. This is the speed of light (300 000 000 m/s).

Electromagnetic waves and communication

As electromagnetic waves travel so fast they are very useful for communication. There are some examples listed below:

Radio waves	TV, radio, and wireless communications
Microwaves	mobile phones and satellite TV
Infrared	remote controls and some cable Internet connections
Visible light	photography and some cable Internet connections

The radio waves used for radio stations have a longer wavelength than those used for TV signals. This means they *diffract* more than TV signals. This allows radio signals to be picked up in places where TV signals can't reach, for example, at the bottom of some valleys.

Mobile phones and microwaves

Mobile phones are very useful for communication and can be especially helpful in emergencies.

All mobile phones use microwaves to send and receive information. Some people are concerned about the effect they have on the body. Research has shown they have a small heating effect on living tissue.

Scientists are not sure whether this is a serious health risk and if it will cause any long-term damage. There is no clear evidence either way; people must balance the possible risks of using mobile phones with the benefits.

Key words

electromagnetic wave, vacuum, electromagnetic spectrum

Questions

1 List the electromagnetic spectrum from shortest wavelength to longest wavelength.

2 Give an example of how radio waves might be used for communication.

3 Describe the possible risks in using a mobile phone.

4 **H** Give an example for a typical wavelength of radio wave and a gamma ray.

Revision objectives

- explain and use the wave equation $v = f \times \lambda$

Student book references

1.24 Waves all around us

Specification key

- P1.5.1 i

Exam tip (AQA)

When using the wave equation, frequency must be measured in hertz (Hz) and wavelength in metres (m).

Key words

speed, frequency, wavelength

The wave equation

The **speed** of a wave, its **frequency**, and its **wavelength** are all linked together in the wave equation:

v	=	f	×	λ
wave speed	=	frequency	×	wavelength
(metres per second, m/s)		(hertz, Hz)		(metres, m)

For example, if a sound wave has a frequency of 6600 Hz and a wavelength of 0.05 m, we can find its speed.

$v = f \times \lambda$

$v = 6600\,\text{Hz} \times 0.05\,\text{m}$

$v = 330\,\text{m/s}$

H Electromagnetic waves

The wave equation can be used with all types of wave, including electromagnetic waves.

All electromagnetic waves travel at the same speed through a vacuum: 300 000 000 m/s.

We can use the wave equation to find the frequency of a radio wave that has a wavelength of 200 m.

$v = f \times \lambda$ so $f = v/\lambda$

$f = v/\lambda$

$$f = \frac{300\,000\,000\,\text{m/s}}{200\,\text{m}}$$

$f = 1\,500\,000$ Hz or 1.5 MHz

Questions

1 Calculate the wave speeds of the following waves:

a water wave with a frequency of 0.5 Hz and a wavelength of 4 m

b sound wave with a wavelength of 60 cm and a frequency of 500 Hz

c wave with a frequency of 1.2 kHz and a wavelength of 80 cm

2 **H** Calculate the wavelength of an electromagnetic wave with a frequency of 3×10^{10} Hz.

Reflection and images

When light is reflected off a mirror is must obey the **law of reflection**.

- *The **angle of incidence** = the **angle of reflection**.*

We see objects because the light they give off, or the light reflected off them, enters our eyes.

When we look into a mirror we see an image of ourselves. This image is formed by the light reflecting off the mirror. These images have three key properties:

Upright	The image is the right way up.
Laterally inverted	The image is flipped around horizontally.
Virtual	The image is not really there; it can't be projected onto a screen.

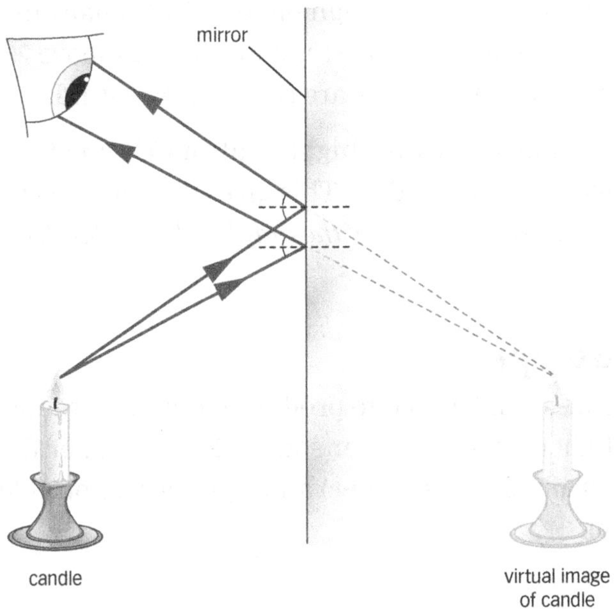

▲ A plane mirror produces an upright, laterally inverted, virtual image.

Revision objectives

- ✓ describe the properties of an image formed inside a plane mirror

Student book references

1.28 Communications and optics

Specification key

✓ P1.5.2

Exam tip AQA

On ray diagrams, remember that all angles are measured to the **normal** line.

Questions

1 Explain why the word FIRE is written backwards on the front of fire engines.

2 Describe the three key properties of an image formed behind a mirror.

3 Draw a diagram to show how an image is formed inside a plane mirror.

Key words

normal, law of reflection, angle of incidence, angle of reflection, upright, laterally inverted, virtual

21: Sound

Revision objectives

- describe the key features of sound waves
- relate the pitch of a sound to its frequency and its loudness to its amplitude
- know that echoes are reflections of sound

Student book references

1.29 Sound waves

Specification key

- P1.5.3

Sound waves

Sound waves are produced whenever an object *vibrates*. These vibrations cause neighbouring air particles to vibrate and the sound waves travel through the air.

Sound waves are *longitudinal waves*. The oscillations are parallel to the direction of energy transfer.

Like all waves, sound waves can be reflected, refracted, and diffracted. A reflection of a sound wave is called an **echo**.

Pitch and volume

If an object vibrates faster it will create more sound waves per second. This creates a sound wave with a higher frequency; it sounds higher in **pitch**. *The higher the frequency, the higher the pitch.*

Some sound waves are too high pitched for humans to hear. They have a frequency above human hearing (above 20 000 Hz). These kinds of sound waves are called **ultrasound**.

A louder sound (one with a higher **volume**) is created when the particles vibrate further. This gives the sound wave a larger amplitude. *The larger the amplitude, the louder the sound.*

Oscilloscopes

Oscilloscopes can be used to produce pictures of sound waves. Higher-pitched, louder sounds have a higher frequency (the waves are closer together) and a greater amplitude (they are taller).

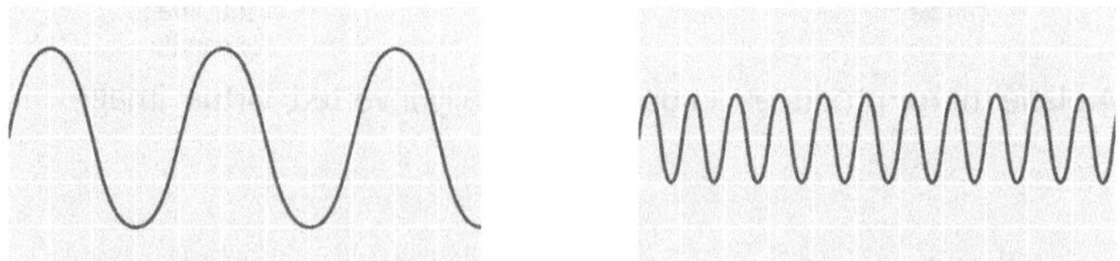

a low-pitch, low-frequency, loud sound

a higher-pitch, higher-frequency, quiet sound

▲ Different sound waves shown on an oscilloscope.

Key words

sound waves, echo, pitch, ultrasound, volume

Questions

1 Describe how a sound wave is formed.

2 Describe how the pitch of a sound is affected by its frequency.

3 Draw diagrams to show two sound waves of the same pitch, but with different volumes.

22: Wave sources and the Doppler effect

Wave sources

Any object that emits a wave can be described as a **wave source**.

Type of wave	Examples of wave sources
sound	speaker, police siren, car engine
light	lightbulb, galaxy
microwaves	satellite, microwave oven

The Doppler effect

When a wave source moves this affects the frequency and wavelength of the wave detected by stationary observers. This is called the **Doppler effect**.

- When the wave source moves *away* from the observer, the waves get stretched out. The wavelength *increases* and the frequency *decreases*.
- When the wave source moves *towards* the observer the waves get all bunched up. The wavelength *decreases* and the frequency *increases*.

This effect can be heard when race cars or police sirens move past an observer. The sound appears higher pitched when the car is moving towards the observer and lower pitched when it has gone past.

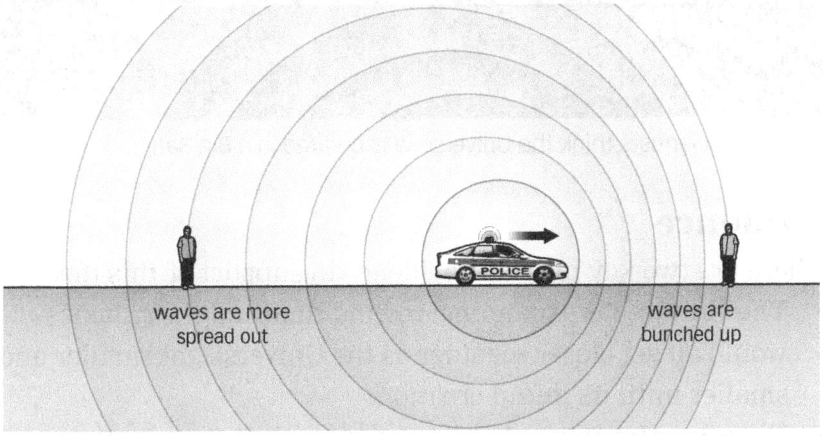

▲ The Doppler effect can be heard when a police car passes by with its siren sounding.

Revision objectives

✓ describe the Doppler effect

Student book references

1.30 The Doppler effect

Specification key

✓ P1.5.4 a

Key words

wave source, Doppler effect

Questions

1 Give an example of a wave source for light, sound, and microwaves.

2 Explain why a race car makes the distinctive 'neeee-awwww' sound when it races passed a stationary observer.

Revision objectives

- describe the key features of the Big Bang theory
- outline the evidence for the Big Bang theory, including red-shift/expanding Universe and cosmic microwave background radiation (CMBR)

Student book references

1.31 Red-shift
1.32 The Big Bang theory

Specification key

✔ P1.5.4 b – e

Exam tip AQA

Make sure you can explain *how* observations of red-shift lead to the idea of an expanding Universe.

The Big Bang theory

The **Big Bang theory** is the current scientific description for the origin of the Universe. It states:

- The Universe began around 14 billion years ago.
- The Universe started from a very small, incredibly hot initial point.
- The Universe then exploded outwards and has been expanding ever since.

▲ Most scientists think the Universe was created in a Big Bang.

Evidence

There are two key pieces of evidence in support of this theory:

- The Universe is expanding: rewind time and the galaxies would all get closer together as the Universe got smaller and smaller until its initial creation.
- **Cosmic microwave background radiation**: scientists are able to detect the heat left over from the Big Bang.

The expanding Universe and red-shift

Scientists use the Doppler effect applied to light to show the Universe is expanding.

When galaxies move away from us the light they emit is stretched: its wavelength increases. As red has the longest wavelength of all the colours this effect is called **red-shift**.

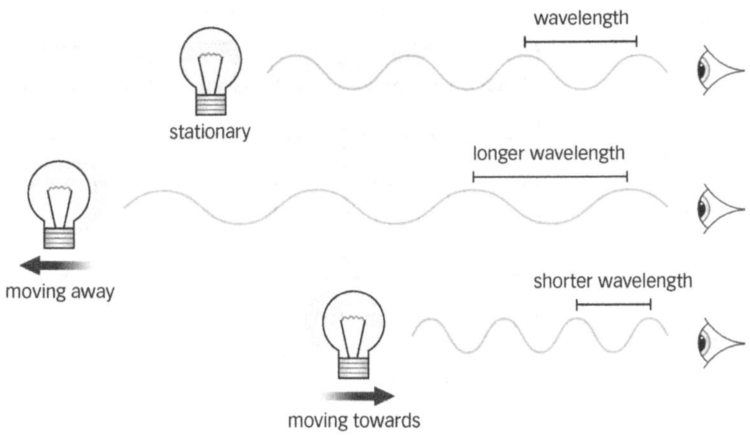

▲ The wavelength of light changes, depending on the motion of the source.

When you look at the light from distant galaxies there are two key observations:

- Most galaxies show a red-shift – they are moving away from us.
- The further a galaxy is away, the greater the red-shift – the faster it is moving.

These two observations allow scientists to conclude that the Universe is expanding.

Cosmic microwave background radiation

The second key piece of evidence is cosmic microwave background radiation (CMBR).

Cosmic microwave background radiation is a form of radiation that fills the entire Universe; it is the same everywhere you look. It is the 'heat' left over from the Big Bang. As the Universe expanded, it cooled. This initial heat is now in the microwave part of the electromagnetic spectrum.

The Big Bang theory is currently the only theory that can explain the existence of the cosmic microwave background radiation.

Key words

red-shift, Big Bang theory, cosmic microwave background radiation

Questions

1 Describe the key features of the Big Bang theory.

2 Explain how the observation of red-shift supports the idea of a Big Bang.

3 What is meant by cosmic microwave background radiation and why is it important to the Big Bang theory?

Questions
Waves

Working to Grade E

1 In each sentence below, highlight the correct **bold**.
- a Waves transfer **matter/energy** from one place to another.
- b Light is an example of a **transverse/longitudinal** wave.
- c The law of reflection states the angle of incidence is equal to the angle of **refraction/reflection**.
- d Radio waves have the **shortest/longest** wavelength of all electromagnetic waves.
- e Gamma rays have the **most/least** energy of all electromagnetic waves.
- f **Infrared/microwaves** are used by most TV remote controls.
- g The higher the pitch of a sound the **higher/lower** its frequency.
- h Most galaxies are moving **towards/away** from us.

2 List all seven types of electromagnetic waves, from highest frequency to the lowest frequency.

3 Draw a labelled diagram to show how a single ray of light is reflected off a plane mirror. Your diagram should include the following labels:
- a ray of incidence
- b angle of incidence
- c normal
- d ray of reflection
- e angle of reflection

4 Electromagnetic waves are useful for communications. Name one example of how the following might be used in communications:
- a radio waves
- b microwaves
- c infrared
- d visible light

5 Highlight the statements below that are **true**. Write corrected versions of the statements that are **false**.
- a Gamma rays have a higher frequency than radio waves.
- b Gamma rays travel faster through a vacuum than radio waves.
- c When waves spread out as they pass through a gap this is called refraction.
- d The best diffraction occurs when the wavelength of the wave is the same size as the gap.
- e The amplitude of a wave is the height of the wave from the top of the peak to the bottom of the trough.
- f Sound waves are examples of transverse waves.
- g A reflection of sound is called an echo.
- h A louder sound has a smaller amplitude.
- i When a sound source moves towards you the wavelength decreases.
- j The light emitted by distant galaxies is stretched as they move away from us. This is called blue-shift.

6 Use wave equation below to find the speed of the following waves:

wave speed = frequency × wavelength

Wave speed	Frequency	Wavelength
	1000 Hz	2 m
	3.2 kHz	0.5 m
	300 Hz	40 cm
	0.9 kHz	12 cm

7 Write definitions for the following wave terms:
- a wavelength
- b frequency
- c amplitude

8 Match the following terms describing the image formed by a plane mirror.

Upright	The image cannot be projected onto a screen.
Laterally inverted	The image is the right way up.
Virtual	The image is flipped around horizontally.

9 Name two pieces of evidence in support of the Big Bang theory.

Working to Grade C

10 Copy and complete the following sentences about the Big Bang theory.
- a The Universe began about 14 ________ years ago.
- b It started from a very________, very hot, very dense initial point.
- c It then ________ outwards and has been ________ ever since.

11 Classify the following waves as either transverse, longitudinal, or could be either.

sound	radio waves	mechanical waves on springs
light	infrared	water waves
X-rays	microwaves	gamma rays

12 Draw a labelled diagram of a transverse wave. Your diagram should include the following labels:
  a amplitude
  b wavelength.

13 Draw a labelled diagram of a longitudinal wave. Your diagram should include the following labels:
  a compression
  b rarefaction
  c wavelength.

14 Explain why sound diffracts through an open doorway but light does not.

15 Complete the following sentences about the Doppler Effect. Your answers should include the following terms: wavelength, frequency, increases, and decreases.
  a When a wave source moves towards an observer ________
  b When a wave source moves away from an observer ________

Working to Grade A*

16 Use your answer above to explain why the engine noise from a race car appears to change pitch as it races past a stationary observer.

17 Using the terms in the box below describe the two different sounds as shown on an oscilloscope screen. You may use the terms more than once.

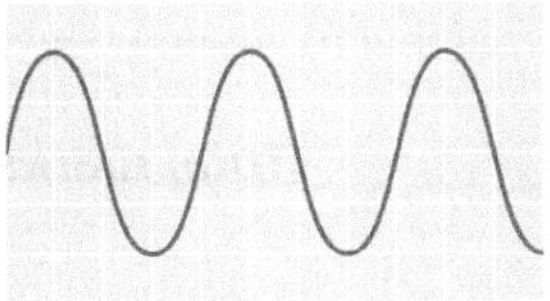

a low pitch, low frequency, loud sound

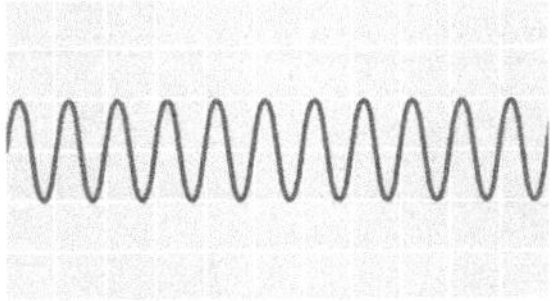

a higher pitch, higher frequency, quieter sound

pitch frequency loud quiet higher lower amplitude

18 In terms of vibrations, describe the differences between transverse and longitudinal waves.

19 Complete the following sentences on sound waves.
  a A sound wave is produced whenever an object ________
  b These ________ cause neighbouring particles to ________
  c Sound waves are examples of ________ waves, so these ________ are ________ to the direction of energy transfer.

20 Draw a diagram showing how radio waves are diffracted as they pass over a hill (an obstacle). Use your diagram to explain why it may be possible to receive a radio signal behind the hill but not a mobile phone signal.

21 Complete the table below using the wave equation.

wave speed = frequency × wavelength

Wave speed (m/s)	Frequency (Hz)	Wavelength (m)
3500	75	
340		0.2
12000		60
3×10^8	150000000	

Examination questions
Waves

1 This question is about waves.

a What do all waves transfer from one place to another?

....

(1 mark)

b Draw straight lines to link each term to its description.

Term
amplitude
wavelength
frequency

Description
the number of peaks passing a point per second
the minimum distance from one peak to another
the maximum height of the wave, from the middle to the peak

(3 marks)

c **i** Describe the oscillations in a transverse wave.

....

....

(2 marks)

ii Give **two** examples of transverse waves.

1 ....

2 ....

(2 marks)

(Total marks: 8)

2 **a** Complete the sentences on reflection below.

When waves bounce off surfaces this is called reflection. The law of reflection states that the angle of .... is equal to the angle of .... All angles are measured to the .... line.

(3 marks)

b **i** Complete the diagrams below to show how waves are diffracted when they pass through gaps of different sizes.

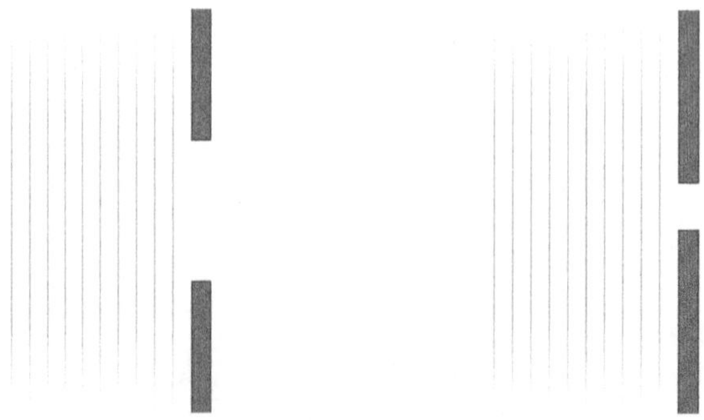

(3 marks)

ii Under what conditions does significant diffraction occur?

....

....

(1 mark)

(Total marks: 7)

3 A flute produces a note with a frequency of 1.2 kHz and a wavelength of 30 cm.

a Calculate the speed of sound and give the unit.

wave speed = frequency × wavelength

....

....

Wave speed ....

(3 marks)

b The flute is used to play the same note at the same volume whilst on a train moving towards a stationary observer.

What effect, if any, does this have on the amplitude and wavelength of the sound heard by the observer in front of the train?

Amplitude: ....

Wavelength: ....

(2 marks)

(Total marks: 5)

4 In this question you will be assessed on using good English, organising information clearly, and using specialist terms where appropriate.

Describe the **two** key pieces of evidence for the Big Bang theory of the origin of the Universe.

....

....

....

....

....

....

....

(6 marks)

(Total marks: 6)

Law of reflection

There are a number of key terms you must be familiar with when discussing any scientific investigation.

In terms of experimental data you might be asked whether it is:

- **Accurate** – meaning close to the true value.
- **Precise** – meaning there is very little spread around the average (mean) value.
- **Repeatable** – meaning that if the experiment was completed again it would produce the same results.
- **Reproducible** – meaning if the investigation was completed by another person or using a different method (different equipment or techniques) it would produce the same results.

The exam might include questions about data collected as part of an investigation. Any investigation will contain errors (or uncertainties). They could be caused by tiny differences in the experiment or limitations caused by things like the resolution of the scale on the equipment, or human errors in things like timings. An experimental error will affect the data collected, moving it away from the true value, reducing its accuracy. There are three types of error:

Random errors	These cause results to be spread above and below the true value. They are unpredictable and cannot be corrected. Repeating measurements and taking an average can reduce the effects of random errors.
Systematic errors	These cause results to differ from the true value by a consistent amount (either always above or always below the true value). Repeating measurements and taking an average does not reduce the effects of systematic errors; instead a different piece of equipment or an alternative technique should be used.
Zero errors	This is an example of a systematic error and it occurs when a piece of equipment does not give a value of zero when it should, for example, if a voltmeter reads 0.2 V when it should read 0 V. All results will be 0.2 V too high. To correct for zero errors, the zero value should be added or subtracted from each reading.

A student investigates how the angle of reflection varies when a ray of light is reflected off a mirror at different angles of incidence.

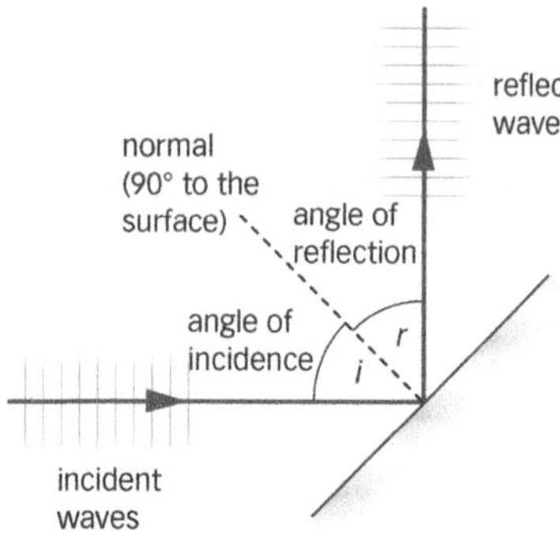

Angle of incidence (°)	Angle of reflection (°)			
	1	2	3	Average
15	15	14	16	15
30	30	35	29	
45	45	45	45	
60	62	65	62	
75	69	75	76	

The law of reflection states:

angle of incidence = angle of reflection

1 Complete the table by calculating the averages (give your answer to the nearest whole degree).

2 Plot an appropriate graph of angle of incidence against the average angle of reflection. Explain whether or not the data supports the law of reflection.

3 Discuss whether or not you think the results are:
  a accurate
  b precise
  c repeatable
  d reproducible

4 a What type of error causes the readings to vary in an unpredictable way (both above and below the true value)?
  b Name two possible sources of error in this investigation.

5 Another student conducted the same experiment but they drew their normal line incorrectly – it was not at 90° to the surface of the mirror. What type of error would this introduce into the results?

6 Explain why it is important for the data produced by a company selling products to be reproducible by independent scientists.

AQA Upgrade

Answering a question with data response

QUESTION

In the UK, electricity is generated using a mixture of renewable and non-renewable energy resources.

1 What does the term 'renewable energy resource' mean? *(1 mark)*

2 These piecharts show the relative proportion of electricity generated from different energy sources.

Describe the key changes from 1970 to 2010. *(3 marks)*

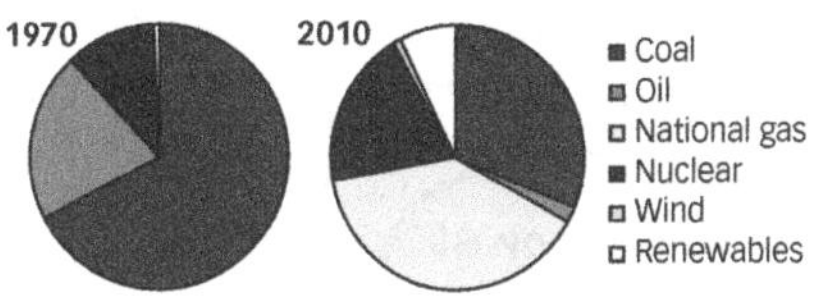

3 The changes in the proportion of different energy sources have altered the risk from manmade global warming. Explain, as fully as you can, how this has changed. *(3 marks)*

G–E

1 It will run out.
2 The sources used have changed. There is now more natural gas.
3 Global warming is caused by sulfur dioxide and this has changed.

Examiner: The candidate has confused non-renewable with renewable. No mark is awarded.

The answer is very vague. The candidate only mentions one energy resource. However, one mark may be awarded as they have noticed the increase in natural gas.

The candidate incorrectly links sulfur dioxide to manmade global warming. No marks are awarded.

D–C

1 You can use it again and again. It will not run out.
2 The amount from coal has dropped. The amount from natural gas has increased a lot.
3 Global warming is caused by the release of CO_2. Less coal is burnt so the amount of CO_2 released has gone down. This reduces the risk.

Examiner: The answer given is not very clear, although it may be awarded a mark. Renewable energy resources can be used again and again as they do not use a fuel which will run out.

Both points are correct and so two marks may be awarded. However, the candidate has not discussed any of the other energy resources. They need to mention all of them to gain all the marks.

The candidate has got a mark for recognising that manmade global warming is due to the release of CO_2 and that this may have dropped as a lower proportion of our electricity comes from burning coal. However, they have not discussed that it has been replaced by energy resources that either do not produce CO_2 (nuclear, wind, and renewables,) or produce less CO_2 (natural gas).

B–A*

1 This type of energy resource does not use a fuel that will run out.
2 There has been an increase in the proportion of electricity generated from wind, other renewables, nuclear and natural gas. There has been a decline in coal and a significant drop in oil.
3 The risk from manmade global warming may have been reduced as a smaller proportion of the electricity comes from burning coal or oil. These both produce large quantities of CO_2. In their place we now use more nuclear, wind, and other renewables, which do not produce CO_2. We also use more natural gas, which produces less CO_2 than coal and oil.

Examiner: Good clear answer.

An excellent answer. Each energy resource is mentioned.

The student has given a clear answer to the question. They clearly identify that the proportion of electricity from sources producing lots of CO_2 has dropped. They have also made it clear that although natural gas does produce CO_2, it is less than other fossil fuels.

Part 2 Course catch-up
Electrical energy and waves

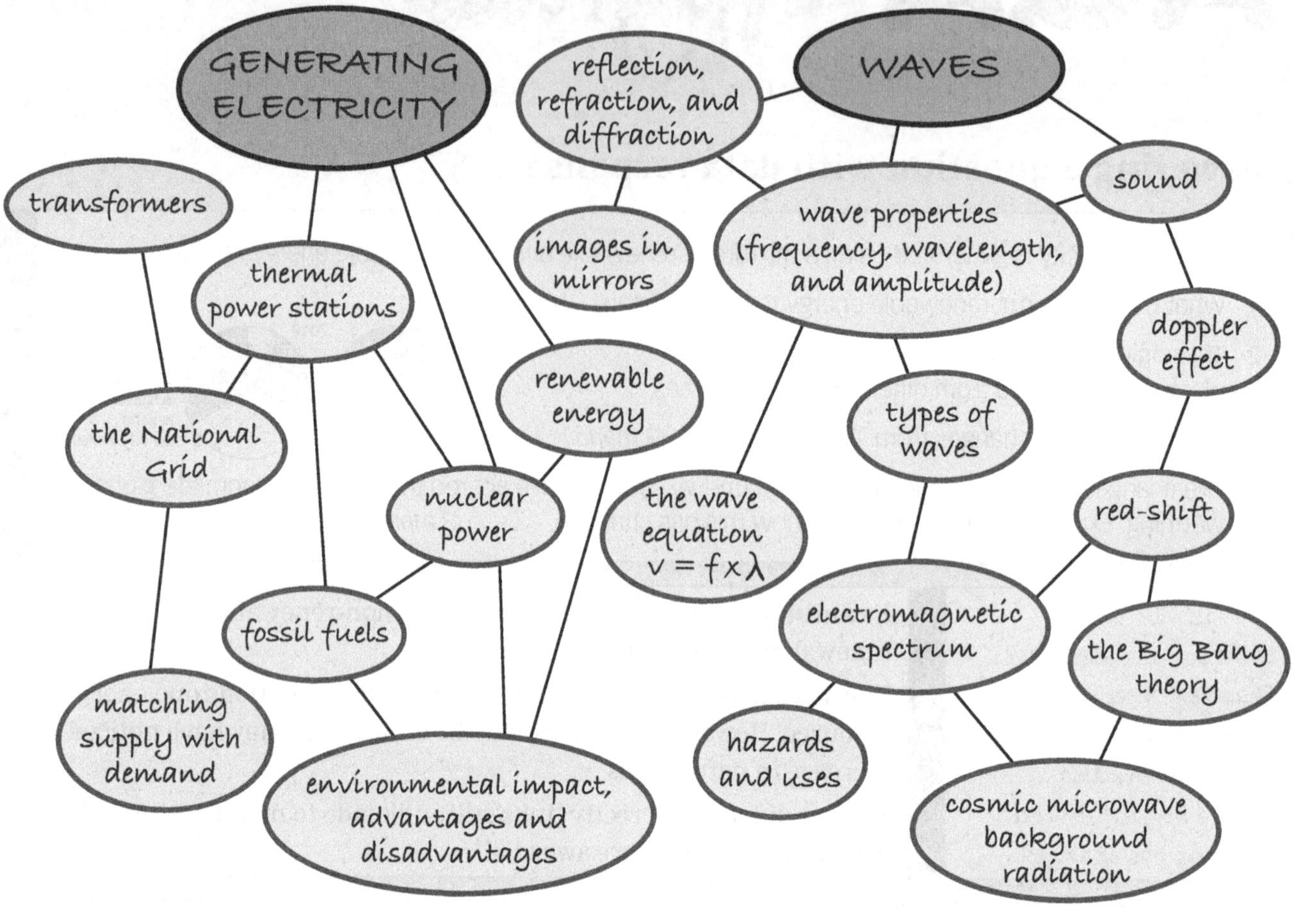

Revision checklist

- In thermal power stations heat is used to turn water to steam. This turns a turbine, which turns a generator to generate electricity.
- Different power stations have different start-up times. Nuclear and coal have the longest, HEP and natural gas have the shortest.
- Electricity is distributed using the National Grid. This connects power stations to homes and businesses.
- Transformers allow electricity to be transmitted at high voltages. This means a lower current can be used, the wires don't get as hot, and so less energy is wasted.
- Fossil fuels produce most of the electricity in the UK. They are a non-renewable energy resource (they will eventually run out).
- Nuclear power can be used to generate electricity. Inside nuclear reactors, nuclear fission takes place releasing heat.
- Renewables do not use a fuel that will run out. Examples include: wind, wave, tidal, solar, biomass, and geothermal.
- All methods of electricity generation offer a number of different advantages and disadvantages.
- Waves transfer energy. There are two types: transverse (oscillations at right angles to energy transfer, for example, light, radio waves, water waves) and longitudinal (oscillations parallel to energy transfer, for example, sound and some mechanical waves on springs). Longitudinal waves contain compressions and rarefactions.
- All waves have an amplitude, wavelength, and frequency.
- The wave equation states:
  wave speed = frequency × wavelength
- Waves can be reflected, refracted, and diffracted (significant diffraction: wavelength = size of gap).
- The law of reflection states:
  angle of incidence = the angle of reflection (measured from the normal line).
- Images formed in plane mirrors are virtual, upright, and laterally inverted.
- Electromagnetic waves can travel through a vacuum. The electromagnetic spectrum (from longest to shortest wavelength is: radio waves, microwaves, infrared, visible, ultraviolet, X-rays, and gamma rays.
- Electromagnetic waves can be used for communication.
- Sound is a longitudinal wave. High frequency means high pitch. Large amplitude means a loud sound. A reflection of sound is called an echo.
- The Doppler effect is the observed change in wavelength when a wave source moves towards or away from an observer. When the source moves towards an observer the wavelength reduces (waves are squashed up); when the source moves away the wavelength increases (waves are stretched out).
- The Big Bang theory states that around 14 billion years ago the Universe exploded from a very small, very hot initial point.
- Evidence includes red-shift (galaxies are moving away from us; the furthest away are moving faster – indicating that the Universe is expanding) and cosmic microwave background radiation (heat left over from the Big Bang).

Speed

The average **speed** of an object tells you how far it moves in a certain time. You calculate average speed with this equation:

$$\text{average speed (metres/second, m/s)} = \frac{\text{distance (metres, m)}}{\text{time (seconds, s)}}$$

So what is the average speed of a car that moves a distance of 180 m in a time of 12 s?

$$\text{average speed} = \frac{180\,\text{m}}{12\,\text{s}} = 15\,\text{m/s}$$

This is only an average speed because the car may be speeding up or slowing down at the time of measurement.

A **speed camera** takes two photographs of the car, 0.5 s apart. The car is moving at 20 m/s, so its position along the road changes by 20 m/s × 0.5 s = 10 m between the two photographs. The faster the car is moving, the further it goes between the photographs.

Velocity

The **velocity** of an object tells you two things:

- how fast it is moving
- the direction of its motion.

The two cars to the left have the same speed of 40 mph, but different velocities. The left car is moving to the right, the right car to the left. If you say that the left car has a velocity of +40 mph, then the right car has a velocity of –40 mph.

Distance–time graphs

Time (s)	Laps	Distance (m)
0	0	0
20	1	300
40	2	600

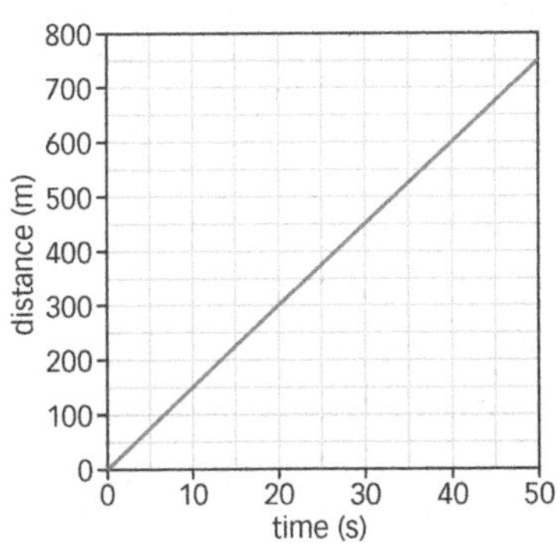

▲ Distance–time graph for a car using the data in the table.

Revision objectives

- ✔ calculate the speed of an object
- ✔ understand the difference between speed and velocity
- ✔ draw and interpret distance–time graphs
- ✔ calculate speed from a distance–time graph

Student book references

2.3 Speed and velocity
2.4 Distance–time graphs

Specification key

✔ P2.1.2 b – d

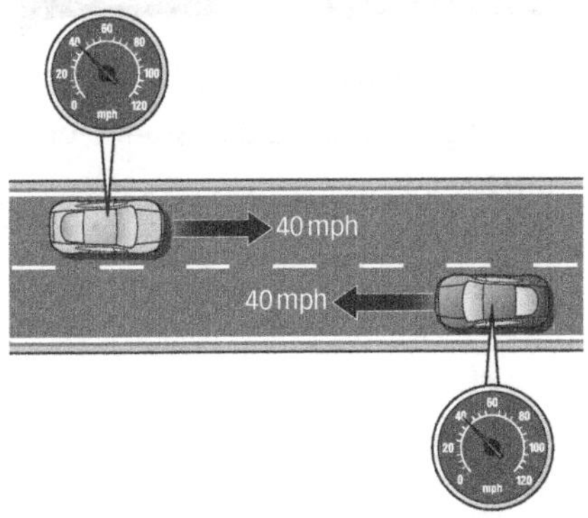

▲ Two cars with the same speed but a different velocity.

Key words

speed, speed camera, velocity, distance–time graph, gradient

A car is moving round and round a track at a steady speed. It has to move a distance of 300 m to get back to where it started. The table shows the reading on a stopwatch for two laps of the circuit. This information is presented as a **distance–time graph**, with time plotted on the x-axis. The car is going at a steady speed, so the graph is a straight line.

H Gradient

Here is how to use the **gradient** (or slope) of the graph to calculate the speed of the car.

- Take any pair of data points (x, y) from the graph: (10 s, 150 m) and (50 s, 750 m)
- Calculate the increase of distance: 750 m – 150 m = 600 m
- Calculate the increase in time: 50 s – 10 s = 40 s
- Calculate the gradient:

$$\text{gradient (speed)} = \frac{\text{increase of distance}}{\text{increase in time}}$$
$$= \frac{600\text{ m}}{40\text{ s}}$$
$$= 15\text{ m/s}$$

Exam tip AQA

Practise using the speed equation to calculate distance or time.

Questions

1 Joe runs a distance of 1200 m in 240 s. Calculate his average speed.

2 The three graphs below show how the distance of three cars from you changes with time.

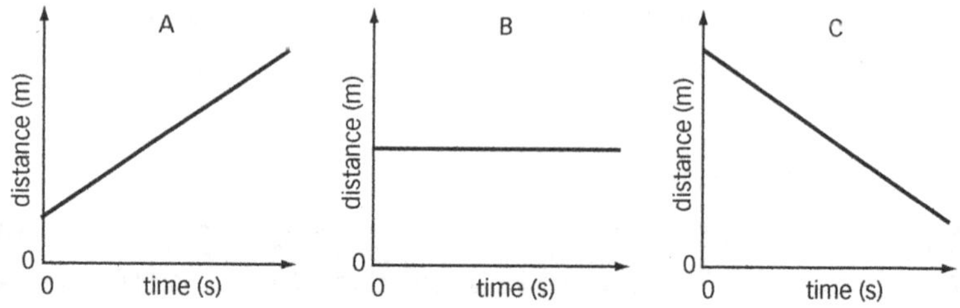

a Which car is not moving?

b Which car is moving towards you?

3 **H** Calculate the speed of runner P from the graph below.

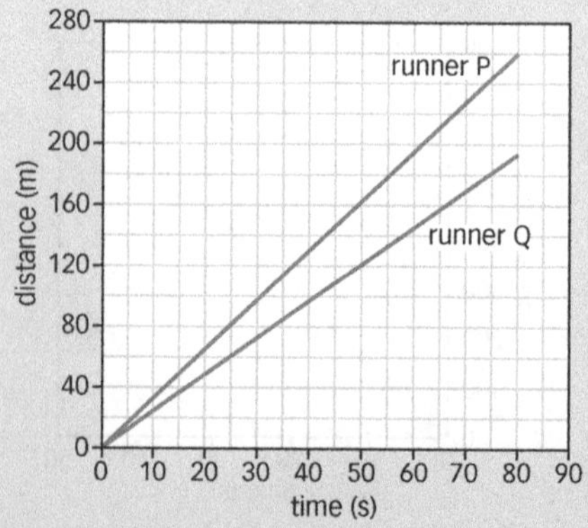

Changing speed

Below is the **velocity–time graph** for a car. This is what it shows:

- The speed increases from zero in the first 15 s, so the car is accelerating.
- The speed is steady at 18 m/s for the next 30 s.
- The speed drops back to zero in the last 20 s, so the car is decelerating.

Calculating acceleration

The **acceleration** of an object tells you how fast its velocity is changing. You calculate acceleration with this equation:

$$a = \frac{v - u}{t}$$

a is the acceleration in metres per second squared (m/s^2)
u is the initial velocity in metres per second (m/s)
v is the final velocity in metres per second (m/s)
t is the time taken for the change in seconds (s)

So what is the acceleration of the car in the first 15 s of its journey?

The graph gives u = 0 m/s, v = 18 m/s, and t = 15 s

$$a = \frac{v - u}{t} = \frac{18\,\text{m/s} - 0\,\text{m/s}}{15\,\text{s}} = 1.2\,\text{m/s}^2$$

This means that the speed of the car increases by 1.2 m/s in every second.

H Using gradients

What is the acceleration of the car as it slows down?

The graph gives u = 18 m/s at a time of 45 s and v = 0 m/s at a time of 65 s.

$$a = \frac{v - u}{t} = \frac{0\,\text{m/s} - 18\,\text{m/s}}{65\,\text{s} - 45\,\text{s}} = \frac{-18\,\text{m/s}}{20\,\text{s}} = -0.9\,\text{m/s}^2$$

The acceleration is negative because the car is slowing down. A negative acceleration is sometimes called a **deceleration**.

Revision objectives

- ✔ calculate the acceleration of an object
- ✔ draw and interpret velocity–time graphs
- ✔ use a velocity–time graph to calculate acceleration or distance

Student book references

2.5 Acceleration
2.6 Velocity–time graphs

Specification key

✔ P2.1.2 e – h

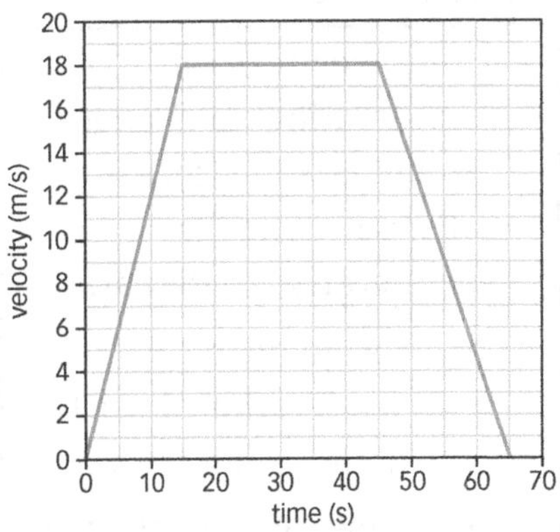

▲ Velocity–time graph for a short car journey.

Key words

velocity–time graph, acceleration, deceleration

Exam tip

AQA

Always use changes of velocity and time when calculating acceleration.

Practise changing $a = \frac{v - u}{t}$ to $a \times t = v - u$ and $t = \frac{v - u}{a}$

Questions

1 The velocity of an accelerating car changes from 2 m/s to 17 m/s in 10 s. Calculate the acceleration of the car.

2 a Calculate the acceleration of car D in the graph below.

b How can you tell from the graph that car E has a greater acceleration?

3 **H** Calculate the distance that car D moves as the time increases from 0 s to 8 s.

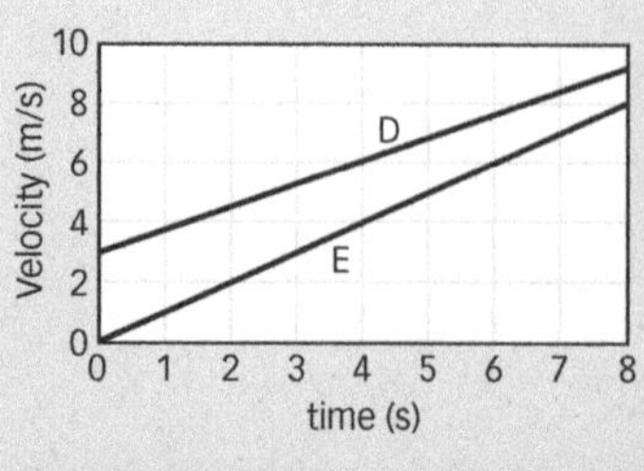

Backwards and forwards

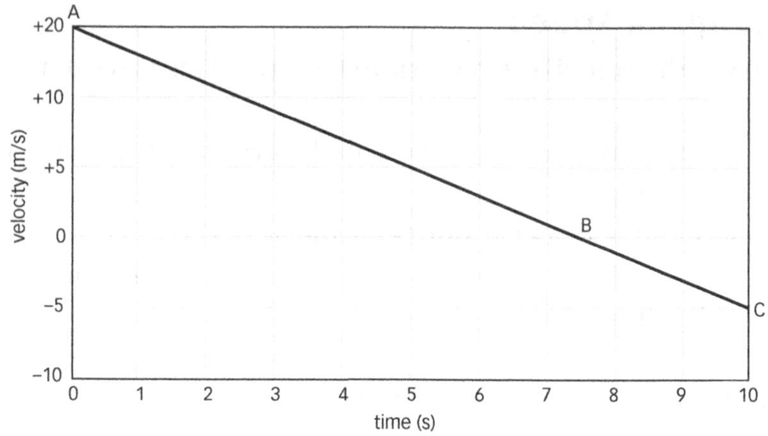

What does the above velocity–time graph for a car show?

- At point A, the car moves forwards with a velocity of +20 m/s.
- The velocity drops steadily to zero in the next 7.5 s as the car slows to a halt at point B.
- For the final 2.5 s the velocity is negative. This means that the car is now going backwards, ending up with a velocity of −5 m/s at point C.

H Distance

You calculate the distance moved by the car during this manoeuvre by finding the area between the line and the time axis of the velocity–time graph.

Remember the area of a triangle is ½ × base × height.

- The area of the triangle under the line AB = ½ × 7.5 s × 20 m/s = 75 m
- The area of the triangle under the line BC = ½ × 2.5 s × −5 m/s = −6.25 m

So the car moved forwards by 75 m, then moved backwards by 6.25 m. The overall distance covered was therefore 75 − 6.25 = 68.75 m.

Forces

A **force** is a push or a pull that changes the shape or motion of an object. All forces have a size (measured in newtons, N) and a direction. Here are some examples:

- Gravity exerts a downwards force of 650 N on a teenager.
- Friction exerts a backwards force of 6000 N on a braking car.
- The ground underneath an elephant exerts an upwards force of 10 000 N on each foot.

Pairs of forces

Every force is the result of one object interacting with another object. So the boy in the diagram interacts with the wall by pushing it to the right with a force of 100 N. The wall reacts by pushing back on the boy with another force of the same size (100 N), but in the opposite direction (left). Each force in a **pair of forces** between different objects has the same size but opposite direction.

Resultant force

When more than one force acts on an object you can combine them to find the **resultant force**. You need to take account of the direction of the forces when you do this. You should:

- add forces that are acting in the same direction
- subtract forces that are acting in opposite directions.

You need to state the direction as well as the size when you calculate a resultant force.

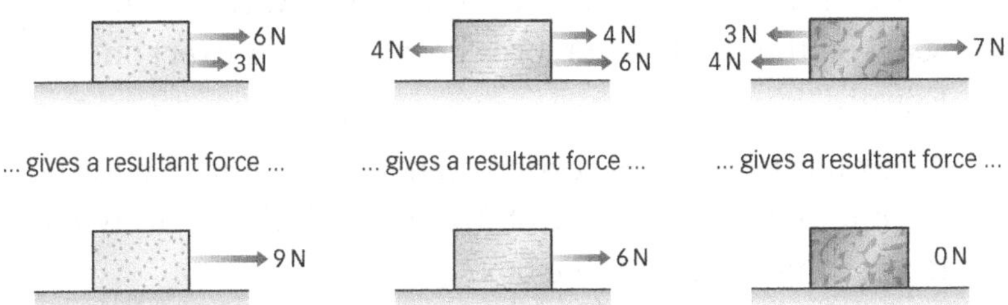

▲ Three forces are replaced by a single resultant force.

Revision objectives

- ✔ understand how forces change the motion of objects
- ✔ understand that forces between objects are equal and opposite to each other
- ✔ calculate the resultant force on an object
- ✔ use the equation *resultant force = mass × acceleration* ($F = m \times a$)

Student book references

2.1 Forces

2.2 Force, mass, and acceleration

Specification key

✔ P2.1.1 ✔ P2.1.2 a

▲ Forces always come in pairs.

Key words

force, pair of forces, resultant force, acceleration, mass

Motion

The resultant force on an object determines its motion.

- If the resultant force is zero the motion does not change. The object carries on moving with the same speed and direction (velocity).
- If the resultant force is in the direction of motion, the object speeds up (accelerates).
- If the resultant force is opposite to the direction of motion, the object slows down.

Acceleration

The **acceleration** of an object depends on its **mass** and resultant force. They are linked by this equation:

$$F = m \times a \text{ or } a = \frac{F}{m}$$

F is the resultant force in newtons (N)
m is the mass in kilograms (kg)
a is the acceleration in metres per second squared (m/s^2)

A car of mass 1500 kg has an acceleration of 6 m/s^2. What is the resultant force on it?

$$F = m \times a = 1500\,kg \times 6\,m/s^2 = 9000\,N$$

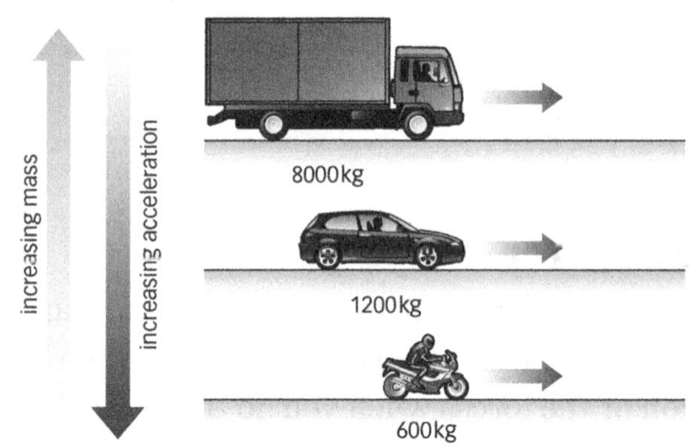

▲ The mass of an object affects its acceleration for the same force.

Exam tip

AQA

Work out the resultant force on an object before deciding how its velocity changes.

Questions

1 Edward sits on a chair. He exerts a downwards force of 600 N on the chair. What force does the chair exert on Edward?

2 A box has three forces acting on it. Forces of 6 N and 12 N push it to the left. A force of 9 N pushes it the right. What is the resultant force on the box?

3 **H** A car has a mass of 900 kg. The engine pushes it forwards with a force of 4000 N. Friction pushes backwards on it with a force of 1000 N. Calculate its acceleration.

Forces on a car

Two horizontal forces act on a car when it moves along a level road:

- the **driving force** pushes the car forwards
- the **resistive forces** push the car backwards.

The driving force is caused by the engine turning the wheels. There are two different resistive forces. The **friction force** appears whenever objects slide against each other, and **air resistance** appears when objects have to push air out of their way.

Balanced forces

If the driving and resistive forces are the same size, then the resultant force on the car will be zero. This is because the two forces act in opposite directions, so cancel out. When this happens, the forces are **balanced** and the car's velocity remains constant. It doesn't speed up or slow down.

Unbalanced forces

For a car to speed up, the resultant force must be in the forwards direction. This means that the driving force must be greater than the resistive forces. If the driving force is smaller than the resistive forces, then the resultant force will be in the backwards direction. This will make the car slow down.

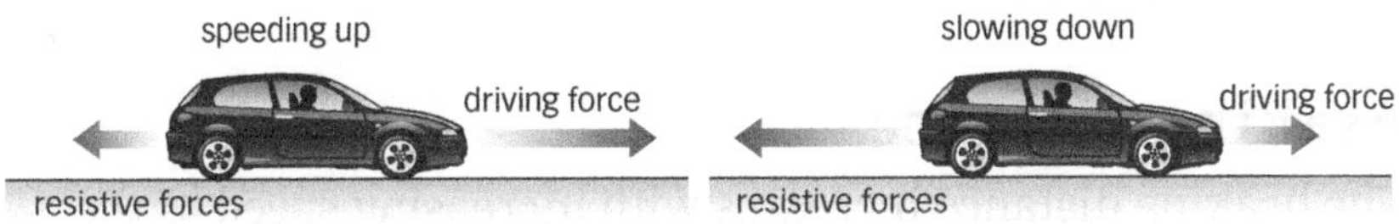

▲ The speed of the car changes if the forces are unbalanced.

Braking force

When the driver wants to stop their car, they do two things:

- take their foot off the accelerator, making the driving force zero
- put a foot on the brake pedal, adding the **braking force** to the resistive forces.

This applies a large resultant force in the backwards direction to the car. The car slows down until it stops.

▲ Forces on a car when the brakes are applied.

Revision objectives

- ✓ know that a constant velocity requires balanced forces
- ✓ understand stopping, braking, and thinking distances for a car
- ✓ understand why braking force increases with speed for a fixed stopping distance
- ✓ state factors that affect stopping distance

Student book references

2.7 Resistive forces
2.8 Stopping distances

Specification key

✓ P2.1.3 a – d, f

▲ The horizontal forces on a moving car.

Key words

driving force, resistive force, friction force, air resistance, balanced, braking force, stopping distance, reaction time, thinking distance, braking distance

Stopping distance

The **stopping distance** is the total distance that a car moves when it is stopped. Once the driver decides to stop there will be a **reaction time** before they put their foot on the brakes. During this time the car continues moving at a steady speed through the **thinking distance**. Once the brakes have been applied, the car moves at a falling speed through the **braking distance**.

stopping distance = thinking distance + braking distance

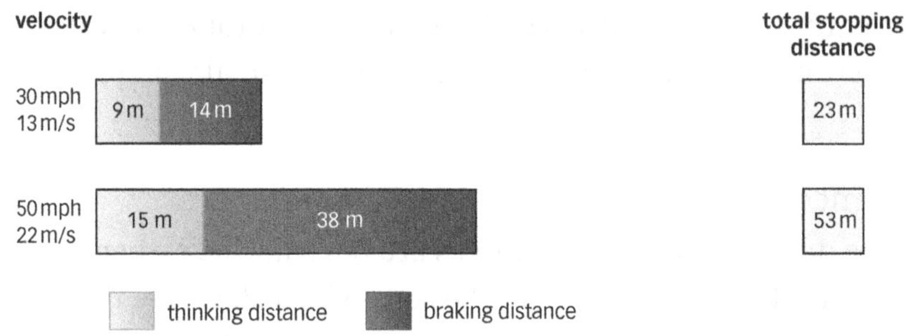

▲ Stopping distance increases with increasing velocity.

Thinking distance

There are ways of increasing the thinking distance:

- driving under the influence of drugs such as alcohol
- distracting the driver with mobile phones or satellite navigation systems.

Any factor that increases the reaction time increases the chance of an accident.

Braking distance

The braking distance increases with increasing speed of the car. This is because the car has to decelerate for longer, so travels further in that time. The braking distance for a given speed can be increased by:

- reducing the friction between road and tyres with ice, snow, or rain on the road
- reducing the braking force by having worn or badly adjusted brakes.

Questions

1 The stopping distance for a car at 70 mph is 96 m. If the thinking distance is 21 m, what is the braking distance?

2 Discuss the factors that can increase the stopping distance of a car.

3 **H** A car starts from rest and accelerates to a steady top speed of 80 mph. If the driving force is a steady 800 N, explain how the resistive forces change in this time.

Exam tip

AQA

Don't forget to include a reason as well as a factor when discussing changes of thinking or braking distance.

Weight

The gravitational force on an object is called its **weight**. You calculate it with this equation:

$$W = m \times g$$

W is the weight of the object in newtons (N)
m is the **mass** of the object in kilograms (kg)
g is the **gravitational field strength** in newtons per kilogram (N/kg)

Since weight is a force it must always have a direction. It always acts towards the centre of the planet. The value of g depends on the size of the planet – on Earth it is about 10 N/kg but on Mars it is only 3.7 N/kg.

Revision objectives

- calculate the weight of an object
- describe the motion of an object falling under gravity
- understand how a falling object reaches a terminal velocity
- draw and interpret velocity–time graphs for falling objects

Student book references

2.9 Motion under gravity
2.10 Terminal velocity

Specification key

✔ P2.1.4

Falling down

Gravity can only accelerate objects downwards when they are unsupported. So when the ball is on the table, its weight is cancelled out by an equal and opposite force from the table. As the forces on the ball are balanced its motion cannot change – it just stays there.

Without the table there is only gravity (and a small amount of air resistance) acting on the ball. The resultant force is its weight, so it accelerates downwards.

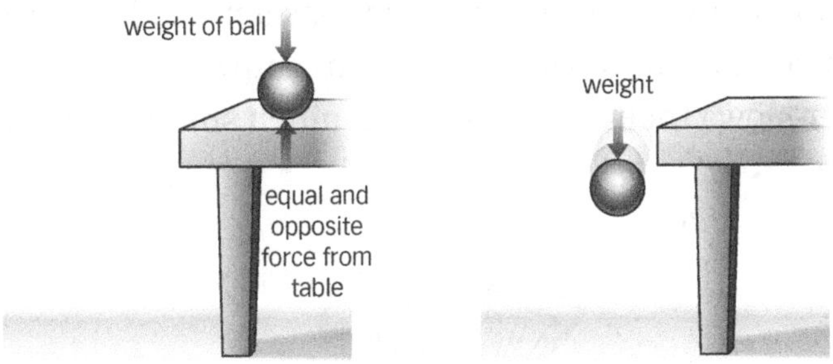

▲ Two equal but opposite forces act on the ball when it is on the table, but there is a resultant force while it falls (small amount of air resistance not shown).

Air resistance

Objects that fall through the air have to push their way through the air. So the air exerts an equal and opposite upwards force on the object: **air resistance**. The size of air resistance can be increased by:

- increasing the speed of the object
- increasing the surface area of the object
- making the shape of the object less streamlined.

So air resistance affects flat, light shapes such as leaves much more than round, heavy ones like balls.

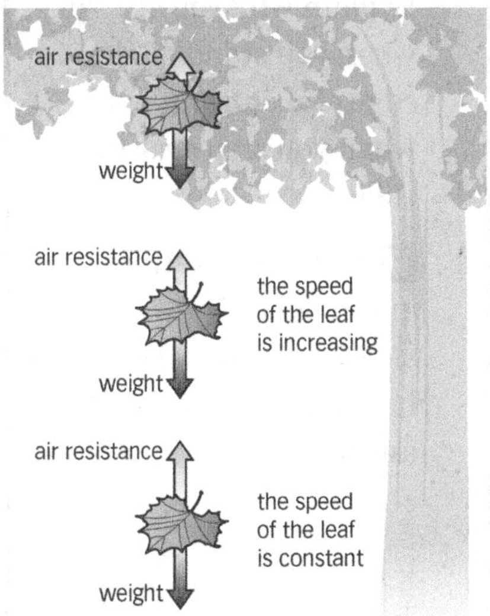

▲ Air resistance on the leaf increases as it speeds up.

Key words

weight, mass, gravitational field strength, air resistance, terminal velocity

Terminal velocity

Air resistance sets a limit to the velocity of a falling skydiver. As the skydiver falls, their weight stays constant but their air resistance increases as they speed up. Since the two forces act in opposite directions, they will eventually become balanced and the skydiver will fall at a steady speed – the **terminal velocity**.

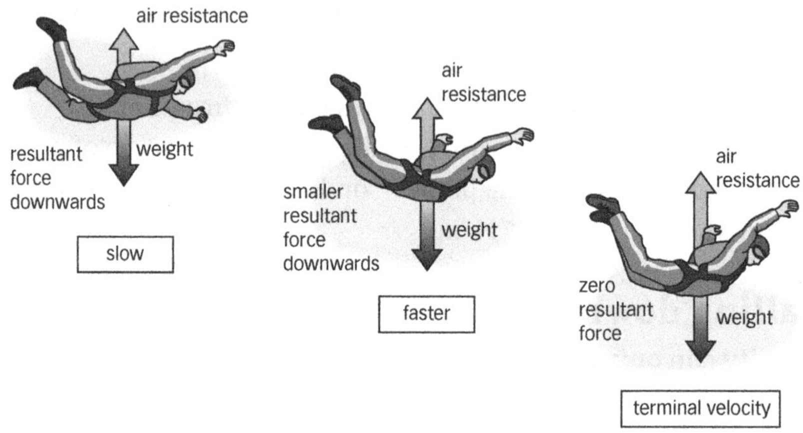

▲ The air resistance on the skydiver increases as they fall through the air.

Exam tip

AQA

Remember that *mass* and *weight* are different things. Moving an object from one planet to another does not affect its mass.

Parachutes

The terminal velocity of a skydiver can be over 100 mph. This is not a safe landing speed. Usually the skydiver opens a parachute before they hit the ground. The parachute has to push a lot of air out of the way, so it has a much higher air resistance than the skydiver. This extra upwards force on the skydiver slows them down to a new, much smaller, terminal velocity.

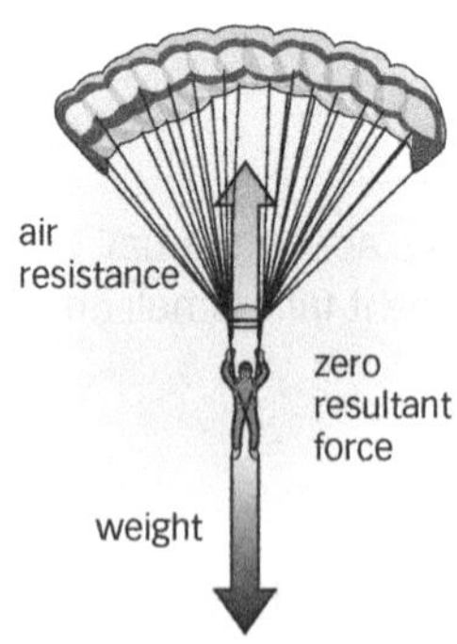

▲ A parachute increases air resistance.

Questions

1 Calculate the weight of a 65 kg person on Mars where $g = 3.7$ N/kg.

2 Explain why you are safe when you stand on the edge of a cliff but not when you step over the edge.

3 **H** The velocity–time graph below is for a skydiver who makes a safe landing. Explain the shape and stages of the graph.

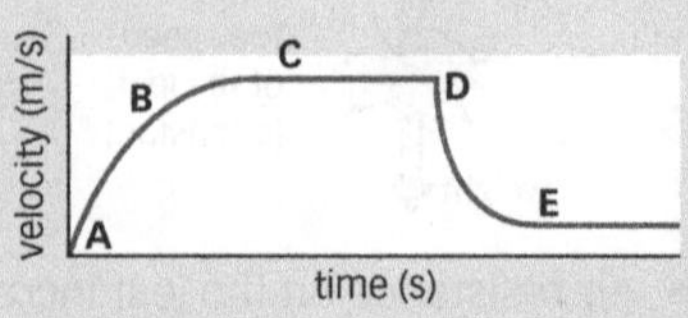

Working to Grade E

1 State what happens to the motion of a car if:
  a the driving force is greater than the resistive forces
  b the driving force is less than the resistive forces
  c the driving force is equal to the resistive forces.

2 Calculate the resultant force on a car of mass 900 kg that accelerates at $3\,m/s^2$.

3 A plane moves 250 m in just 5 s. How fast is it moving?

4 Use the velocity–time graph of a car, below, to complete the sentences that follow. Use these words (some may be used more than once):
accelerates decelerates steady zero

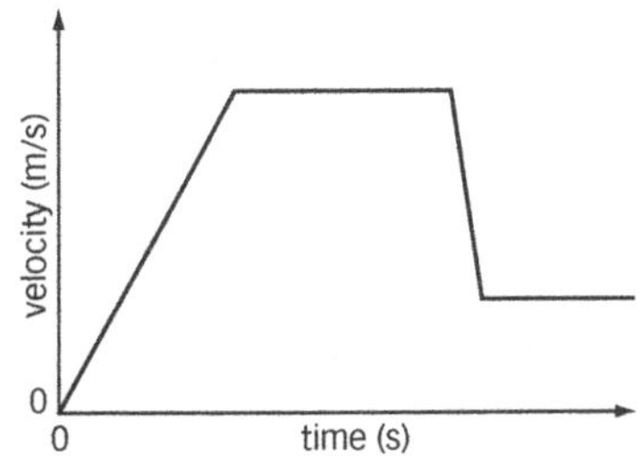

The car starts off with ________ speed. It then ________ to a ________ speed. Then it ________ to a ________ speed.

5 State **two** factors that could increase the stopping distance of a car.

6 Complete the sentences below for a skydiver. Choose from these words: **acceleration air resistance balanced unequal velocity weight**
As the skydiver speeds up, her ________ remains constant but her ________ increases.
When these two forces are ________ she is at her terminal ________ .

Working to Grade C

7 Three forces act on a brick, as shown below. Calculate the size and direction of its acceleration.

8 Calculate the weight of the brick (g = 10 N/kg) and explain why the brick's vertical acceleration is zero.

9 A car of mass 750 kg moves at steady speed of 10 m/s when the driving force is 250 N. What is the deceleration of the car when the driver takes her foot off the accelerator?

10 A speed camera takes two photos of a passing car 0.25 s apart. The car is 5.6 m away from the camera in the first photo and 12.4 m away in the second photo. Is the car going faster than the speed limit of 30 m/s?

11 Use this distance–time graph of a car to state how its speed is changing with time.

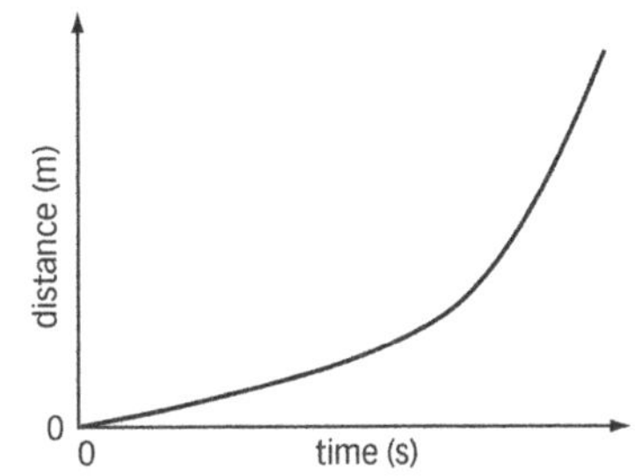

12 Sketch the distance–time and velocity–time graphs for a person who behaves as follows:
- runs away from you at a steady speed
- then stops for a while
- then walks back to you at a steady speed.

13 State the meaning of the following terms: braking distance, stopping distance, and thinking distance.

Working to Grade A*

14 Use this girl's distance–time graph to calculate her velocity when the time is 1 s, 2 s, and 3 s.

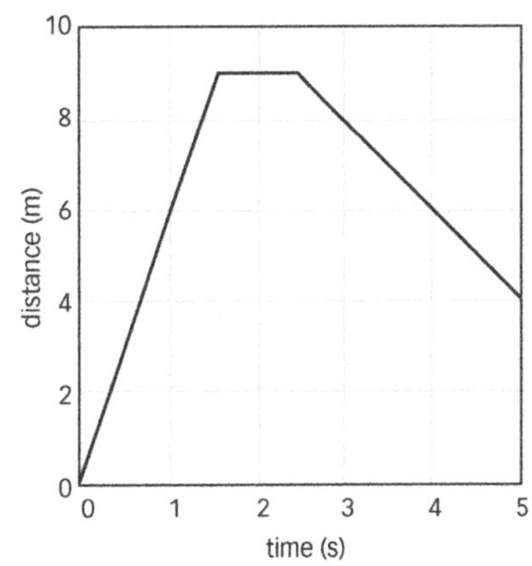

15 Use this car's velocity–time graph to calculate how far it went.

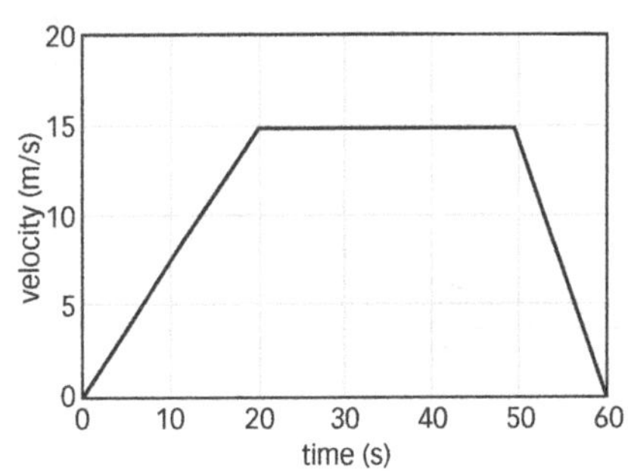

Examination questions
Force and motion

1 The graphs in List A show how the distances of three vehicles change with time.

The statements in List B describe different motions.

Draw one line from each graph in List A to the description of the motion represented by that graph in List B.

List A
Distance–time graphs

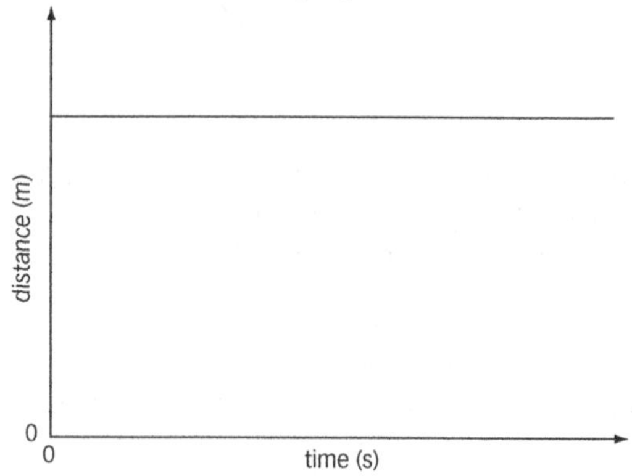

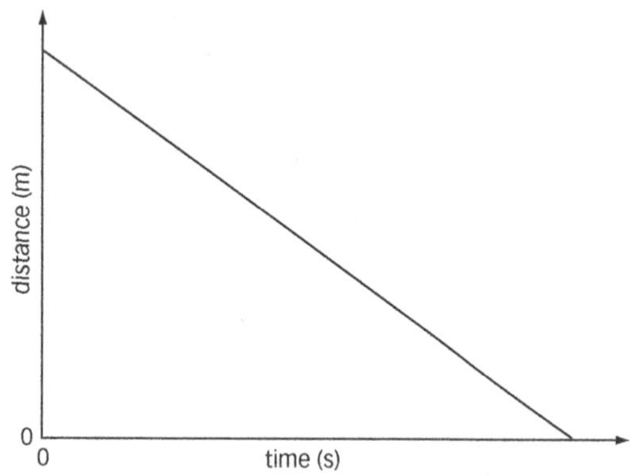

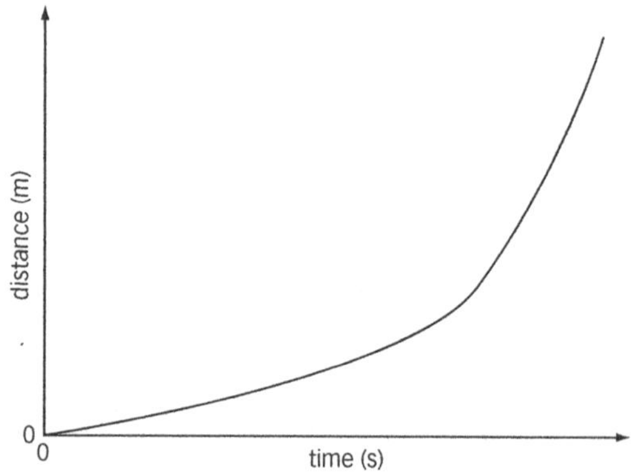

List B
Descriptions of motion

constant acceleration

constant deceleration

constant zero velocity

constant non-zero velocity

(3 marks)

(Total marks: 3)

2 The diagram shows the four forces acting on a car that is moving along a level road.

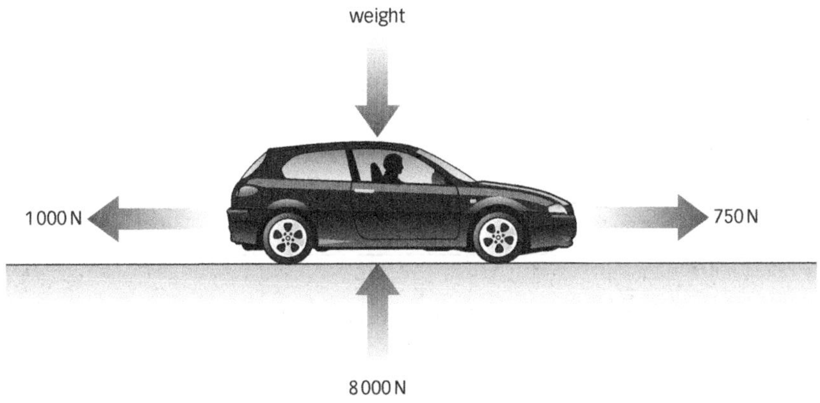

a Explain why the weight of the car must be 8000 N.

....

....

(2 marks)

b Calculate the resultant force on the car.

Show clearly how you work out your answer.

....

....

Resultant force = ... N

(2 marks)

H

c Calculate the acceleration of the car when the forces shown in the diagram act on it.

....

....

....

Acceleration = ... m/s^2

(3 marks)

d Explain how the velocity of the car changes with time when the forces shown in the diagram act on it.

....

....

....

(2 marks)

(Total marks: 9)

3 The table below provides data on thinking and braking distances for a car that does an emergency stop on a dry, level road.

Speed in m/s	Thinking distance in m	Braking distance in m
10	6	8
20	12	32
30	18	72

a Calculate the stopping distance of the car at a speed of 20 m/s.

....

Stopping distance = ... m
(1 mark)

b Use the data in the table above to calculate the reaction time of the driver.

....

....

Reaction time = ... s
(2 marks)

c **i** Explain why the braking distance of the car increases as its speed increases.

....

....

....

....

(3 marks)

ii Explain **one** further factor that affects the braking distance.

....

....

....

(2 marks)
(Total marks: 8)

Work

Whenever an object moves in the direction of an applied force, work is done on it. You calculate the **work done** with this equation:

$$W = F \times d$$

W is the work done on the object in joules (J)
F is the force applied to the object in newtons (N)
d is the distance moved by the object in the direction of the force in metres (m)

So how much work is done on a 150 N weight when it is raised vertically through a distance of 2 m?

$$W = F \times d = 150\,\text{N} \times 2\,\text{m} = 300\,\text{J}$$

Energy transfer

Every time work is done, some energy is transferred. So when the 150 N weight is raised by 2 m, 300 J of energy is transferred from the weightlifter to the weight. 300 J of chemical energy in the weightlifter's muscles transfers to 300 J of **gravitational potential energy** in the weight.

work done = energy transferred

When the weight is lowered back to the ground, it transfers 300 J of gravitational potential energy back to the weightlifter as **heat** in his muscles.

Work against friction

Moving objects have **kinetic energy**. Whenever moving objects slide past each other, there is a frictional force opposing the motion. So work is done whenever friction is present. This work transfers kinetic energy of the moving objects to heat.

Elastic potential energy

When a force squashes or stretches an object, work is done on the object. That work transfers **elastic potential energy** to the object. When the force is removed, that energy is transferred, often as kinetic energy.

Revision objectives

- ✔ understand that work is done when an object is moved against a force
- ✔ use the equation *work done = force × distance moved in the direction of the force* (*W* = *F* × *d*)
- ✔ understand that work done is equal to energy transferred
- ✔ describe the energy transfers when a force is used to change the shape of a spring
- ✔ use the equation *force = spring constant × extension* (*F* = *k* × *e*)

Student book references

2.11 Hooke's law

2.12 Work done and energy transferred

Specification key

- ✔ P2.1.5
- ✔ P2.2.1 a – d

Key words

work done, gravitational potential energy, heat, kinetic energy, elastic potential energy, Hooke's law, extension, spring constant

Hooke's law

Hooke's law says that the extension of a spring is directly proportional to its **extension**. This is represented in this equation.

$$F = k \times e$$

F is the force extending the spring in newtons (N)
k is the **spring constant** of the spring in newtons per metre (N/m)
e is the extension of the spring in metres (m)

Bungee rope has a spring constant of 250 N/m. So how much force is needed to increase the length of a bungee rope from 25 m to 30 m?

$$F = k \times e = 250\,\text{N/m} \times (30\,\text{m} - 25\,\text{m}) = 1\,250\,\text{N}$$

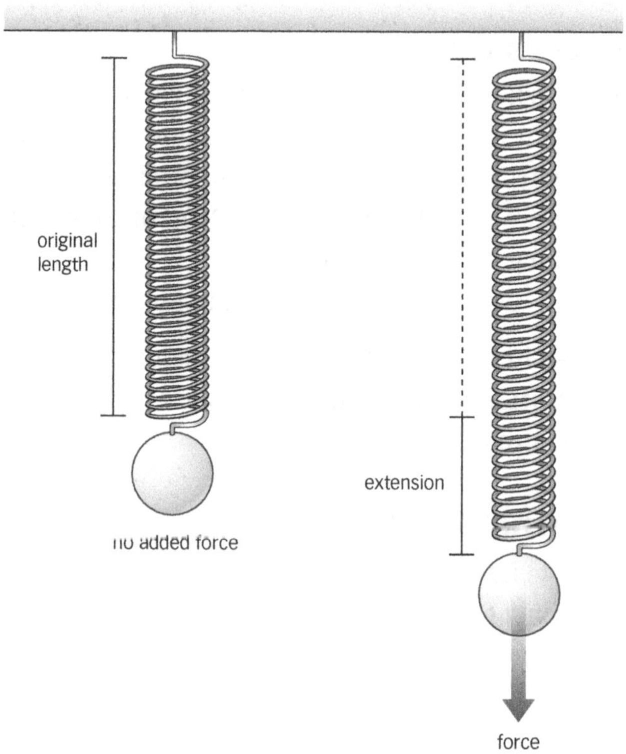

▲ The extension of a spring is its change of length due to the applied force.

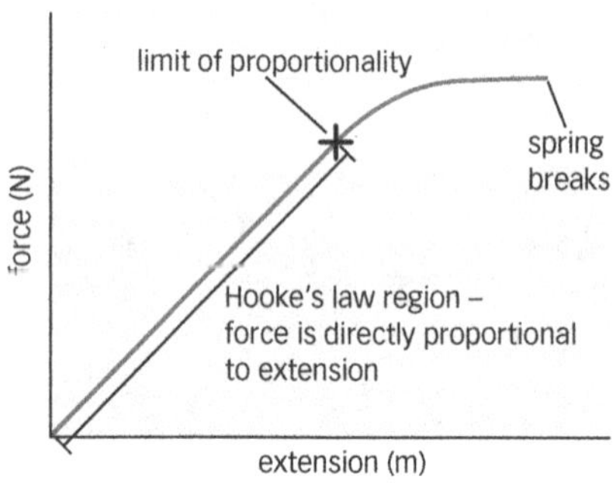

▲ Hooke's law can only be used reliably if the spring isn't stretched too much.

Questions

1 Jim weighs 800 N. He uses the stairs to climb a vertical height of 6 m. How much gravitational potential energy does he gain?

2 How much kinetic energy is transferred to heat when a car brakes in a distance of 40 m by a braking force of 6 000 N?

3 **H** Calculate the spring constant of the elastic band whose length is increased from 10 cm to 25 cm by an applied force of 50 N.

Exam tip

AQA

The force and distance must be in the same direction when you calculate work done. Don't confuse the extension of a spring with its length.

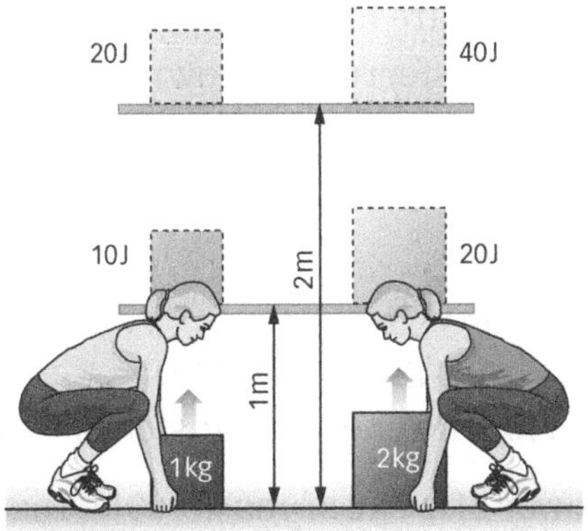

▲ Changes of gravitational potential energy are affected by mass and height.

Gravitational potential energy

Whenever an object is moved up it gains **gravitational potential energy** (GPE). You can calculate the change of GPE with this equation:

$$E_p = m \times g \times h$$

E_p is the change of GPE of the object in joules (J)
m is the **mass** of the object in kilograms (kg)
g is the gravitational field strength in newtons per kilogram (N/kg)
h is the vertical change of height in metres (m)

So how much GPE does a boy of mass 50 kg lose when he drops a vertical height of 0.5 m when he falls off his chair?
(g = 10 N/kg on Earth)

$$E_p = m \times g \times h = 50\,\text{kg} \times 10\,\text{N/kg} \times 0.5\,\text{m} = 250\,\text{J}$$

Kinetic energy

Moving objects have **kinetic energy** (KE). You can calculate kinetic energy with this equation:

$$E_K = \tfrac{1}{2} \times m \times v^2$$

E_K is the kinetic energy of an object in joules (J)
m is the mass of the object in kilograms (kg)
v is the **velocity** of the object in metres per second (m/s)

So what is the kinetic energy of a 50 kg cheetah moving at 30 m/s?

$$E_K = \tfrac{1}{2} \times m \times v^2 = \tfrac{1}{2} \times 50\,\text{kg} \times (30\,\text{m/s})^2 = 0.5 \times 50 \times 900 = 22\,500\,\text{J}$$

Revision objectives

- ✔ understand what affects the gravitational potential energy of an object
- ✔ understand what affects the kinetic energy of an object
- ✔ use the equations $E_p = m \times g \times h$ and $E_K = \tfrac{1}{2} \times m \times v^2$
- ✔ understand that power is the rate of doing work
- ✔ use the equation $P = \frac{E}{t}$

Student book references

2.13 Power
2.14 Gravitational potential energy and kinetic energy

Specification key

✔ P2.2.1 e – g

Key words

gravitational potential energy, mass, kinetic energy, velocity, power

Power

Some energy transfers are much quicker than others. The rate at which energy is transferred is known as **power**. You can calculate it with this equation:

$$P = \frac{E}{t}$$

P is the power in watts (W)
E is the transferred energy in joules (J)
t is the time taken for the energy transfer in seconds (s)

So what is the power of a car of mass 900 kg that can accelerate from 0 m/s to 32 m/s in 8 s?

Start off by calculating the energy transferred to kinetic energy:

$$E_K = \tfrac{1}{2} \times m \times v^2 = \tfrac{1}{2} \times 900\,\text{kg} \times (32\,\text{m/s})^2 = 0.5 \times 900 \times 1024 = 460\,800\,\text{J}$$

Then calculate the power:

$$P = \frac{E}{t} = \frac{460\,800\,\text{J}}{8\,\text{s}} = 57\,600\,\text{W}$$

H Transfer time

The power of a device allows you to work out how long you will need to use it. Suppose you want to use a microwave oven to reheat a mug of coffee. The microwave will need to transfer 114 000 J of energy as heat to the mug. How long will it take if the microwave's power is 950 W?

$$P = \frac{E}{t} \text{ so } P \times t = E \text{ and } t = \frac{E}{P}$$

$$t = \frac{114\,000\,\text{J}}{950\,\text{W}} = 120\,\text{s}$$

Exam tip AQA

Write out every step of a calculation before you use a calculator. Practise rearranging the equations for KE, GPE, and power.

Questions

1 Jo transfers 7200 J to GPE per minute as she climbs a mountain. What is her power?

2 Pat lifts 12 bricks, each of mass 2 kg, up a vertical height of 18 m on a building site. How much energy does he transfer to the bricks as GPE?

3 **H** A car of mass 800 kg has a KE of 160 kJ. How fast is it moving?

Momentum

The **momentum** of an object allows you to predict its change of motion when it collides with another object. You calculate its size with this equation:

$$p = m \times v$$

p is the momentum of the object in kilogram metres per second (kg m/s)
m is the mass of the object in kilograms (kg)
v is the velocity in metres per second (m/s)

The momentum has the same direction as the velocity.

Conservation of momentum

The total momentum of a set of interacting objects never changes, providing that the objects only interact with each other. This principle of **momentum conservation** allows you to calculate the effect of collisions or explosions.

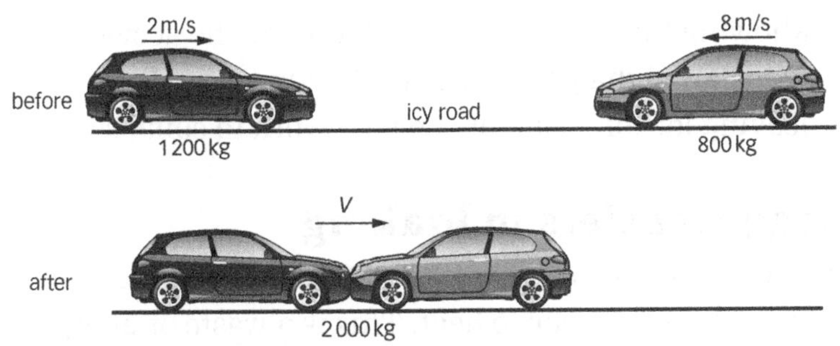

▲ The situation before and after the collision of two cars.

For example, suppose that two cars skid together and have a head-on collision on an icy road. The conservation of momentum allows you to calculate the final velocity V of the cars after they have collided and joined together.

Start off by calculating the total momentum of each car before the collision.

left car: $p = m \times v = 1200\,\text{kg} \times +2\,\text{m/s} = +2400\,\text{kg m/s}$
right car: $p = m \times v = 800\,\text{kg} \times -8\,\text{m/s} = -6400\,\text{kg m/s}$

(The velocities are in opposite directions, so one must be chosen to be negative.)

Then calculate the total momentum:

$$(+2400) + (-6400) = -4000\,\text{kg m/s}$$

Revision objectives

- ✓ use the equation $p = m \times v$ to calculate momentum
- ✓ apply the law of conservation of momentum
- ✓ describe the energy transfers for a braking car
- ✓ explain the benefits of air bags and crumple zones for car safety

Student book references

2.8 Stopping distances
2.12 Work done and energy transferred
2.15 Momentum

Specification key

✓ P2.1.3 e ✓ P2.2.1 c
✓ P2.2.2

Key words

momentum, momentum conservation, seatbelt, crumple zone, airbag, regenerative braking

After the collision the two cars are locked together and behave like a single object of mass 1200 + 800 = 2000 kg. Provided there is no friction with the icy road, the momentum of this object must be –4000 kg m/s.

$$p = m \times v \text{ so } \frac{p}{m} = v$$

$$V = \frac{-4000\,\text{kg m/s}}{2000\,\text{kg}} = -2\,\text{m/s}$$

So the velocity of the cars after the collision is 2 m/s to the left.

Car safety

When a car has a head-on collision, the people inside have to stop moving. Something has to exert a backwards force on them to reduce their velocity to zero. Normally a **seatbelt** applies this decelerating force. The **crumple zone** at the front of the car increases the time for its velocity to drop to zero. This increase in time reduces the deceleration of the people, and reduces the force needed from the seatbelt.

The time for a collision can be increased in a number of ways:

- allowing the seatbelt to stretch during the accident
- using an **airbag** to slow down heads gradually
- leaving lots of room for the bodywork to collapse.

Energy transfers in braking

When a car is stopped, friction in the brakes transfers the kinetic energy of the car to heat. This is a waste of energy as the heat eventually spreads into the air and cannot be used for anything else. Some cars use **regenerative braking** instead. This slows down the car by transferring the kinetic energy of the car to electricity that charges up a battery. The battery can then transfer this energy back to kinetic energy when the car speeds up again.

Exam tip AQA

Remember to take account of directions when calculating total momentum.

Questions

1 Sue has a mass of 52 kg. What is her momentum when she runs at a speed of 7 m/s?

2 Explain how the crumple zone of a car increases the safety of the driver when a car crashes.

3 **H** A gun of mass 2 kg fires a bullet of mass 0.02 kg with a speed of 300 m/s. Calculate the recoil velocity of the gun.

Questions
Work and energy

Working to Grade E

1 A spring has a spring constant of 60 N/m. Calculate the force required to increase its length by 0.25 m.

2 Complete this table with the correct units for each quantity.

Quantity	Unit
kinetic energy	
momentum	
power	
work	

3 Complete the sentences for a braking car.

When the brakes are applied on a level road, the _______ energy of the car transfers to _______ in the brakes. If the car is going uphill at the time, some of the _______ energy transfers to _______ potential energy.

4 A crane can do 100 000 J of work in 20 s. What is its power?

5 A plane of mass 2 000 kg falls a vertical distance of 50 m. What is its change of GPE? (g = 10 N/kg)

6 State **three** features of cars that increase the safety of the driver in a crash.

7 Calculate the momentum of 0.5 kg ball when it has a speed of 20 m/s.

Working to Grade C

8 Explain why a seatbelt increases the safety of the driver when a car crashes.

9 A crane lifts a load of mass 250 kg through a vertical height of 30 m in a time of 15 s.

Calculate the power of the crane.

10 A car of mass 1100 kg accelerates from 0 m/s to 30 m/s in a time of 12 s. Calculate the power of the car.

11 State the law of momentum conservation. Include the conditions under which it applies.

12 State Hooke's law. Include the conditions under which it applies.

13 A spring's length increases from 0.26 m to 0.30 m when an extra force of 32 N is applied. Calculate the spring constant of the spring.

14 Which of these quantities have both a size and a direction?

acceleration force kinetic energy
momentum power velocity

15 Explain why the use of regenerative braking increases the fuel efficiency of a car.

Working to Grade A*

16 A trolley of mass 2 kg moves towards a stationary trolley of mass 3 kg with a velocity of 1.5 m/s. The trolleys collide and stick together. Calculate the velocity of the joined trolleys after the collision, stating any assumptions you have to make.

17 A ball of mass 1.6 kg is released from rest and falls down a deep well through a vertical height of 20 m. Calculate the speed of the ball just before it hits the water. State any assumptions you have to make (g = 10 N/kg).

1 This diagram shows a car moving up a ramp at a steady speed.

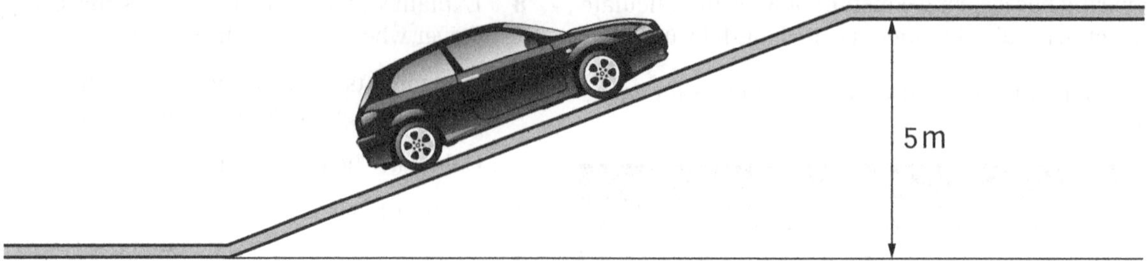

a Draw an arrow on the diagram to represent the weight of the car.

(1 mark)

b The car has a mass of 1200 kg. Calculate the weight of the car.

gravitational field strength = 10 N/kg

Write down the equation you use, and then show clearly how you work out your answer.

....

....

Weight = ... N

(2 marks)

c The ramp raises the car up by 5 m.

Calculate the work done by the car as it moves from the bottom of the ramp to the top.

Write down the equation you use, and then show clearly how you work out your answer.

....

....

Work done = ... J

(2 marks)

d Which **one** of these quantities increases as the car moves up the ramp at a steady speed? Circle your answer.

GPE	KE	momentum	weight

(1 mark)

(Total marks: 6)

2 A car with a mass of 900 kg travels along a level road.

It accelerates from rest to a speed of 15 m/s in a time of 5 s.

a Calculate the kinetic energy of the car at its final speed.

Write down the equation you use, and then show clearly how you work out your answer.

....

....

kinetic energy = ... J

(2 marks)

b Calculate the power developed by the car in the time of 5 s.

Write down the equation you use, and then show clearly how you work out your answer.

....

....

power = ... W

(2 marks)

c *In this question you will be assessed on using good English, organising information clearly, and using specialist terms where appropriate.*

The car crashes into a solid wall.

Explain how the crumple zone of the car increases the safety of the driver in the crash.

....

....

....

....

....

....

....

....

....

....

....

....

(6 marks)

(Total marks: 10)

3 A marksman shoots a bullet into a block of wood.

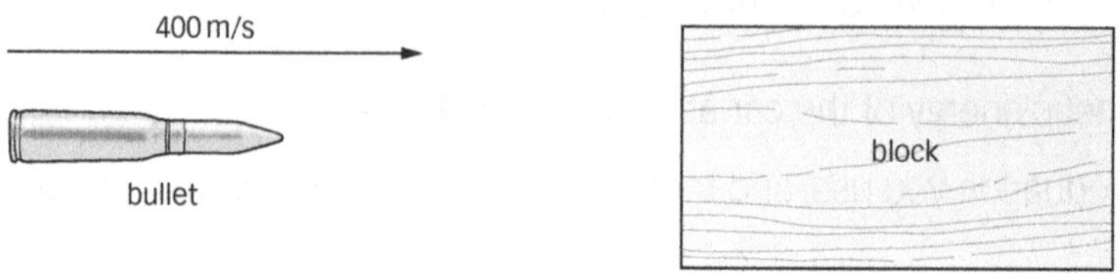

a The bullet has a mass of 0.025 kg. Calculate the momentum of the bullet.

Write down the equation you use, and then show clearly how you work out your answer.

....

....

momentum = ... kg m/s
(2 marks)

b The bullet enters the block and joins onto it. The block is on a friction-free mounting.

i Which one of these quantities remains the same as the bullet enters the block?

Tick (✓) **one** box.

Total momentum ☐

Total heat energy ☐

Total kinetic energy ☐

(1 mark)

ii The block has a mass of 2.0 kg.

Calculate its velocity once the bullet has stuck into it.

Write down the equation you use, and then show clearly how you work out your answer.

....

....

velocity = ... m/s
(2 marks)
(Total marks: 5)

How Science Works
Energy and distance

Designing an investigation and making measurements

In this module there are several opportunities to design investigations and make measurements. These include the acceleration of objects by forces and the behaviour of springs.

As well as demonstrating your investigative skills practically, you are likely to be asked to comment on investigations done by others. The example below offers guidance in this skill area. It also gives you the chance to practise using your skills to answer the sorts of questions that may well come up in exams.

Comparing the skidding distance of different cylinders

Skill – Understanding the experiment

Bill tested the hypothesis that the kinetic energy of a cylinder is proportional to the distance it skids to a halt.

He placed cylinders with their flat side on a level table and propelled them through a light gate.

The light gate measured the speed of each cylinder.

Each cylinder was allowed to skid to a halt after it had passed through the light gate.

Bill measured the distance between the light gate and the centre of the halted cylinder.

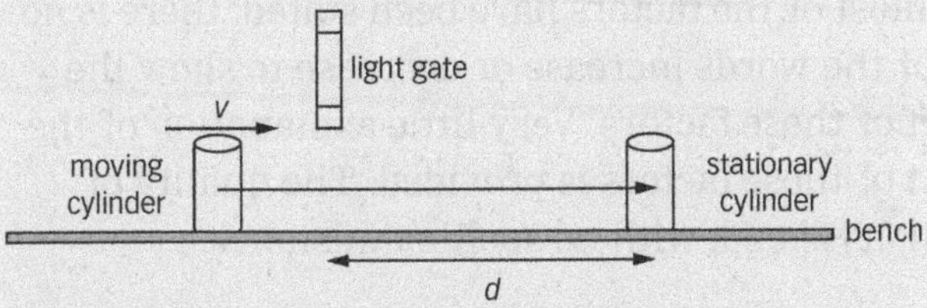

Bill's results are in the table below.

Mass of cylinder (kg)	Initial speed, *V* (m/s)	Skid distance, *d* (m)
0.2	3.5	1.23
0.4	2.2	0.56
0.2	1.5	0.27
0.3	3.3	0.98
0.1	2.5	0.76

1 Identify the independent and dependent variables.

In an investigation:
- the independent variables are the ones that are changed by the scientist
- the dependent variable is the one that is measured for each change of the independent variables.

2 Suggest an important control variable for the investigation.

A control variable is one that the investigator thinks might affect the outcome, so they try to keep this variable the same all the way through.

Skill – Using data to draw conclusions

3 What does Bill need to calculate from his results?

Bill has two independent variables that need to be combined to find one of the variables mentioned in his hypothesis.

4 What is the best graph for Bill to draw to see if his hypothesis is correct?

If one quantity is proportional to another, then a scatter graph for the two quantities should be a straight line through the origin.

5 What should Bill do about results that don't fit the same pattern as the others?

Unless there is a very good reason for ignoring data that is well outside the pattern, it should not be ignored. The best thing is to repeat the experiment again to double check the data.

Skill – Societal aspects of scientific evidence

6 Could Bill apply his results to a real situation such as skidding cars?

Bill would need to make estimations from his results to take account of the faster speeds and greater mass of a real car. He might have greater confidence in this if his cylinders and the table had been made from comparable materials.

AQA Upgrade

Answering an extended writing question

QUESTION

In this question you will be assessed on using good English, organising information clearly, and using specialist terms where appropriate.

1 Explain the factors that determine the distance needed to stop a car in an emergency. *(6 marks)*

G–E

When the driver notices the emergency they have to think about putting there foot on the brake before actually doing it, this is the thinking time and the car keeps moving in this time. Then the brakes take over and the speed of the car quickly drops to nothing, this is the braking distance which gets bigger the faster the car is going. It takes longer for the car to stop if the ground is wet, or the driver has been drinking or is using there mobile or is on drugs or too old.

Examiner: This is a poor-quality answer, typical of an E-grade candidate. It is worth 2 marks. There is very little use of technical terms and very little explanation is provided for the statements of fact. It is unclear which distance is affected by which factor. Some spelling is incorrect and sentence structure is often poor.

D–C

There are two stages in stopping a car. The braking distance is how far the car goes while it is actually slowing down. This depends on the speed of the car and how much friction there is between the tyres and the road. The thinking distance is how far the car goes before it starts to slow down. This depends on the reaction time of the driver, which is affected by tiredness and drugs.

Examiner: This is a medium-quality answer, typical of a D-grade candidate. It earns 3 marks. Although correct technical terms have been used, and most of the factors have been stated, there is no use of the words increase or decrease to show the effect of these factors. Very little explanation of the effect of these factors is provided. The quality of English is good, with no spelling mistakes.

B–A*

The stopping distance is equal to the thinking distance added to the braking distance. The thinking distance is how far the car moves before it starts to slow down, while the driver is reacting to the emergency but before they have got their foot on the brake. The thinking distance is equal to the speed multiplied by the reaction time, so gets longer if either or both the speed and reaction time are increased. Reaction times can be increased if the driver isn't paying attention, drugged up or drunk. Braking distance depends on the speed of the car, its mass, and on the friction in the brakes and the road surface. Reducing the friction reduces the force decelerating the car, and so reduces the deceleration. The time needed for the brakes to stop the car is its speed divided by deceleration, and the longer the time is, the further the car will go. Poor friction can be the result of rain or poor maintenance of the car. Increasing the mass of a car increases the energy which must be transferred by the brakes, so the brakes must be applied for longer.

Examiner: This is a high-quality answer, typical of an A-grade candidate. It is worth 6 marks.

All parts of the question have been explained in sufficient detail. The conclusion on the effect of mass is incorrect, but the candidate has not been penalised for this common error. The candidate has used correct specialist terms and the spelling, punctuation, and grammar are very good.

Part 1 Course catch-up
Motion and energy

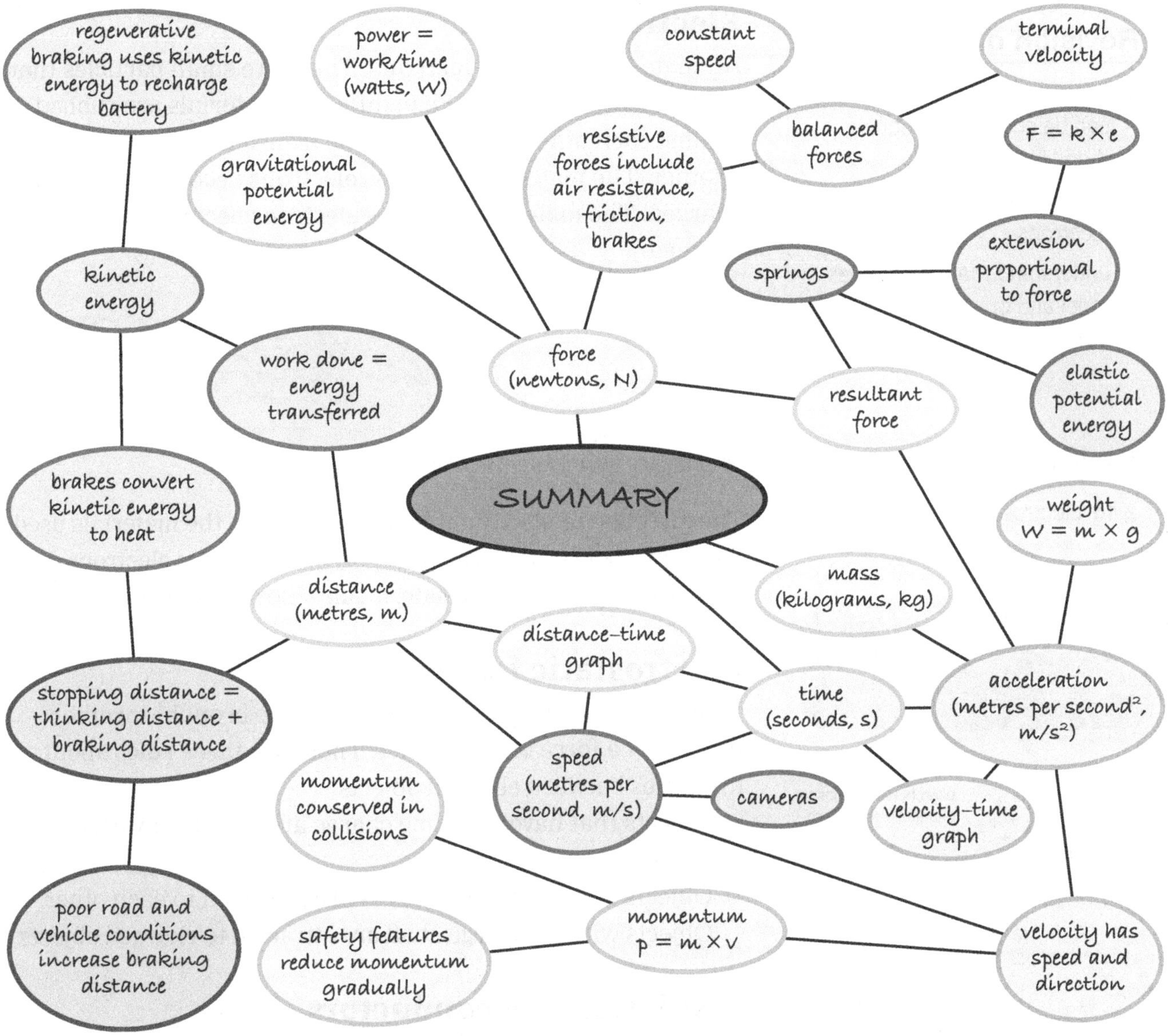

Revision checklist

- Forces are pushes and pulls. Objects exert equal and opposite forces on one another. Resultant force is the sum of all the forces acting on an object.
- Resultant forces change the motion of objects, causing them to accelerate. Resultant force = mass × acceleration.
- Speed is a measure of how fast something is moving. Speed = distance/time. This principle is used in speed cameras.
- Velocity describes direction as well as speed.
- The gradient of a distance–time graph represents speed. Acceleration is a change in speed, and can be positive (speeding up) or negative (slowing down).
- The gradient of a velocity–time graph represents acceleration. The area under a velocity–time graph represents distance travelled.
- A vehicle must overcome the forces of friction and air resistance in order to start moving. When these are balanced by the vehicle's driving force, the vehicle is travelling at a steady speed.
- Stopping distance (thinking distance plus braking distance) is affected by speed, road conditions, vehicle condition, and driver reaction time.
- Weight = mass × gravitational field strength.
- As an object falls under gravity, its velocity increases until its weight is balanced by the force of air resistance. The object then reaches a terminal velocity (steady speed).
- Forces can change the shape of objects. Squashing or stretching a spring gives it elastic potential energy. Hooke's law dictates that the force applied to an object is directly proportional to its extension, up to a certain point.
- Work done is calculated using the equation, work done = force × distance moved in the direction of the force.
- Power = work done/time taken.
- Gravitational potential energy (GPE) is defined by mass, height above the ground, and the Earth's gravitational field. GPE is transferred into kinetic energy (KE) when an object moves.
- A moving object's KE is defined by its mass and its speed.
- The momentum of a moving object is defined by its mass and its velocity.
- Car safety devices increase the time taken for the change in momentum experienced in a crash.

Revision objectives

- describe how some materials can be charged by rubbing them
- explain static electricity with electrons
- understand that like charges repel and opposite charges attract

Student book references

2.16 Electrostatics

Specification key

✔ P2.3.1

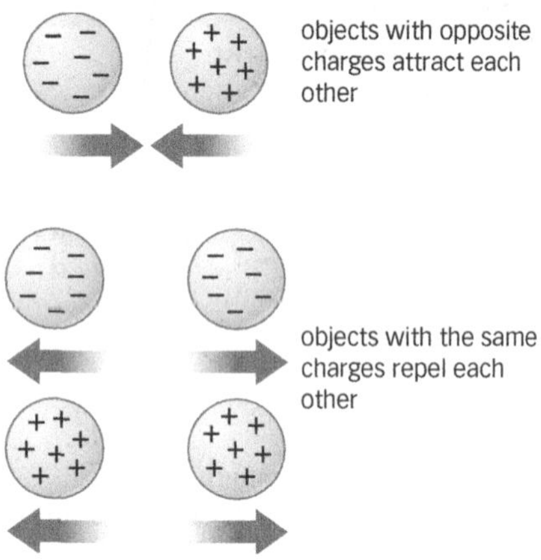

▲ Attraction and repulsion of charged objects.

Key words

electron, charge, negative, positive, insulator, conductor

Exam tip

Remember that electrons are always negative.

Electron transfer

All materials contain **electrons**. These are small particles that carry negative **charge**. When different materials are rubbed against each other, electrons can be transferred from one to another. The material that gains electrons becomes **negatively** charged. The material that loses electrons becomes **positively** charged.

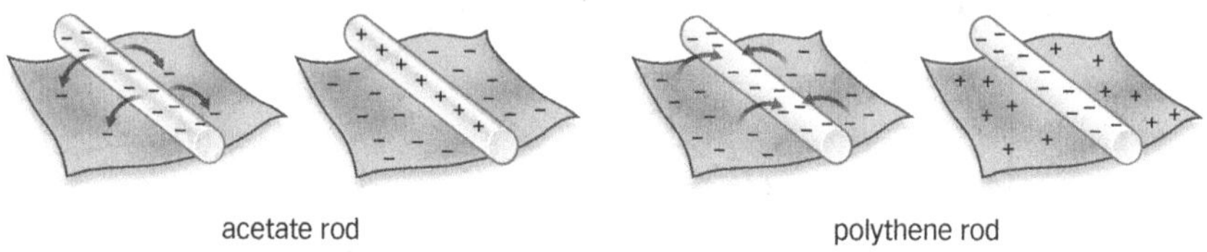

▲ Rubbing two different insulators with a woollen cloth.

The direction of electron transfer depends on the materials used. So when wool is rubbed against polythene, it loses electrons. If wool is rubbed against acetate, it gains electrons instead.

Electrostatic forces

When two electrically charged objects are brought together they exert a force on each other. There are three rules about the forces between charged objects:

- Objects that have the same charge are repelled by each other.
- Objects with different charges are attracted to each other.
- Objects with no charge at all are attracted to charged objects.

Insulators and conductors

Materials can only be charged this way if they are **insulators**. This means that once the electrons have been transferred, they cannot move through the material back to where they started. Electrons can move easily through **conductors**, such as metals, so it is difficult to charge them by rubbing.

Questions

1 What is the difference between a conductor and an insulator?

2 A glass rod is rubbed with a cloth. Electrons transfer from the cloth to the glass. State the charge of the rod and the cloth at the end of this process.

3 **H** A girl rubs a balloon on her hair. This makes her hair stand on end, but also move towards the balloon. Explain these observations.

Current in circuits

The **cell** in the circuit below pushes electrons around it. The lamp, ammeter, and connecting wires are all conductors, so the electrons can move easily through them. This means that there is a flow of negative charge in the circuit, a **current**. The size of the current in a component tells you how quickly the **charge** is passing through it. You calculate it with this equation:

$$I = \frac{Q}{t}$$

I is the current in amperes (A)
Q is the charge passing through in coulombs (C)
t is the time taken in seconds (s)

So if 480 C passes through the lamp in just 120 s, what is the current in it?

$$I = \frac{Q}{t} = \frac{480\,\text{C}}{120\,\text{s}} = 4\,\text{A}$$

Conventional current

Early scientists guessed that charge in a circuit flowed from the positive terminal of a cell to its negative terminal. This is called the direction of **conventional current**. Nowadays we know that the electrons actually flow the other way, but current is still shown as a flow from positive to negative.

Potential difference

The cell applies a **potential difference** across the circuit. It does this by transferring energy to charge that passes through it. As that charge flows around the circuit it transfers energy to each component that it passes through. You calculate potential difference with this equation:

$$V = \frac{W}{Q}$$

V is the potential difference across a component in volts (V)
W is the energy transfer to the component in joules (J)
Q is the charge passing through the component in coulombs (C)

So if 270 J of energy transfer to a mobile phone when 30 C of charge pass through, what is the potential difference across it?

$$V = \frac{W}{Q} = \frac{270\,\text{J}}{30\,\text{C}} = 9\,\text{V}$$

Revision objectives

- ✔ understand that electric current is the rate of flow of charge
- ✔ calculate the size of an electric current
- ✔ understand potential difference
- ✔ recognise standard circuit symbols
- ✔ draw and interpret circuit diagrams

Student book references

2.17 Current and potential difference
2.18 Circuit diagrams

Specification key

✔ P2.3.2 a – c

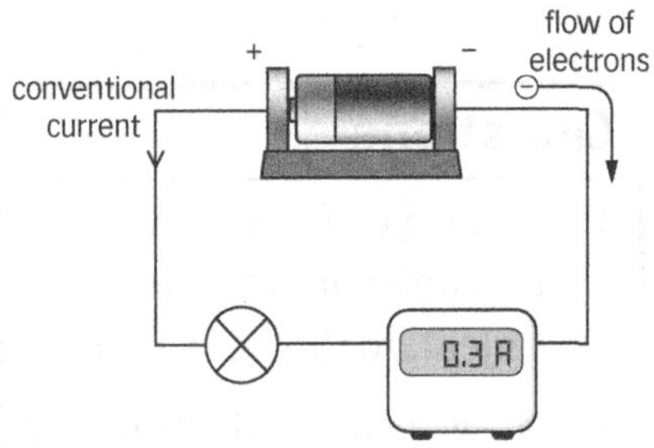

▲ Electron flow in a simple circuit.

Key words

cell, current, charge, conventional current, potential difference, circuit diagram, circuit symbol

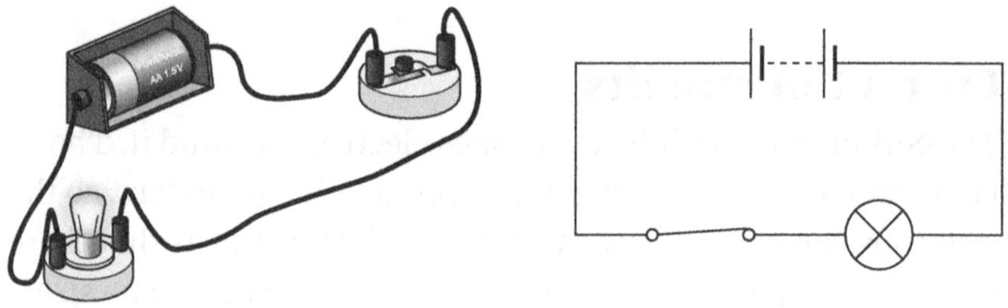

▲ The circuit diagram shows how to assemble the circuit.

Circuit diagrams

Real electrical circuits are usually represented in **circuit diagrams.** Each component is drawn with the correct **circuit symbol**. This can help you to understand how a circuit works.

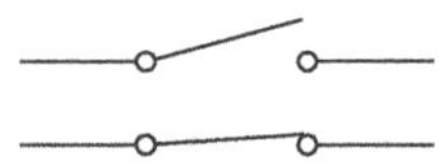	open switch closed switch
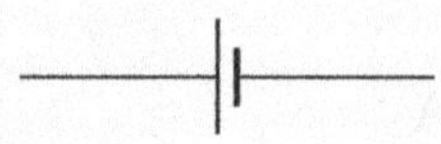	cell
	battery
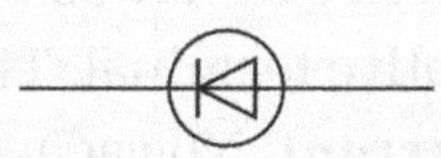	diode
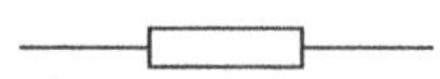	resistor
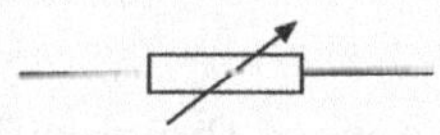	variable resistor
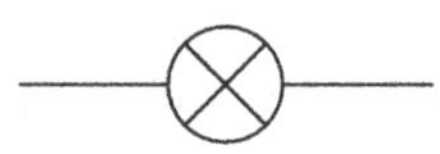	lamp
	fuse
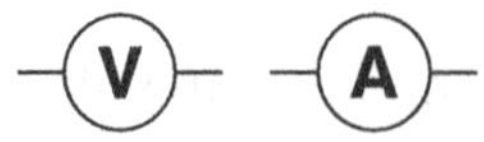	voltmeter ammeter
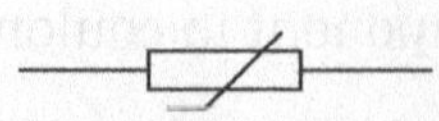	thermistor
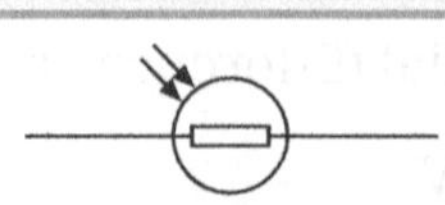	light-dependent resistor (LDR)
	light-emitting diode (LED)

▲ Some circuit components and their symbols.

Exam tip AQA

Make sure that you use the correct symbols when you draw circuit diagrams.

Questions

1 A charge of 27 C flows through a lamp in 9 s. Calculate the current in it.

2 Draw a circuit diagram for a cell connected in series to an ammeter, a resistor, and a diode.

3 **H** The current of 0.5 A in a resistor is switched on for a time of 30 s. If the potential difference across the resistor is 12 V, how much energy is transferred to the resistor in that time?

Resistance

The **resistance** of a component indicates how difficult it is for charge to flow through it. The resistance of a component can be calculated with this equation:

$$V = I \times R$$

V is the potential difference across the component in volts (V)
I is the current in the component in amperes (A)
R is the resistance of the component in ohms (Ω)

To measure the resistance you need to connect an ammeter before the component and connect a voltmeter across both ends of it, as shown in the diagram below.

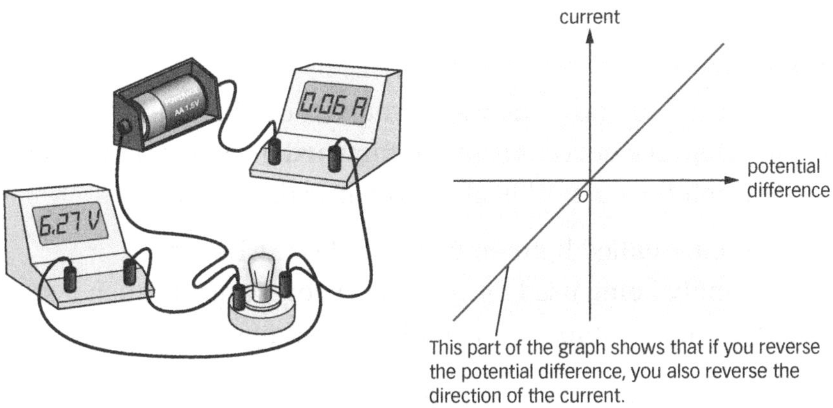

▲ Measuring the current–potential-difference graph for a resistor at constant temperature, illustrating that the current through a resistor is directly proportional to the potential difference across it.

So if the potential difference across a resistor is 3 V when the current in it is 0.5 A, what is its resistance?

$$V = I \times R \text{ so } I \times R = V \text{ and } R = \frac{V}{I}$$

$$R = \frac{3\,\text{V}}{0.5\,\text{A}} = 6\,\Omega$$

Resistors

A **resistor** is usually a thin wire of a conducting material, such as a metal. Its current–potential-difference graph is a straight line through the origin, provided that the temperature of the resistor does not change. This means that its resistance is constant, whatever the current in it. The resistance of a resistor is often quoted in kilo-ohms (kΩ): 1 kΩ = 1000 Ω. The current in such a resistor is likely to be measured in milliamps (mA): 1 A = 1000 mA.

Revision objectives

- ✔ calculate current, potential difference, and resistance
- ✔ draw and interpret current–potential-difference graphs for resistors
- ✔ explain how to find the resistance of a component
- ✔ draw and interpret current–potential-difference graphs for lamps and diodes
- ✔ describe the behaviour of light-dependent resistors and thermistors

Student book references

2.19 Current–potential-difference graphs
2.22 Lamps and light-emitting diodes (LEDs)
2.23 Light-dependent resistors (LDRs) and thermistors

Specification key

✔ P2.3.2 d – f, h, m – q

Key words

resistance, resistor, filament lamp, diode, forward, reverse, light-dependent resistor, thermistor

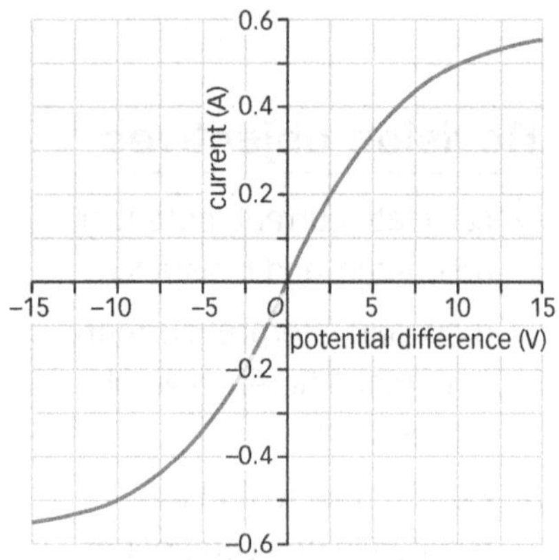

▲ Current–potential-difference graph for a filament lamp.

Lamps

A **filament lamp** emits light when there is enough current in it. The charge flows through a thin wire, heating it up enough for it to glow brightly. The increase in temperature increases the resistance of the wire, so its current–potential-difference graph is not a straight line.

H The metal in the lamp consists of ions and electrons. When there is a current, the electrons have to flow past the ions, which are fixed in position. As the temperature of the metal increases, the ions vibrate more, getting in the way of the electrons. So the resistance increases as the wire heats up.

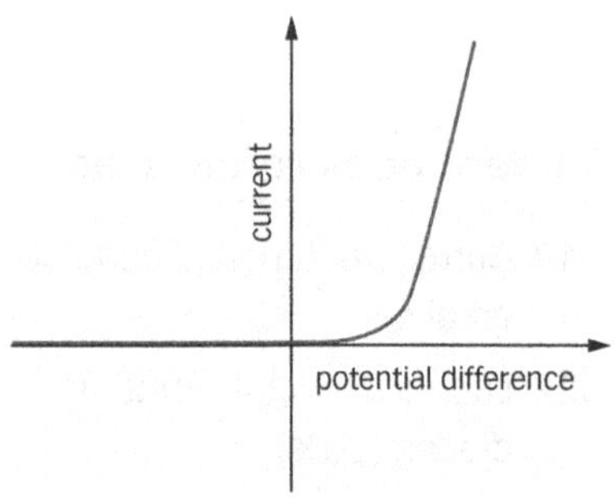

▲ Current–potential-difference graph for a diode.

Diodes

Charge can only flow one way through a **diode**. The resistance is low when the current is in the **forward** direction, but is very large when the current is in the **reverse** direction.

Some diodes called light-emitting diodes (LEDs) are increasingly being used for lighting. They transfer much less energy as heat compared with filament lamps.

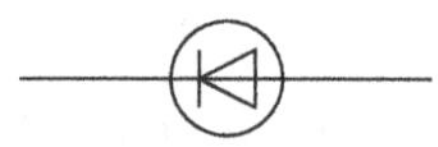

▲ Charge flows easily from right to left through this diode.

Sensors

Some resistors can be used as sensors in electrical circuits.

- A **light-dependent resistor** (LDR) has a resistance that decreases with increasing light intensity.
- A **thermistor** has a resistance that decreases as the temperature increases.

Exam tip AQA

Practise changing the subject of the equation $V = I \times R$.
Learn the current–potential-difference graphs for resistors, diodes, and lamps.

Questions

1 What is the potential difference across a 5.6 Ω resistor when it has a current of 0.25 A?

2 Sketch the current–potential-difference graph for a diode and state what it means for the resistance of the diode.

3 **H** Sketch the current–potential-difference graph for a filament lamp. Explain its shape.

Series

In a **series** circuit, there is only one way for electrons to get round the circuit. They have to pass through each component in turn.

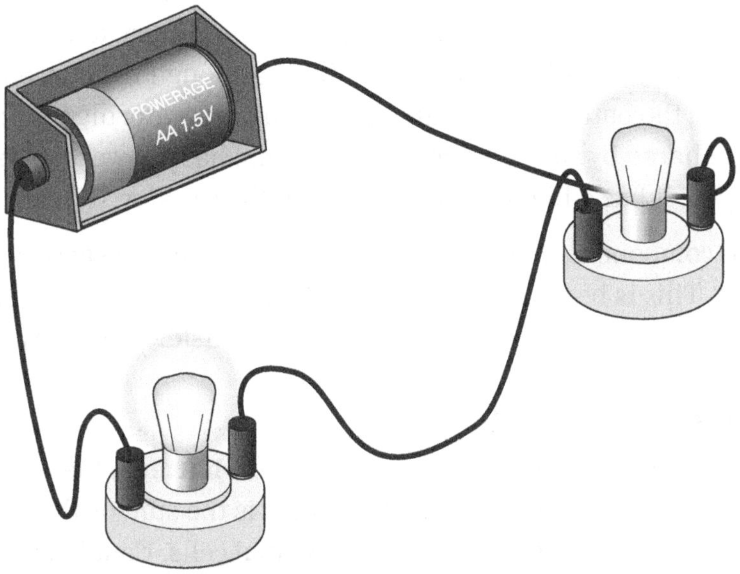

▲ Two lamps in series with a cell.

Current and potential difference

In a series circuit:

- all the components have the same **current**
- the components share the **potential difference** from the supply.

This is because each electron has to pass through each component in turn. So as an electron flows from one terminal of the supply to the other, all of its energy has to be shared amongst the components it passes through.

Resistance

Each component in a series circuit will have a **resistance**. By adding all of their resistances together you find the **total resistance** of the circuit. This allows you to calculate the current in the circuit.

So what is the current in this circuit?

The total resistance = 5 Ω + 10 Ω + 15 Ω = 30 Ω

$$V = I \times R \text{ so } I \times R = V \text{ and } I = \frac{V}{R}$$

$$I = \frac{6\,\text{V}}{30\,\Omega} = 0.2\,\text{A}$$

Revision objectives

- ✔ recognise series and parallel circuits
- ✔ explain how current and potential difference are shared in series circuits
- ✔ explain how current and potential difference are shared in parallel circuits
- ✔ calculate the resistance of resistors connected in series
- ✔ understand the effect of connecting cells in series

Student book references

2.17 Current and potential difference

2.20 Series circuits

2.21 Parallel circuits

Specification key

✔ P2.3.2 h – l

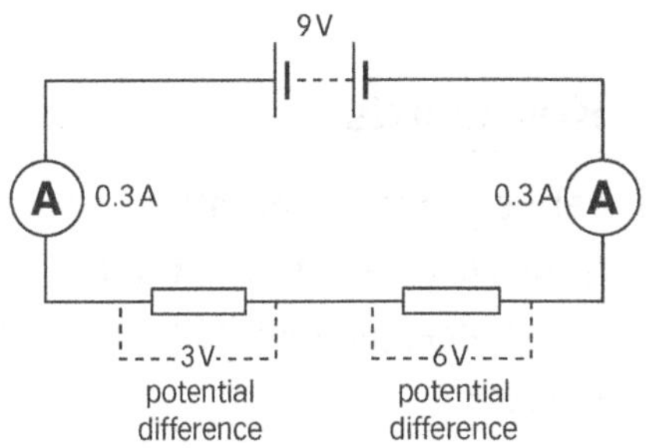

▲ All components have the same current, but only a share of the supply's potential difference.

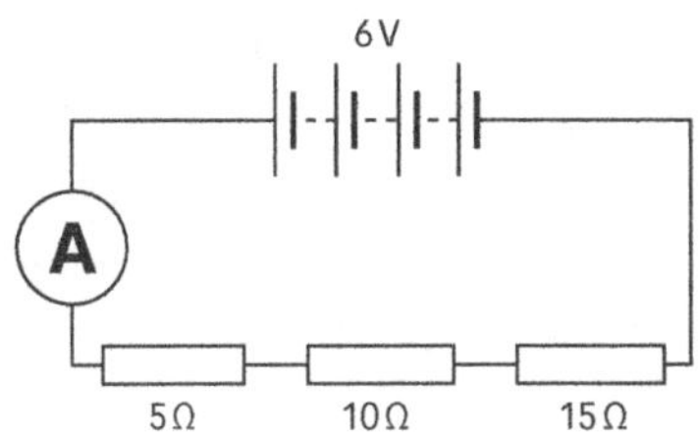

▲ What does the ammeter read?

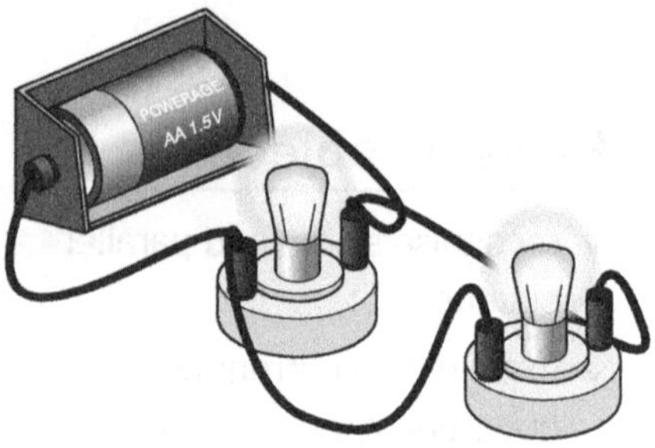

▲ Two lamps in parallel with a cell

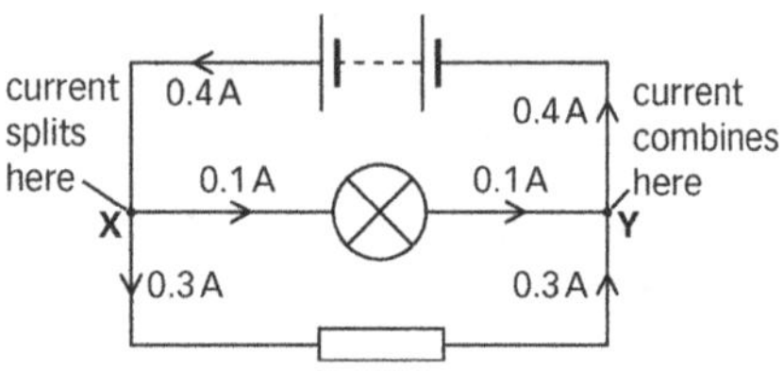

▲ All components have the same potential difference but share the current.

Parallel

In a **parallel** circuit, there is more than one way for the electrons to get round the circuit.

Current and potential difference

In this circuit, electrons flow through either the resistor or the lamp on their way from one terminal of the battery to the other. They can't flow through both. So although the current leaving the battery is the same as the current entering it, it has to be shared by the components. The lamp has a lower current because it has a higher resistance than the resistor.

Both components have the same potential difference across them. This is because they are directly connected to the supply – there is nothing else for an electron to transfer its energy to.

Batteries of cells

When **cells** are stacked in series to make a **battery**, the potential difference across its terminals is the sum of the potential differences across the individual cells. Usually, all of the cells are the same way round. If any cells are the wrong way round, you have to subtract their potential difference from the total. Connecting cells in parallel doesn't increase the potential difference, but does make a battery that lasts longer.

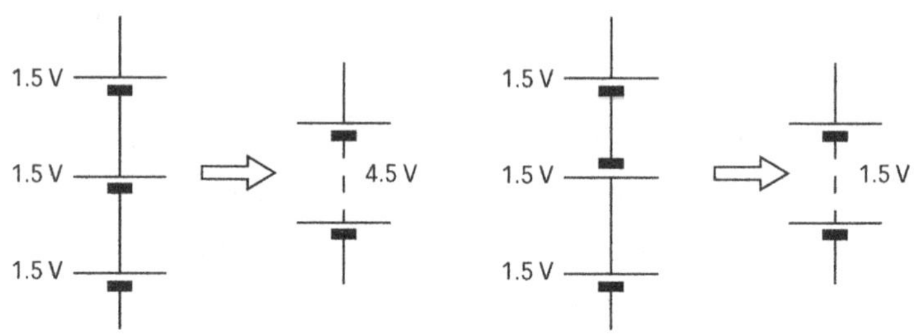

▲ Two batteries of three cells.

Key words

series, current, potential difference, resistance, total resistance, parallel, cell, battery

Exam tip

AQA

Remember that an ammeter has a low resistance and goes in series with a component, but a voltmeter has a high resistance and goes in parallel with a component.

Questions

1 A resistor is connected in series with a cell and an ammeter. A voltmeter is connected in parallel with the resistor. Draw the circuit diagram.

2 Resistors of 6Ω and 3Ω are connected in series with a $1.5\,V$ cell. By calculating the total resistance, find the current and potential difference for each resistor.

3 **H** Resistors of 6Ω and 3Ω are connected in parallel with a $1.5\,V$ cell. By calculating the current in each resistor, find the total resistance of the circuit.

Direct and alternating current

If the power supply of a circuit is a battery, then it has **direct current (d.c.)**. The current is always in the same direction, from the positive terminal of the battery to the negative one.

If the power supply of a circuit is a generator, then it has **alternating current (a.c.)**. The current keeps changing direction, first one way, then the other.

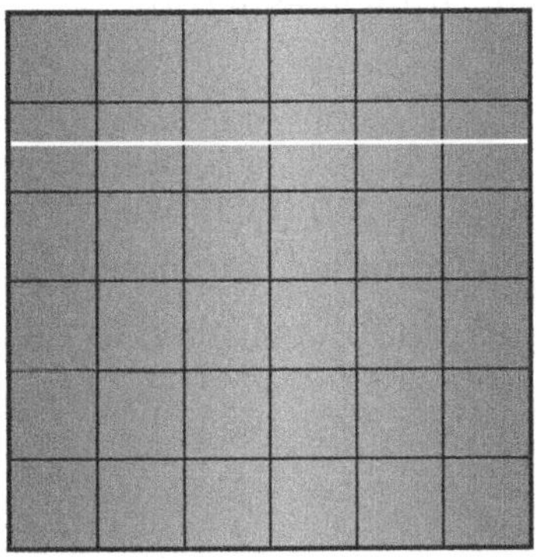

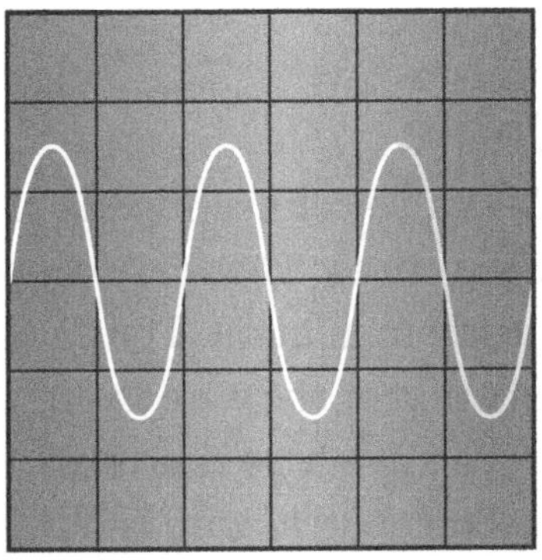

▲ Oscilloscope traces for d.c. and a.c. supplies.

Oscilloscope

An **oscilloscope** is an instrument that shows how potential difference changes with time. When the oscilloscope is connected to a d.c. supply, the **trace** on the **screen** is a horizontal line. An a.c. supply gives a wavy line as the potential difference alternates between positive and negative values.

Mains electricity

Mains electricity in the UK is supplied at 230 V a.c. with a **frequency** of 50 hertz or Hz. This means that the potential difference goes through 50 cycles of positive and negative values in each second.

Revision objectives

- understand the difference between alternating and direct current
- know that mains electricity in the UK is 230 V a.c at 50 Hz
- use an oscilloscope to measure a.c. supply frequency
- understand the structure of a UK three-pin plug
- explain the use of fuses and circuit breakers for electrical safety
- understand why devices are earthed

Student book references

2.24 Direct current and alternating current

2.25 Mains electricity in the home

Specification key

✔ P2.4.1

H

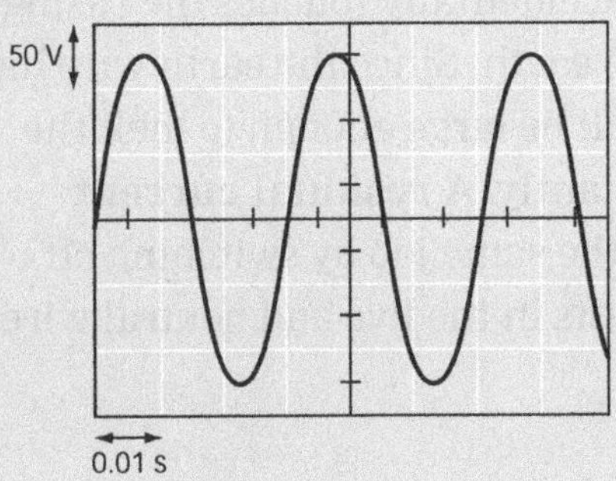

▲ Screen trace for an a.c. supply.

Finding frequency

The trace shows that one complete cycle of change takes up three squares.

The **timebase** of the oscilloscope is set to 0.01 s per square. So the time for one cycle (the **time period**) = 3 × 0.01 = 0.03 s.

$$\text{frequency (Hz)} = \frac{1}{\text{time period (s)}} = \frac{1}{0.03\,\text{s}} = 33\,\text{Hz}$$

The trace also shows that the potential difference alternates between +125 V and –125 V.

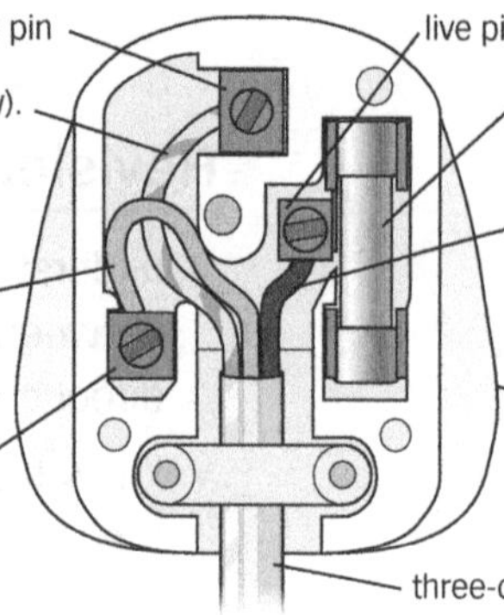

▲ The inside of a UK three-pin plug.

UK plugs

UK plugs have three pins that connect with the mains supply.

- The **live** pin carries current at 230 V a.c. from the supply.
- The **neutral** pin allows current to return at a low voltage to the supply.
- The **earth** pin allows current to the ground when something goes wrong.

Cable

The cable connecting the plug to the device can have two or three **cores**. These are copper wires surrounded by coloured plastic insulation. The colour of the insulation is linked to the function of the wire inside it.

- The live wire is brown.
- The neutral wire is blue.
- The earth wire is striped yellow and green.

Two-core cables can only be used with devices that are double insulated. This means that if the live wire comes loose it can't connect with the user of the device.

Fuses

Every plug must contain a **fuse**. This is a short length of thin wire in a glass or ceramic tube. It is inserted between the live pin and the live wire. If there is too much current in the live wire, the fuse wire heats up and melts, breaking the circuit. So the fuse is a fast switch that automatically turns off the supply if the current gets dangerously big. A **circuit breaker** is a type of fuse that can be reset by pressing a button.

Earth

Many useful devices have metal casings that are connected to the earth wire. If the live wire accidentally touches the casing, the current can safely escape to earth. Since the earth wire has a low resistance, the current will be large enough to melt the fuse, turning off the supply instantly. A **residual current circuit breaker (RCCB)** does the same job by switching off the supply as soon as the currents in the live and neutral wires are not the same.

Key words

direct current (d.c.), alternating current (a.c.), oscilloscope, trace, screen, frequency, timebase, time period, live, neutral, earth, cores, fuse, circuit breaker, residual current circuit breaker (RCCB)

Exam tip

AQA

Remember that an oscilloscope trace is a potential-difference–time graph. It may look like a wave, but it isn't one.

Questions

1 Describe the structure of a three-core cable and explain the choice of materials for it.

2 What is different between d.c. and a.c. supplies?

3 **H** Explain how the fuse and earth wire in a plug make a device safe to touch.

Power

The power of a device tells you the rate at which the supply transfers energy to it. You calculate it with this equation:

$$P = I \times V$$

P is the power of the device in watts (W)
I is the current in the device in amperes (A)
V is the **potential difference** across the device in volts (V)

So what is the maximum power of a device that is connected to the 230 V mains supply through a 5 A fuse?

$$P = I \times V = 5\,\text{A} \times 230\,\text{V} = 1150\,\text{W or } 1.15\,\text{kW}$$

Hot wires

The wires in the cable that carry the current between the supply and a device have a small resistance. There is therefore a small potential difference across each wire, and consequently the current transfers energy to heat in the cable. The resistance of the cable has to be kept low enough to stop it getting too hot – thick cables have a lower resistance than thin ones (but cost more!).

Power can also be calculated using:

$$\underset{\text{(power in watts, W)}}{P} = \frac{E\ \textbf{(energy}\text{ in joules, J)}}{t\ \text{(time in seconds, s)}}$$

H Energy transfer

The energy transferred to a device can be calculated from the potential difference across it and the charge that passes through it.

$$E = V \times Q$$

E is the energy transferred to the device in joules (J)
V is the potential difference across the supply in volts (V)
Q is the charge through the device in coulombs (C)

So how much energy transfers to heat in a cable that has a potential difference of 2.3 V across it when it carries a current of 13 A for an hour?

$$I = \frac{Q}{t} = \text{so } Q = It = 13\,\text{A} \times 3600\,\text{s} = 4.68 \times 10^4\,\text{C}$$

$$E = Q \times V = 4.68 \times 10^4\,\text{C} \times 2.3\,\text{V} = 1.08 \times 10^5\,\text{J}$$

Key words

energy, potential difference, power

Revision objectives

- ✔ use the heating effect of current to explain cable size
- ✔ calculate the power of a device
- ✔ calculate energy transfer from charge and potential difference

Student book references

2.26 Current, charge, and power

Specification key

✔ P2.4.2

Exam tip AQA

Always use standard form when you have to calculate with very large or very small numbers. Remember that 1 kW = 1000 W.

Questions

1 Explain the difference between a 5 A cable and a 13 A cable.

2 Calculate the current in a 3 kW kettle when it is connected to the 230 V mains supply.

3 **H** A mobile phone charger transfers 3600 J of energy to a phone in 20 minutes at a potential difference of 6 V. How much charge passes through the phone in that time?

Questions
Electricity

Working to Grade E

1 A balloon is rubbed against hair. The balloon becomes positively charged. What happens to the hair?

2 What is an electric current?

3 Draw the circuit diagram for a resistor, lamp, and switch in series with a battery.

4 Describe what this circuit diagram shows.

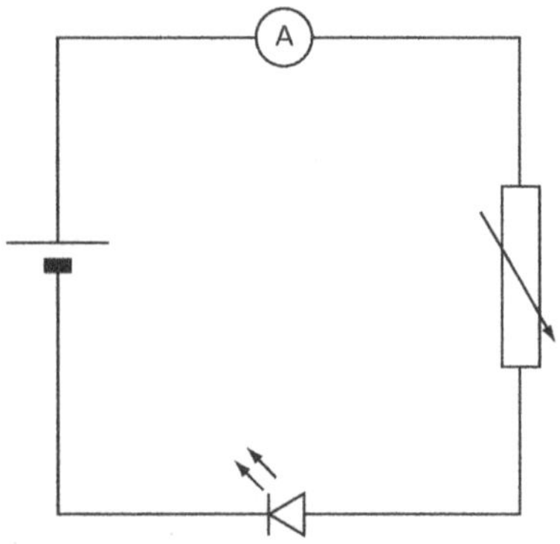

5 Calculate the potential difference across a 30 Ω resistor when it carries a current of 6 A.

6 Draw the circuit diagram for a voltmeter and resistor in parallel with a battery.

7 Name the component that can be used to detect light.

8 Complete the table for a cable connected to a UK three-pin plug.

Colour of insulation	Name of wire
blue	
	live

9 Calculate the power of a device that draws a current of 3 A from the mains supply.

Working to Grade C

10 Electrons transfer from a balloon to hair when they are rubbed together. What charge do the balloon and hair have after this transfer?

11 A charge of 1200 C flows through a TV in 10 minutes. What is the current in the TV?

12 A resistor is connected to a battery. Draw a circuit diagram to show how meters should be connected to allow the calculation of the resistance of the resistor.

13 Identify the components A, B, and C from their current–potential-difference graphs.

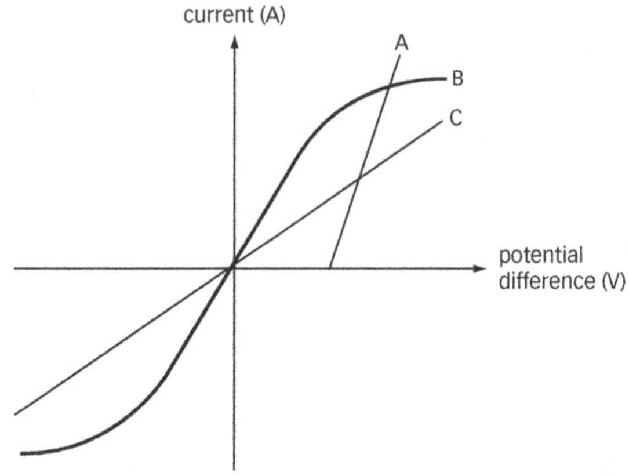

14 The current in the 12 Ω resistor is 4 A. What are the currents in the 6 Ω resistor and the battery in the diagram below?

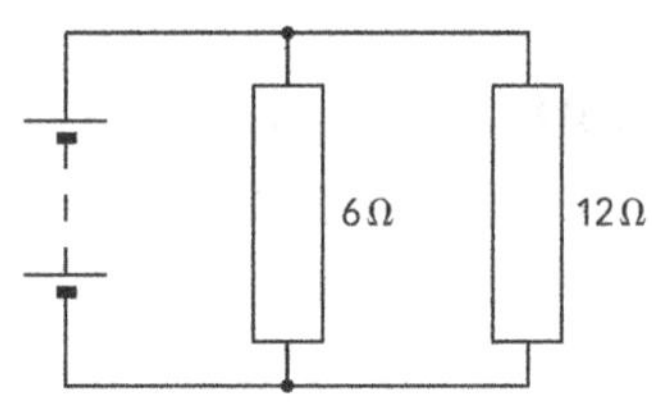

15 Explain why three-pin plugs are equipped with fuses.

Working to Grade A*

16 Calculate the maximum voltage and frequency of the a.c. power supply used for this oscilloscope trace. The timebase is set to 0.02 s/div and the vertical scale to 50 V/div.

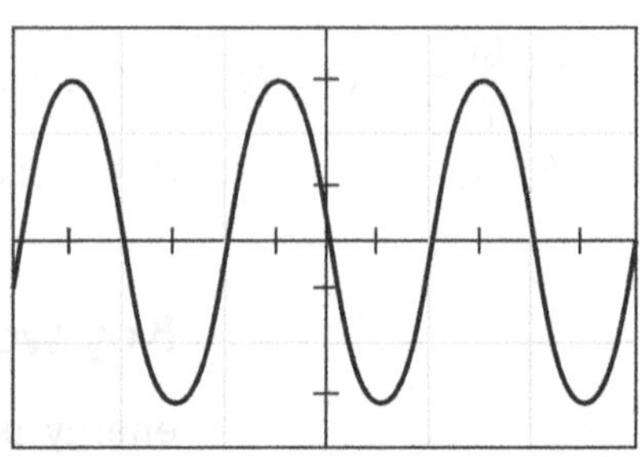

Examination questions
Electricity

1 a Use words from the box to label the components A, B, and C in the diagram.

ammeter	**resistor**	**voltmeter**	**battery**	**switch**

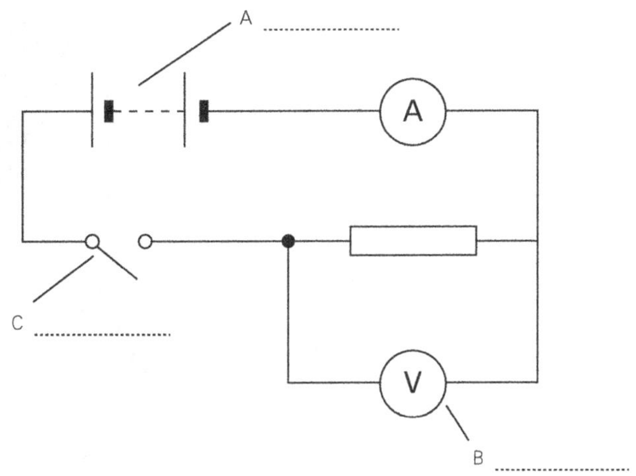

(3 marks)

b The current in the 5 Ω resistor is 0.4 A.

Calculate the potential difference across the resistor.

Write down the equation you use, and then show clearly how you work out your answer.

....

....

potential difference = ... V

(2 marks)

c Plot a current–potential-difference graph for the resistor in part b on the axes below.

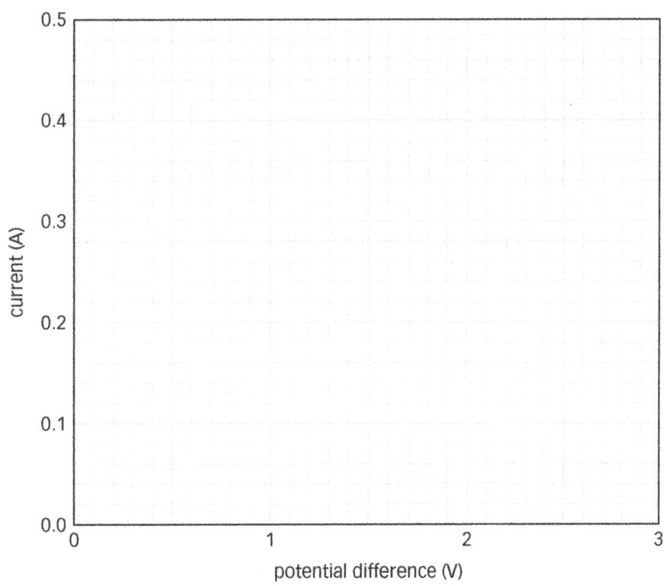

(2 marks)

(Total marks: 7)

2 A kettle is connected to the mains supply by a cable and three-pin plug.

a The statements in List A describe the function of the wires in the cable.

The colours in List B give the colours of the insulation of the wires.

Draw **one** line from each statement in List A to the correct colour in List B.

List A **Function of the wires**	**List B** **Insulation colour**
Makes the kettle safe	Red
	Blue
Carries current at 230 V	
	Brown
Carries low-voltage current	Green and yellow

(3 marks)

b The current in the kettle is 7 A when it is switched on.

Calculate the power of the kettle.

Write down the equation you use, and then show clearly how you work out your answer.

....

....

power = ... W

(3 marks)

c What is the best size of fuse to have in the kettle plug from part b?

Circle **one** value from the box.

1A	**3A**	**5A**	**13A**

(1 mark)

d Explain why there is a fuse in the plug.

....

....

....

....

(3 marks)

e When the fuse is inserted into the plug it is a conductor.

The fuse must be replaced when it becomes an insulator.

i Describe the difference between a conductor and an insulator.

....

....

....

(2 marks)

ii A student uses a cell and a lamp to test a fuse.

Draw a suitable circuit in the space below.

Use the correct symbols for each component.

(4 marks)

(Total marks: 16)

Revision objectives

- describe the structure of an atom in terms of neutrons, protons, and electrons
- explain the changes to an atom when it gains or loses electrons
- understand the meaning of the term isotope
- describe how new evidence caused scientists to change their model of an atom

	Relative charge	Relative mass
Proton	+1	1
Neutron	0	1
Electron	−1	0.0005

Student book references

2.27 The atom and the nucleus

Specification key

- P2.5.1

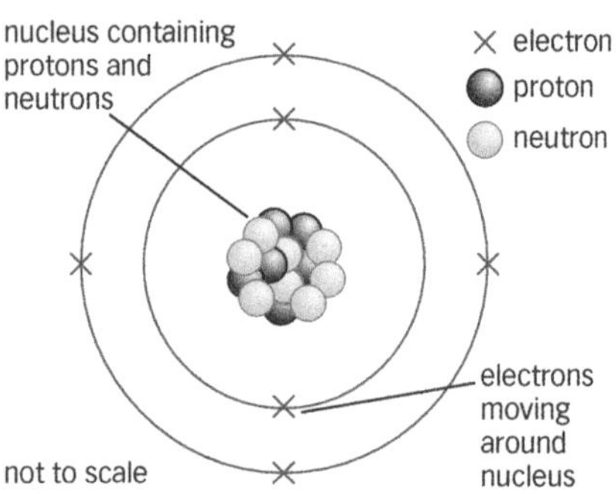

Key words

atom, nucleus, electron, proton, neutron, atomic number, mass number, isotope, ion

Atoms

An **atom** is the smallest part of a substance. We now believe that every atom is made from a small, heavy **nucleus** surrounded by **electrons**. The nucleus contains **protons** and **neutrons**. Most of the space in the atom is taken up by the electrons.

Each atom is specified by two quantities:

- the **atomic number** is the number of protons in the nucleus
- the **mass number** is the number of particles in the nucleus.

Isotopes

The chemical properties of an atom are determined by its electrons. Every atom has to have the same number of electrons and protons to give it an overall charge of zero. However, the number of neutrons in the nucleus is not fixed. So each element can have a number of **isotopes**, each with the same atomic number but a different mass number.

So what are the particles in an atom of the isotope ${}^{60}_{27}Co$?

The atomic number tells you that each atom must have 27 protons and 27 electrons. The mass number allows you to work out the number of neutrons: 60 – 27 = 33.

Atoms can gain or lose electrons to become **ions**. The charge of the ion depends on the number of electrons gained or lost.

Changing ideas

At one time scientists thought that the protons in an atom were spread evenly amongst the electrons. This was called the plum-pudding model. In 1911, Ernest Rutherford invented the modern model to explain the results of an experiment. One of his students fired alpha particles (helium nuclei) at a thin leaf of gold. Most particles passed straight through the foil, as expected, but a few bounced off it. This could not be explained by the plum-pudding model. It could only happen if each atom contained a small, heavy, charged lump – the nucleus.

Questions

1 Name the **three** different particles in each atom.

2 Calculate the numbers of each particle in an atom of ${}^{90}_{38}Sr$.

3 **H** How many electrons are there in a positive ion of the isotope ${}^{12}_{6}C$?

Unstable atoms

Many isotopes are unstable. Their atoms **decay** at random, emitting three types of **ionising radiation**:

- **alpha** particles (α), each one made up of two neutrons and two protons, like a helium nucleus
- **beta** particles (β), each one made of a high-speed electron from the nucleus
- **gamma** rays (γ), each one a high-frequency electromagnetic wave.

We are exposed to this radiation all of the time. This **background radiation** comes from the **radioactive** materials in our surroundings, both natural and artificial.

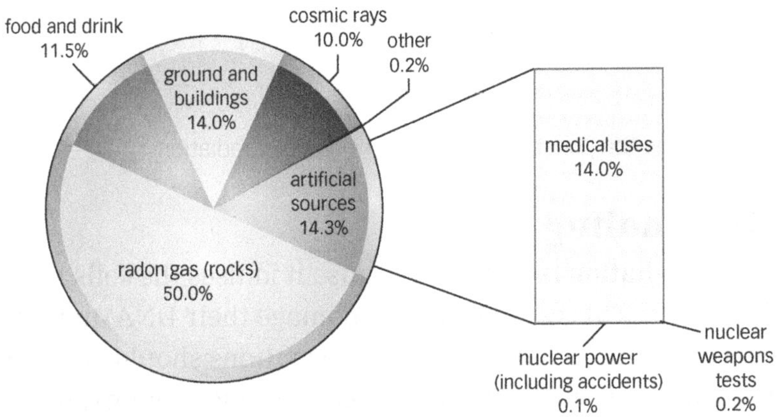

▲ Sources of background radiation in the UK.

Revision objectives

- ✔ describe radioactive decay
- ✔ state sources of background radiation
- ✔ use an activity–time graph to measure half-life
- ✔ understand the effect of electric and magnetic fields on radiation
- ✔ understand the changes in the nucleus that give rise to radiation
- ✔ compare the penetrating properties of alpha, beta, and gamma radiation
- ✔ describe how to handle radioactive sources safely

Student book references

2.28 Radioactive decay and half-life

2.29 Alpha, beta, and gamma radiation

Specification key

✔ P2.5.2 a – f, h

Half-life

The radiation from radioactive materials is easy to detect because it knocks electrons out of atoms. When this **ionisation** takes place inside an insulator, the small electric current created can be detected. The output of a detector tells you about the **activity** of the source, and the rate at which its atoms decay. Since each atom can only decay once, the activity of a source decreases with time. The time taken for the activity to halve is called the **half-life**. Each radioactive isotope has a different half-life.

The half-life of cobalt-60 is 5 years. If a source has an activity of 800 today, what will the activity be in 20 years' time?

Time in years	0	5	10	15	20
Activity	800	½×800 = 400	½×400 = 200	½×200 = 100	½×100 = 50

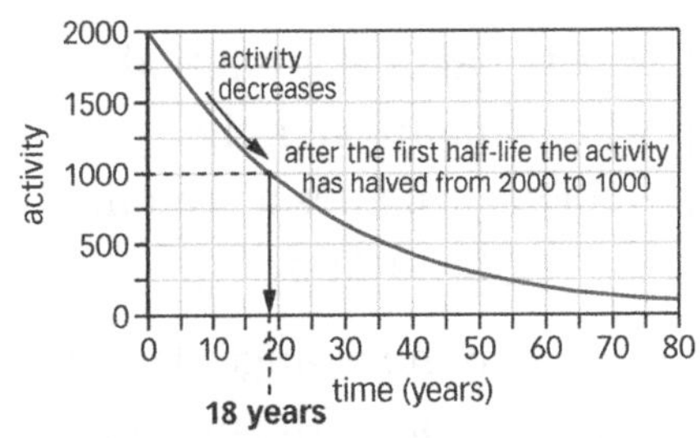

▲ The activity–time graph for a source with a half-life of 18 years.

Key words

decay, ionising radiation, alpha, beta, gamma, background radiation, radioactive, ionisation, activity, half-life

Exam tip

AQA

Write down all of the steps you go through when you do calculations with half-life.

H Nuclear equations

Equations are used to show the effect of radioactive decay on a nucleus. The equations are balanced; the mass and atomic numbers always add up to the same value on both sides of the arrow.

The emission of an alpha particle removes two neutrons and two protons from a nucleus.

$$^{222}_{86}\text{Rn} \rightarrow {}^{218}_{84}\text{Po} + {}^{4}_{2}\alpha$$

A beta particle is emitted when a neutron in the nucleus becomes a proton.

$$^{90}_{38}\text{Sr} \rightarrow {}^{90}_{39}\text{Po} + {}^{0}_{-1}\beta$$

There are no changes to the composition of the nucleus when a gamma ray is emitted.

$$^{60}_{27}\text{Co} \rightarrow {}^{60}_{27}\text{Co} + {}^{0}_{0}\gamma$$

Penetrating power

The distance that an ionising radiation can pass through matter is determined by its mass and charge. The more ions that a particle creates, the less distance it can pass through matter. Alpha particles are the most ionising because they are charged and heavy. Beta particles are less ionising because they are light. Gamma rays are the least ionising of the three because they have no charge.

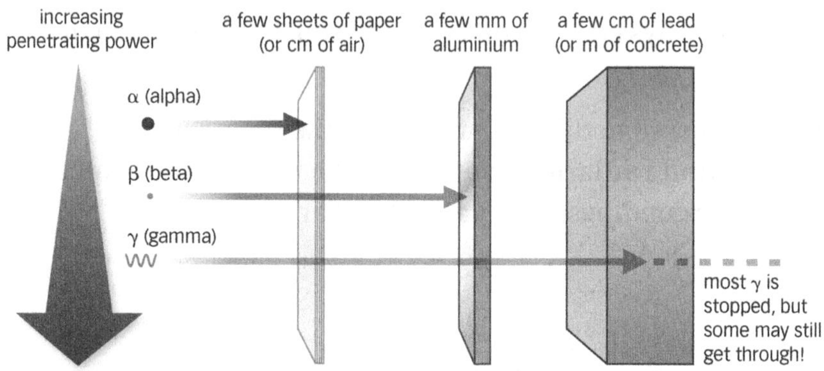

▲ Comparing the penetration of different types of radiation.

Safe handling

Ionising radiation is harmful because it ionises the cells in living tissue. This can kill cells or damage their DNA and make them cancerous. So the following precautions should be taken when handling radioactive materials to reduce your exposure:

- keep as far away as you can
- use them for the shortest time possible
- use protective clothing to stop you ingesting them
- use shielding to absorb the radiation before it gets to you.

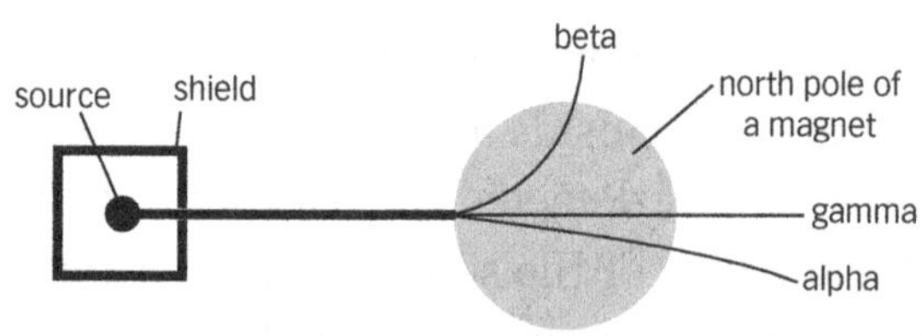

▲ The effect of a magnetic field on radiation.

Questions

1 Describe **three** safety precautions when handling radioactive materials.

2 Radiation from a source passes through a sheet of paper but is blocked by a few millimetres of aluminium. Explain the type of radiation.

3 **H** A radioactive source has an activity of 200 at 1 o'clock. By 4 o'clock the activity drops to just 25. Calculate the half-life of the source.

Alpha particles

The smoke detector below contains an alpha particle source. Alpha particles ionise the air in the chamber next to the source, turning the air from an insulator into a conductor. So a potential difference across the chamber results in a current that can be detected. Any smoke that enters the chamber reduces the ionisation of the air. The resulting drop in current is detected and triggers the alarm. The source needs to have a long half-life to avoid false alarms!

Beta particles

Beta particles are ideal for measuring the thickness of sheets of paper in a paper mill. Alpha particles would be stopped completely by the paper and gamma rays would go straight through it.

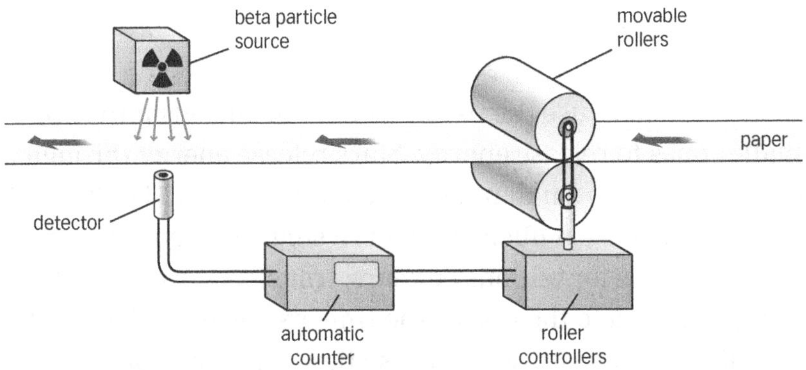

▲ Automatic thickness control of paper.

Any increase in thickness of the paper reduces the rate at which beta particles reach the detector. This can be fed back to the rollers to reduce the thickness back to the target value.

Gamma rays

Medical **tracers** containing gamma ray sources are used to create images of organs inside the body. This is because only gamma rays are easily able to pass through the body. The tracer is injected into the body and gamma ray detectors around the body record where the tracer goes. The tracer needs to have a short half-life so that the patient is only radioactive for a few days!

Revision objectives

- describe the use of radioactive sources for detecting smoke, measuring thickness, and medical tracing
- describe the processes of nuclear fusion and fission
- compare the advantages and disadvantages of using fission and fusion to produce energy

Student book references

2.30 Uses of radiation

2.31 Fission and fusion

Specification key

✔ P2.5.2 g ✔ P2.6.1
✔ P2.6.2 a – b

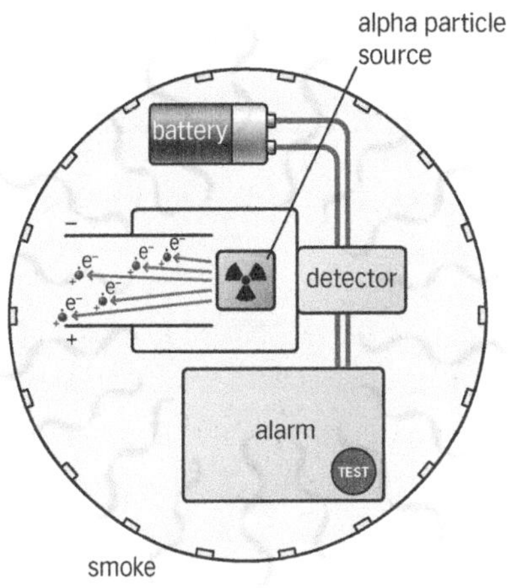

▲ A smoke detector.

Key words

tracers, fission, chain reaction, fusion

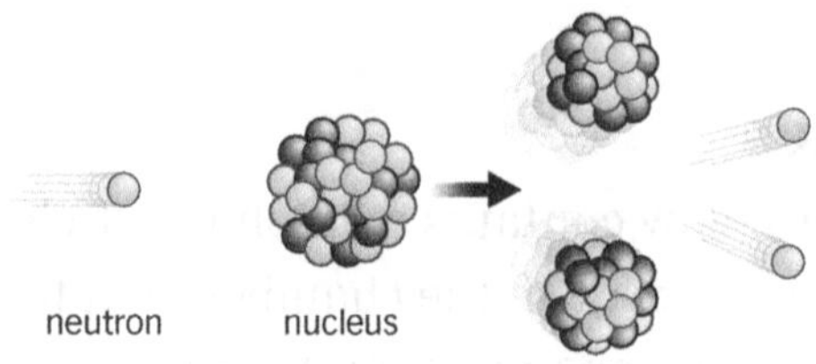

▲ When the nucleus absorbs a neutron it splits into two.

Fission

Two radioactive materials (uranium-235 or plutonium-239) can be used to produce energy in a nuclear reactor. They split (**fission**) into two smaller nuclei when they absorb a neutron. This releases a lot of energy as heat, which can be used to boil water to steam and spin a turbine. Each fission produces two or more neutrons, each of which can go on to produce the fission of another nucleus. If this **chain reaction** is carefully controlled it can result in a steady release of energy.

Fusion

Nuclear reactors use the fission of a large nucleus into two smaller ones to release energy. Stars release energy through the **fusion** of two small nuclei into larger nuclei. The Sun fuses four hydrogen nuclei to make a single nucleus of helium. It has done this for billions of years, transferring most of the energy released to the rest of the Universe as light. The nuclei that fuse have a positive charge, so they repel each other. A very high temperature is required to give the particles enough energy to get close enough for fusion to take place. This is proving difficult to achieve on Earth.

▲ The fusion of two small nuclei can release energy.

Exam tip AQA

Use the properties of a type of radiation to justify its use in an application.

Questions

1 Name **two** substances that are used as fuel in a fission reactor.

2 Explain why a medical tracer should be a gamma ray source with a short half-life.

3 **H** Explain why a long-lived beta source is used to control the thickness of paper in a paper mill.

Birth

All new stars are created the same way.

- A large cloud of gas called a **nebula** starts to collapse under its own weight.
- Gravity pulls the particles (mostly hydrogen) closer to each other, heating the cloud.
- A glowing hot ball of gas called a **protostar** forms at the centre.
- The protostar gets hotter as more material falls into it.
- A **star** forms when the temperature at the centre is high enough for **fusion** reactions.

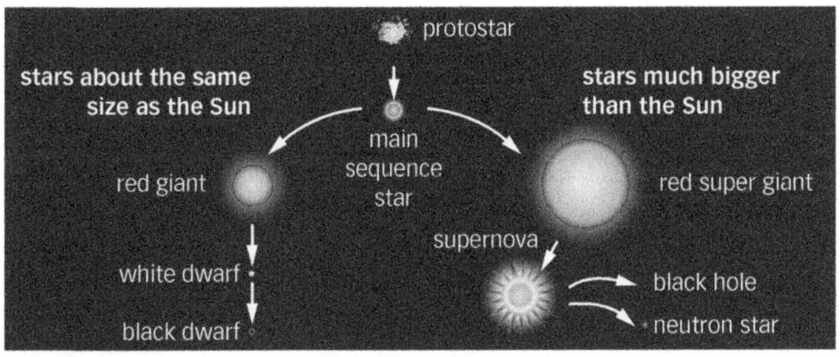

The life cycle of a star.

Death

The energy released by the fusion of hydrogen nuclei into helium stops a star from collapsing. The outward push of the energy flowing to the surface balances the inwards push of gravity. This balance keeps the star stable. This **main sequence** part of the star's life ends when it runs out of hydrogen fuel at its centre. Small stars, like our Sun, last several billion years before swelling up into a **red giant** and then cooling to a **white dwarf** as fusion reactions stop. Large stars have shorter main sequences and turn into **red super giants**. These can fuse helium nuclei into heavier elements. A heavy enough star can convert its nuclei into iron before it explodes as a **supernova**, creating new elements (and elements heavier than iron) and spreading them through space. All of the elements on Earth, apart from hydrogen and helium, were made this way. The material left behind after a supernova collapses under its own weight until it forms a dense **neutron star**. Sometimes a neutron star is heavy enough to collapse forever, becoming a **black hole**.

Exam tip

AQA

Remember that what happens at the end of its main sequence depends upon the mass of a star.

Revision objectives

- ✔ explain the formation of stars
- ✔ describe what happens when a star approaches the end of its life
- ✔ describe the complete life cycle of a star including the production of new elements

Student book references

2.32 Star life cycles

Specification key

✔ **P2.6.2 c – f**

Key words

nebula, protostar, star, fusion, main sequence, red giant, white dwarf, super red giant, supernova, neutron star, black hole

Questions

1. Here are some stages in a star's life. Put them in the correct order, starting with the earliest: protostar, nebula, white dwarf, red giant star.
2. Explain how stars form in space.
3. **H** Explain why a star is only stable during its main sequence.

Questions
Radioactivity

Working to Grade E

1 Complete this table for the particles in an atom.

Name	Mass	Charge
	0	−1
	1	1
		0

2 Name the **two** particles in a nucleus.

3 State **three** sources of background radiation.

4 Name the radiation that is most easily stopped.

5 State **three** precautions to take when handling radioactive materials.

6 Name the best type of radioactive source for a medical tracer.

7 Complete these sentences for a nuclear reactor.

The nuclei of the ______ fuel split into two when they absorb a ______. This is called nuclear ______.

8 Put these stages of star formation in the correct order, ending with the last: black hole, main sequence, protostar, supernova, super red giant.

Working to Grade C

9 Calculate the number of electrons, protons, and neutrons in one atom of $^{22}_{10}Ne$.

10 State the similarities and differences between the isotopes $^{22}_{10}Ne$ and $^{20}_{10}Ne$.

11 A source has a half-life of 5 hours. If its activity is 1000 now, what will it be in 10 hours' time?

12 Explain why radioactive sources can be harmful.

13 Explain **three** different precautions to take when handling radioactive materials.

14 State which types of radiation can pass through paper.

15 Explain why a medical tracer should be a gamma ray emitter with a half-life of a few hours.

16 Explain the stages in the life of a star like the Sun.

Working to Grade A*

17 The activity of a source drops from 512 to 32 in just 8 hours. What is its half-life?

18 Complete the symbol $^{\_}_{\_}Np$ for the product of the alpha decay of $^{241}_{95}Am$.

19 Explain the changes in a nucleus when it emits a beta particle.

Examination questions
Radioactivity

1 The table shows the average radiation dose that a person in various places in the UK receives from background radiation in a year.

The doses are measured in millisieverts (mSv).

UK location	Annual dose in mSv
Cornwall	9
East Anglia	1
London	2

a Give **two** sources of background radiation.

1 ....

2 ....

(2 marks)

b Which of these is the correct reason why background radiation is harmful?

Tick (✓) **one** box.

It is in all of the food that you eat. ☐

It damages cells by ionising them. ☐

It can't be detected without instruments. ☐

It contains three different sorts of radiation. ☐

(1 mark)

c A radiographer works with radiation in a London hospital.

She is only allowed to receive a total dose of 20 mSv of radiation in a year.

Her average dose from the radiation at work is 0.02 mSv per hour.

Calculate the number of hours she is allowed to work each year.

....

....

(3 marks)

(Total marks: 6)

2 This diagram represents an atom of the element lithium.

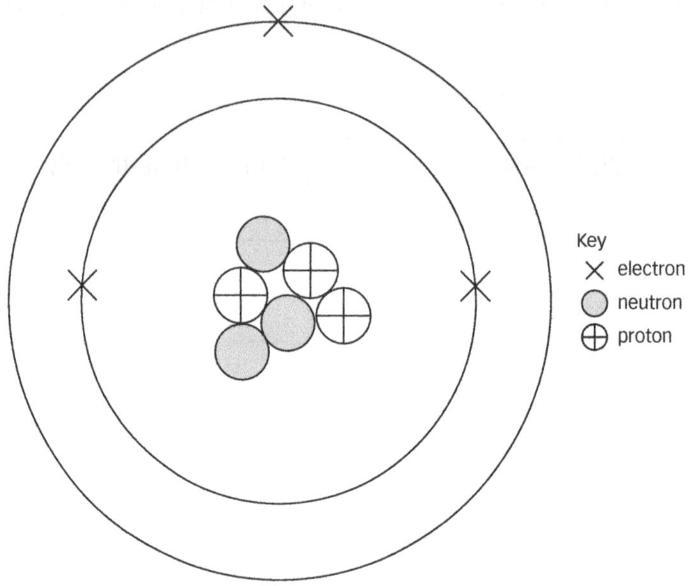

a Complete the symbol for this isotope of lithium.

.... Li
....

(2 marks)

b Another isotope of lithium has a mass number of 7. It is called lithium-7.

Complete the diagram below to represent an atom of this isotope.

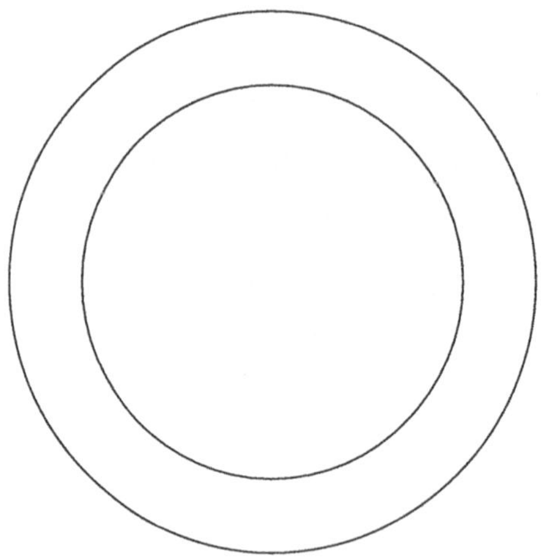

(3 marks)

c When lithium-7 absorbs a neutron it breaks into a pair of alpha particles.

Use a word from the box to complete the sentence.

fission	**fusion**	**radioactive**	**star**

This is an example of a .... reaction.

(1 mark)

d A smoke detector contains a radioactive source.

Radiation from the source ionises air in the detector.

Any smoke in the detector reduces this ionisation.

Explain why the source needs to:
- emit alpha particles
- have a long half-life.

....

....

....

....

(3 marks)

e The people who assemble smoke detectors need to take safety precautions.

Describe and explain **one** precaution that they should take.

....

....

....

(2 marks)

f List A contains the names of three different types of radiation.

List B describes these types of radiation.

Draw **one** line from each name in list A to its description in list B.

List A **Types of radiation**	**List B** **Description**
	Helium nucleus
Beta	
	Hydrogen nucleus
Alpha	
	High-speed electron
Gamma	
	Electromagnetic wave

(3 marks)
(Total marks: 14)

3 a This diagram shows stages in the life cycle of a star.

Use words from the box below to complete the diagram.

main sequence	**neutron star**	**protostar**	**super red giant**
	supernova	**white dwarf**	

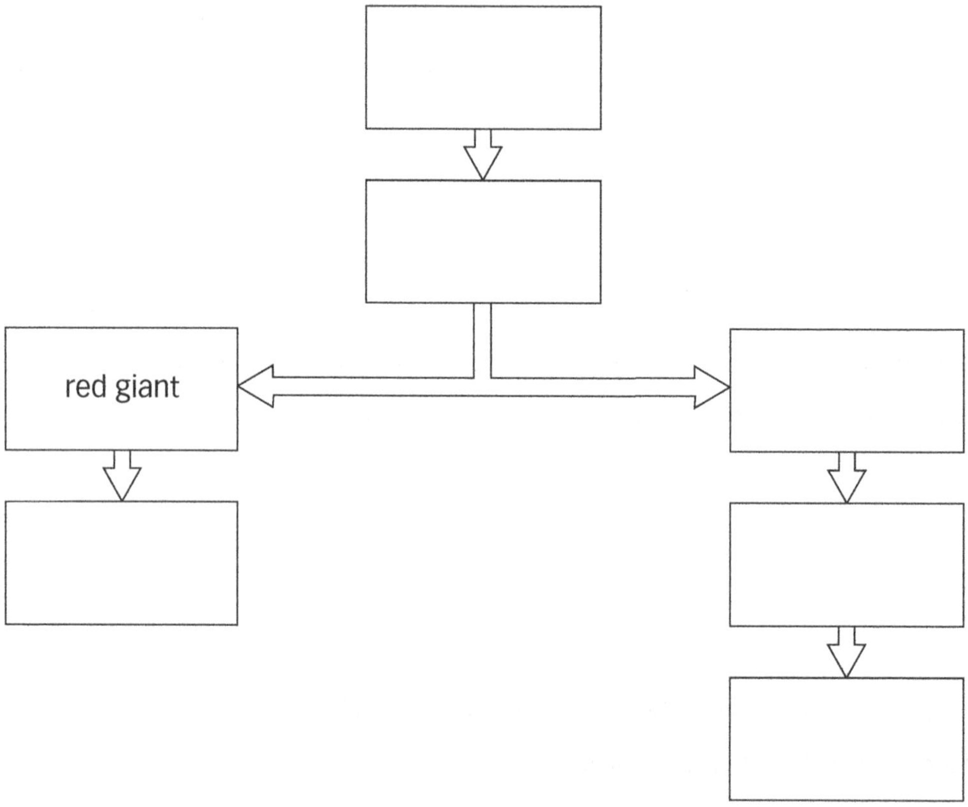

(5 marks)

b A main-sequence star emits a lot of energy as light.

Describe the reaction in the core of the star that produces this energy.

....

....

....

(3 marks)

c Scientists believe that the Universe contained only hydrogen and helium when it was formed. Explain where all the other elements have come from.

....

....

....

....

(3 marks)

(Total marks: 11)

Designing an investigation and making measurements

In this module there are some opportunities to design investigations and make measurements. These include measurements of half-life and the penetrating power of radiation.

Although you are unlikely to demonstrate your investigative skills practically, you are likely to be asked to comment on investigations done by others. The example below offers guidance in this skill area. It also gives you the chance to practise using your skills to answer the sorts of questions that may well come up in exams.

Comparing the usefulness of different thicknesses of shielding

Skill – Understanding the experiment

Sue tested the hypothesis that doubling the thickness of lead shielding halves the rate at which gamma rays get through it.

She placed the radioactive source near a detector, with the lead sheets in between. For each lead sheet in place, she recorded how many gamma rays were detected in each minute. Three measurements were made for each thickness of lead.

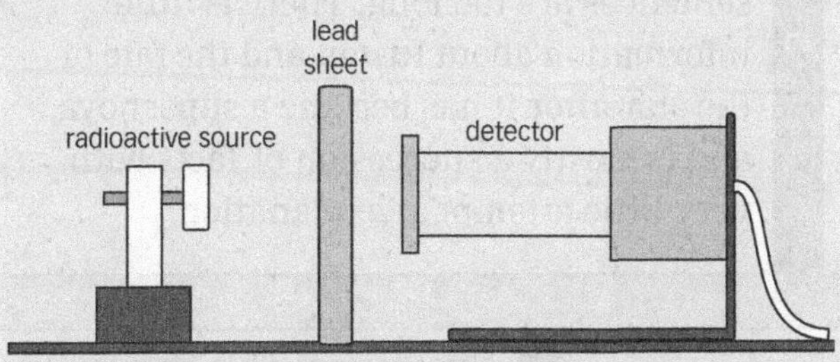

Sue's results are in the table below.

Lead sheet thickness (mm)	Gamma rays (per minute)		
	First trial	Second trial	Third trial
1.0	100	111	107
2.0	79	84	90
4.0	47	60	52
8.0	20	17	23

1 Identify the independent and dependent variables.

In an investigation:

- the independent variables are the ones that are changed by the scientist
- the dependent variable is the one that is measured for each change of the independent variables.

2 Suggest an important control variable for the investigation.

A control variable is one that the investigator thinks might affect the outcome, so they try to keep this variable the same all the way through.

Skill – Using data to draw conclusions

3 How should Sue combine the data from the three trials?

The best way of combining the data from different measurements of the dependent variable is to calculate the average.

4 How can Sue use the data to test her hypothesis?

Each sheet of lead has double the thickness of the previous one. So Sue should divide the average detector reading by the previous one. If the answer is always 0.5, then her hypothesis is correct. A different answer that is still the same for all thicknesses would suggest that her hypothesis could be correct for a different thickness. She could plot a scatter graph of the detector reading against the shielding thickness to find out if there is still a halving law, but not for the thicknesses that she has chosen.

Skill – Evaluating the experiment

5 What should Sue do about the large variation in results for each setting of the independent variable?

The range of data is often reduced by making more measurements. She could do this by either counting gamma rays for more than a minute, or making more measurements for a minute each time (more trials).

AQA Upgrade

Answering an extended question

In this question you will be assessed on using good English, organising information clearly, and using specialist terms where appropriate.

1 All stars go through a life cycle. Describe and explain the life cycle of a star that is much heavier than the Sun. *(6 marks)*

QUESTION

G–E

Well, the star is exploding, then vanish into a black dwarf, because it is too hevy to get away from itself. It starts off a gas which gets hotter and hotter then turns into a star when the gas starts to burn. It explodes when it runs out of fule.

Examiner: This answer only earns 1 mark, so is typical of an F-grade candidate. The spelling and grammar are poor, information is presented in a confusing order, and only some of the science is correct. There is incorrect use of a technical term: 'fusion' should be used instead of 'burn'.

D–C

The star begins as a protostar, this is a gas which gets smaller and smaller and hotter and hotter until the hydrogen starts to turn into a helium. This is main sequence and lasts for a long time until all of the hydrogen is gone. The star grows into a red giant and then explodes when it has a core of iron. Lots of different elements are made in the explosion, these get spread around and eventually get pulled together to make another star, only this time with planets around it.

Examiner: This answer earns 3 marks, typical of a C-grade candidate. It contains a lot of correct information, presented in a logical order with correct spelling. Some sentences are too long. There is little information about fusion and the fate of the star after it has become a supernova, and is mostly a succession of facts with very little attempt at explanation.

B–A*

A cloud of hydrogen gas shrinks as gravity pulls all of its particles towards each other. This transfers GPE to heat, so as the cloud shrinks its temperature increases until the centre is hot enough for hydrogen nuclei to fuse into helium nuclei. This process releases a lot of energy as gamma rays. The outwards flow of this energy stops the star from shrinking any more. When all of the hydrogen in the core has been converted to helium, it contracts until the helium can fuse into heavier elements. The outer layers of the star swell up to form a super red giant. When the core is solid iron, fusion stops and so it collapses under its own weight to make a black hole. The outer layers explode as a supernova, fusing nuclei together to make elements heavier than iron.

Examiner: This answer earns 6 marks, typical of an A*-grade candidate. Each step in the evolution of a star has been correctly named, described, and explained. Information is presented in a logical order (start to finish), with no errors of grammar or spelling.

Part 2 Course catch-up
Electricity and radiation

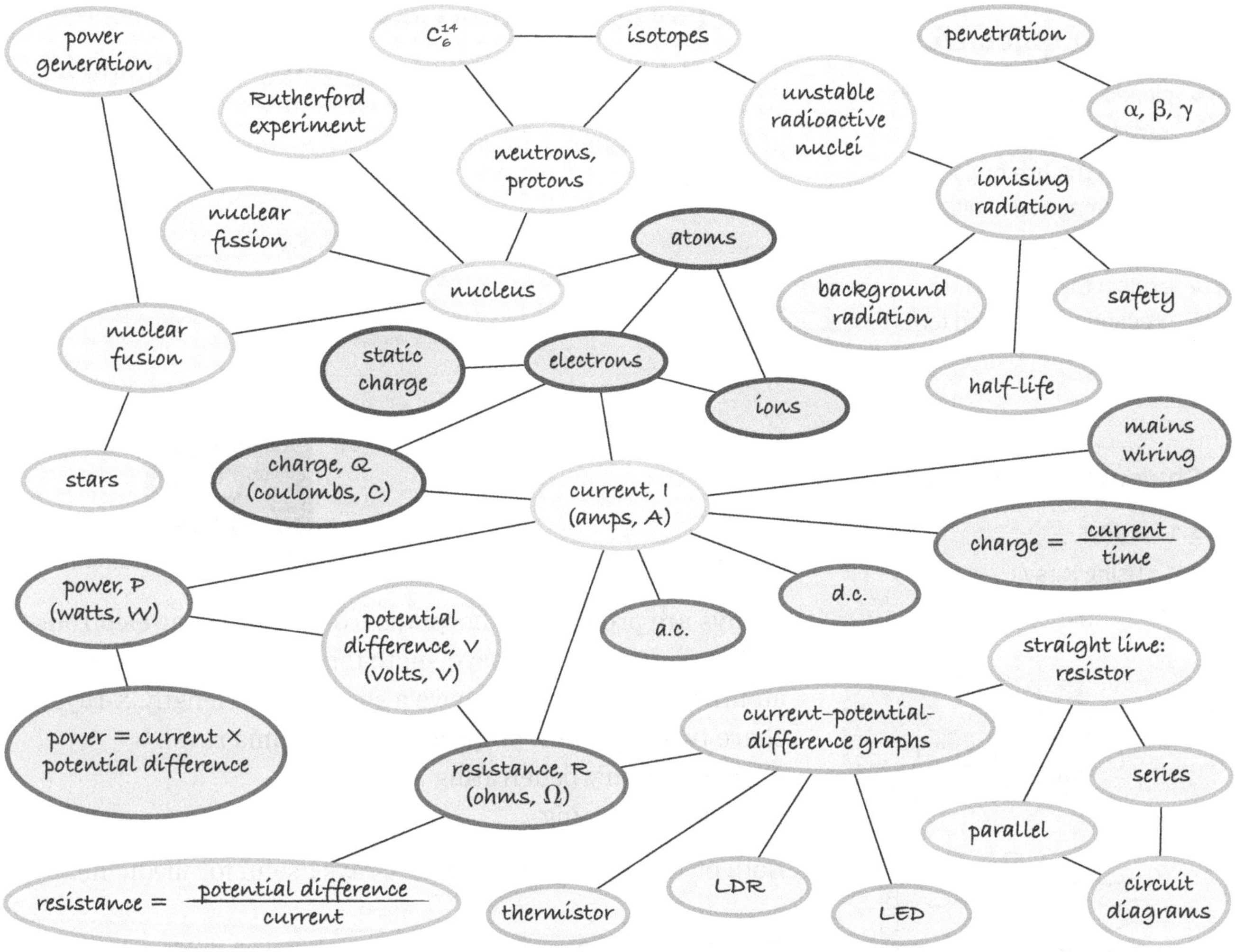

Revision checklist

- Some materials gain an electrostatic charge when rubbed together. Opposite charges attract, like repel.
- Electric current is the flow of charge around a circuit.
- The potential difference between two points in an electronic circuit is the work done (energy transferred) per coulomb of charge that passes through the points.
- Circuit symbols represent electrical components.
- Resistance is a measure of how difficult it is for electrons to pass through a component.
- Current must pass through all components in a series circuit one after the other. Current in a parallel circuit can take more than one route.
- The resistance of a filament lamp increases as its temperature increases.
- A light-emitting diode (LED) produces light when a current flows through it, and is efficient and long-lasting.
- The resistance of a light-dependent resistor (LDR) varies with intensity of light. LDRs are used in switches.
- The resistance of a thermistor varies as its temperature changes. Thermistors are used in temperature sensors.
- Electric current has two forms: direct current (d.c.), usually produced by batteries or cells; and alternating current (a.c.), such as UK mains electricity (230 V a.c. with frequency 50 Hz).
- UK three-pin plugs contain a live wire (brown), a neutral wire (blue), an earth wire (green and yellow), and a fuse. Fuses, earth wires, and circuit breakers are safety devices.
- When an electrical charge flows through a resistor, energy is transferred. Larger devices need larger power cables. The power of a device is its rate of energy transfer.
- Atoms have a small central nucleus of protons (positively charged) and neutrons (no charge) surrounded by negatively charged electrons in orbit. Positively or negatively charged ions are created when atoms gain or lose electrons.
- Isotopes are atoms with the same number of protons (same atomic number) but a different number of neutrons.
- Radioactive decay is the breakdown of the nucleus of an atom to form ionising radiation. Half-life is the average time taken for activity (decays per second) to halve.
- Nuclear fission is used in nuclear reactors to produce electricity.
- Nuclear fusion produces energy in stars.

Revision objectives

- place X-rays correctly in the electromagnetic spectrum
- explain the use of X-rays to make images and diagnoses in medicine
- explain the safety precautions required for X-rays

Student book references

3.1 X-rays

3.2 Using X-rays

Specification key

✔ P3.1.1

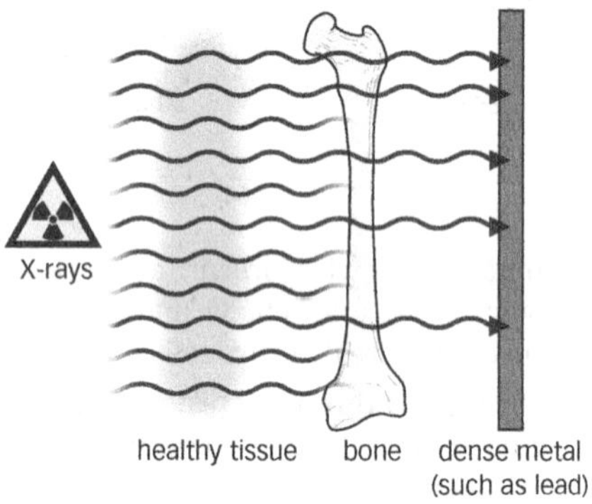

▲ X-rays are easily transmitted through healthy tissue; bone absorbs some X-rays, and lead absorbs most X-rays.

Electromagnetic waves

There are many different types of **electromagnetic wave**. Although they all have the same speed in a vacuum (the speed of light), the energy that they carry depends on their **wavelength**.

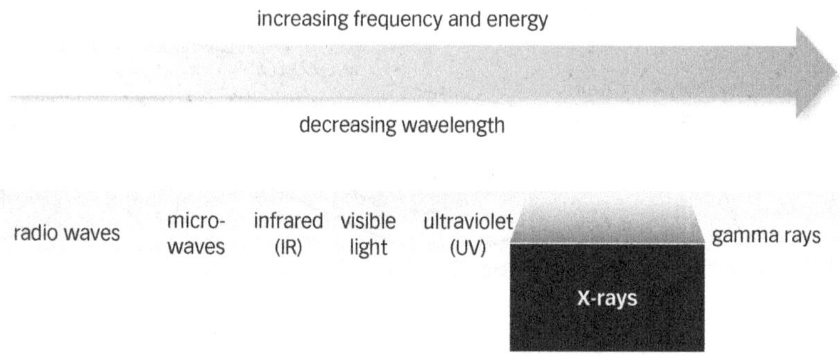

▲ X-rays are at the high-energy end of the electromagnetic spectrum.

X-rays are produced in hospitals from fast-moving electrons and have a very short wavelength (about the same size as an atom). Only gamma rays have a shorter wavelength. X-rays share two important properties with gamma rays:

- they are very penetrating
- they are ionising.

Both of these properties make X-rays useful for medicine.

Penetration

As X-rays pass through matter, they are **absorbed**, knocking electrons off atoms (**ionisation**). High-density materials, such as metals and bone, are better at doing this than low-density materials, such as skin and muscle.

Ionisation

Human cells are damaged when they absorb X-rays. The ionisation of the cell can alter its DNA, making it into a cancer. People who work with X-rays must therefore take these precautions:

- stand behind lead or concrete shielding
- leave the room while the X-ray machine is on
- wear a monitoring badge
- limit the amount of time that they spend working with X-rays.

The damaging effect of X-rays is sometimes put to use in **radiotherapy**. This uses thin beams of X-rays to destroy cancer tumours deep inside the body, without the need for surgery.

Photos

Dentists routinely use **photographic film** to make X-ray images of people's teeth. The film needs to be wrapped in black plastic because it is sensitive to light. The film is placed at one side of the teeth and the X-ray source at the other side. When the source is switched on, the intensity of X-rays reaching each part of the film depends on the density of the material in the way:

- Metal fillings completely absorb X-rays.
- Tooth and bone partially absorb X-rays.
- Skin, muscle, and gum hardly absorb X-rays at all.

The film needs to be processed chemically to fix the image. White regions show where the X-rays didn't reach the film. The rest of the film turns black or grey, depending on the dose of X-rays that reached it. The image can be used to show the dentist any decay inside a tooth.

CT scans

X-rays can be used to make images of more than just bones. A computed tomography **(CT) scan** can create images of internal organs, such as livers and kidneys, on a computer screen. A beam of X-rays passes through the patient and the intensity recorded by a **charge-coupled device (CCD)**. The beam and detector are slowly rotated around the patient so that X-rays eventually pass through in all directions. The computer combines all of the information to generate an image of the slice of patient that the X-rays passed through.

Key words

electromagnetic wave, wavelength, X-ray, absorbed, ionisation, radiotherapy, photographic film, CT scan, charge-coupled device (CCD)

Questions

1 What is the advantage of imaging a broken bone with X-rays?

2 Explain how an image of a broken bone can be created using X-rays.

3 **H** Explain the use of X-rays to diagnose and treat a cancer tumour deep inside the body.

Exam tip AQA

Don't confuse X-rays with X-ray images.

Revision objectives

- state that ultrasound is a sound wave above 20 kHz
- describe how ultrasound can be produced
- explain medical uses of ultrasound
- compare the advantages and disadvantages of using ultrasound and X-rays for medical scans

Student book references

3.3 Ultrasound
3.4 Medical uses of ultrasound

Specification key

✔ P3.1.2

Sound

A **sound wave** is created whenever part of a material is made to vibrate. The wave carries the vibrations through the material. The material can be solid, liquid, or gas. The **frequency** of the wave in hertz (Hz) is the number of complete vibrations of the source in one second. Humans can hear sounds in air with frequencies between 20 Hz and 20 000 Hz (20 kHz). Sound that has a frequency above this range is called **ultrasound** – it is widely used to image internal organs in the human body.

Vibrating crystals

Pulses of ultrasound for medical scans are produced by making special crystals vibrate at the required high frequency. Regular electrical pulses across the **crystal** generate short bursts of ultrasound that move away from the crystal through the medium. Any sudden change in density of the medium causes some of the ultrasound to be reflected back to the crystal. As the reflections are absorbed by the crystal it makes electrical signals. So the crystal acts as both a **transmitter** and **receiver** of ultrasound.

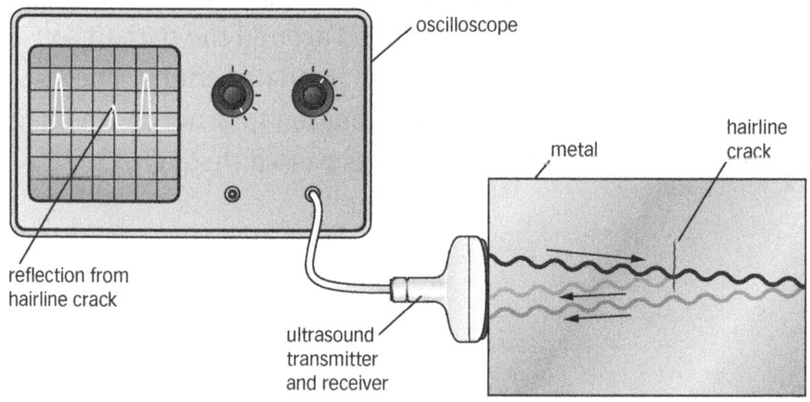

▲ Any change of density of the medium reflects some ultrasound back to its source.

Scanning

Ultrasound is routinely used to scan pregnant women to make images of their unborn babies. A pulsed ultrasound transmitter is held against the skin above the baby. As each pulse passes a boundary inside the woman's body, some of it is reflected back to the transmitter. The depth of the boundary is half the total distance travelled by the pulse. You can use this equation to calculate the total distance travelled by the ultrasound.

$$d = v \times t$$

d is the total distance travelled by the ultrasound in metres (m)
v is the speed of the ultrasound in metres per second (m/s)
t is the time delay for the reflected pulse in seconds (s)

The average speed of sound in the human body is 1500 m/s. So if the time between sending out a pulse of ultrasound and receiving a reflection is 60 microseconds, how far below the skin is the reflecting boundary?

$$d = v \times t = 1500\,\text{m/s} \times 60 \times 10^{-6}\,\text{s} = 9.0 \times 10^{-2}\,\text{m}$$

The wave travels 9.0×10^{-2} m in total, so the reflecting boundary must be half of this distance (4.50×10^{-2} m) below the skin.

Safe images

For each pulse fired into the mother from the transmitter, there are many reflected pulses, one for each boundary inside her. This information can be used by a computer to build up an image of the baby. The technique is similar to a CT scan, but without using X-rays. This is good, as X-rays may harm the unborn baby by ionising its cells. Ultrasound is a non-ionising radiation, so it is much safer.

Other medical uses

High-intensity beams of ultrasound can also be used to break up painful kidney stones into small pieces so that they flush out with the patient's urine.

Questions

1 What is ultrasound?

2 Explain how ultrasound can be used to make an image of an unborn baby.

3 **H** A pulse of ultrasound is reflected off a bone 10 cm below the skin. If ultrasound travels at a speed of 1.5 km/s, what is the time delay between transmission and reception of the pulse?

Exam tip AQA

The need to halve the distance travelled by the wave is often forgotten by students in an exam – remember your calculation of $d = v \times t$ will give you the distance the wave travels to get there **and** back. You will only be calculating the reflection.

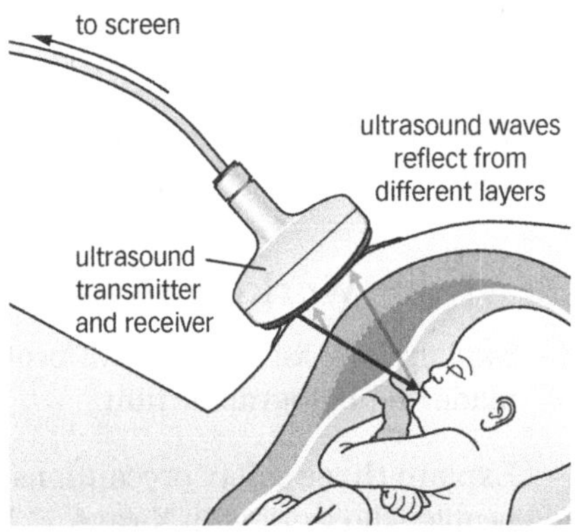

▲ Using ultrasound to image an unborn baby.

Key words

sound wave, frequency, ultrasound, crystal, transmitter, receiver

Exam tip AQA

Remember that ultrasound has to pass through something – it can't pass through a vacuum like X-rays can.

Questions
X-rays and ultrasound

Working to Grade E

1 Which of the following objects has about the same size as the wavelength of X-rays?

atom electron microbe nucleus

2 Why are unborn babies scanned by ultrasound instead of X-rays?

3 Suggest **three** safety precautions for people who work with X-rays.

4 Which of the following frequencies could be for ultrasound?

1 Hz 10 Hz 10 kHz 100 kHz

5 What are the differences between a CT scan image and an X-ray image on photographic film?

Working to Grade C

6 Explain how X-ray images of broken bones can be made on photographic film.

7 Explain **three** safety precautions required for people who work with X-rays.

8 What is ultrasound?

9 Describe how a CT scan is obtained.

10 Explain how ultrasound can be used to image an unborn baby.

Working to Grade A*

11 The reflection of an ultrasound pulse sent into a material is received after a delay of 40 microseconds. If the speed of ultrasound in the material is 2.5 km/s, how deep in the material is the reflecting boundary?

1 a An X-ray image is going to be made on photographic paper of a broken arm.

The following sentences explain the process of making the image. The sentences are in the wrong order.

Q X-rays pass into the arm.
R The X-ray source is switched on.
S X-rays ionise parts of the photographic film.
T The photographic film is wrapped in black plastic.
U The film is developed in chemicals to fix the image.
V The broken arm is placed on top of the photographic film.

Arrange these sentences in the correct order. Start with the letter **T**.

T → ☐ → ☐ → ☐ → ☐ → ☐

(4 marks)

b Explain why the radiographer leaves the room while the X-ray source is switched on.

....

....

....

....

(3 marks)
(Total marks: 7)

2 The picture shows a pregnant woman having her unborn baby scanned by ultrasound.

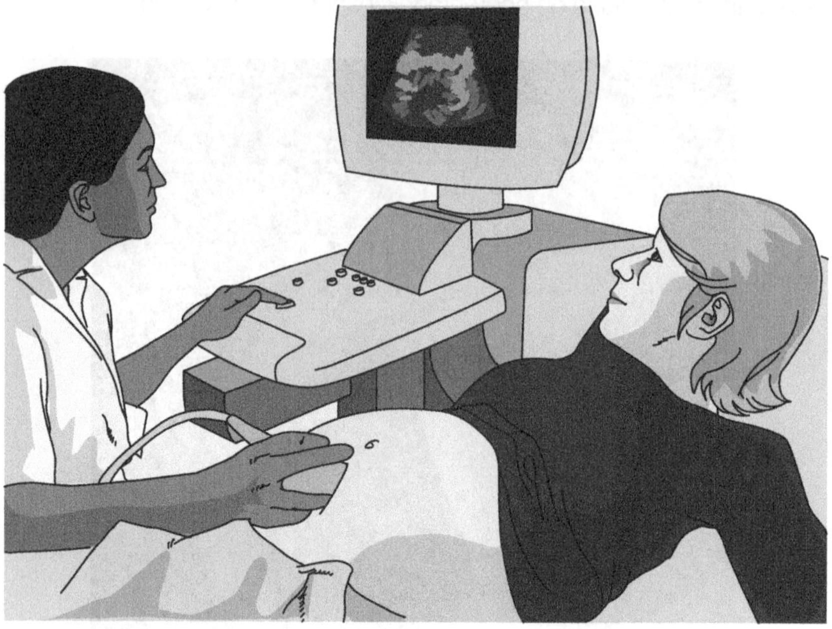

a What is ultrasound?

....

....

....

(2 marks)

b Explain why ultrasound is used for the scan instead of X-rays.

....

....

....

....

(3 marks)

c Explain how the image can be obtained by using ultrasound.

....

....

....

....

....

....

(4 marks)

(Total marks: 9)

Changing direction

When light travels from one medium into another its speed changes. This can cause **refraction**, a change of direction of the light at the boundary between the two different mediums. The direction is measured as an angle to a construction line (the **normal**) at right angles to the boundary. The light refracts towards the normal if it slows down, but away when it speeds up.

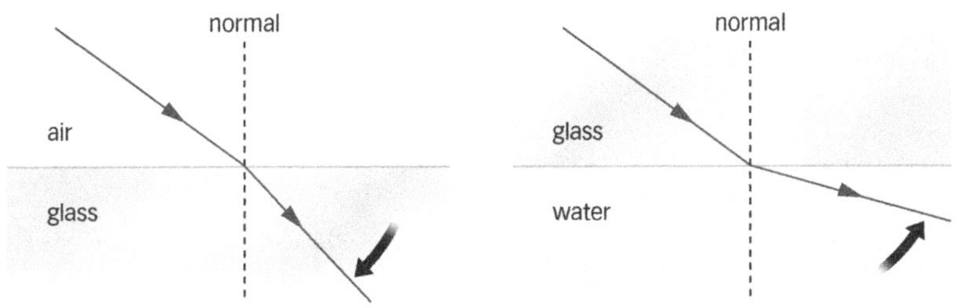

▲ The light refracts towards or away from the normal.

Refractive index

For light passing into or out of air, the **refractive index** (how fast light travels through the material) of the other medium determines the amount of refraction. The speed of light in a material is related to its refractive index. This equation, called Snell's law, can be used to calculate angles:

$$\text{refractive index} = \frac{\sin i}{\sin r}$$

i is the angle of incidence of the light
r is the angle of refraction of the light

So if light is incident on a plastic block at 45° and refracted at 30°, what is the refractive index of the plastic?

$$\text{refractive index} = \frac{\sin i}{\sin r} = \frac{\sin 45}{\sin 30} = 1.4$$

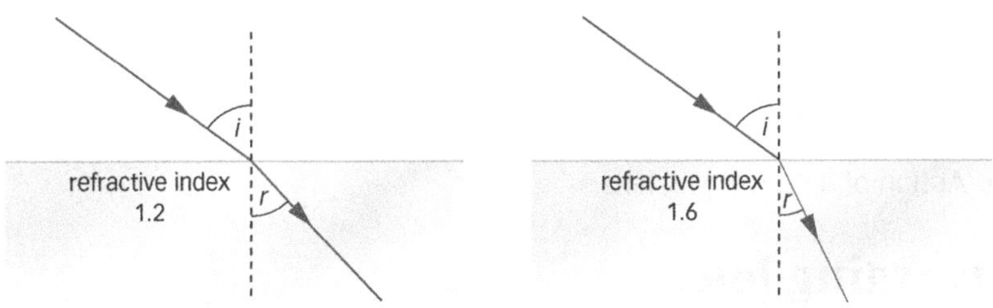

▲ Increasing the refractive index increases the change of direction.

Exam tip AQA

Remember that *i* and *r* are always measured from the ray to the normal.

Revision objectives

- ✔ describe the process of refraction
- ✔ use Snell's law
- ✔ understand the term 'refractive index'

Student book references

3.5 More on refraction

Specification key

✔ P3.1.3 a and c

Key words

refraction, normal, refractive index

Questions

1 Draw a diagram to show what happens to light when it passes from air into glass.

2 Explain why light refracts when it changes medium.

3 **H** Light is incident at 45° to a plastic block of refractive index 1.6. Calculate the angle of refraction.

Revision objectives

- recognise the difference between converging and diverging lenses
- use refraction to explain the operation of a lens
- describe the nature of an image formed by a lens

Student book references

3.6 Introduction to lenses

3.7 Describing images

Specification key

✔ P3.1.3 b and d

Using refraction

All lenses use refraction of light to make **images**. The refraction happens in two stages: when the light enters the lens and when it leaves. The light bends towards the normal on the way in and away from the normal on the way out.

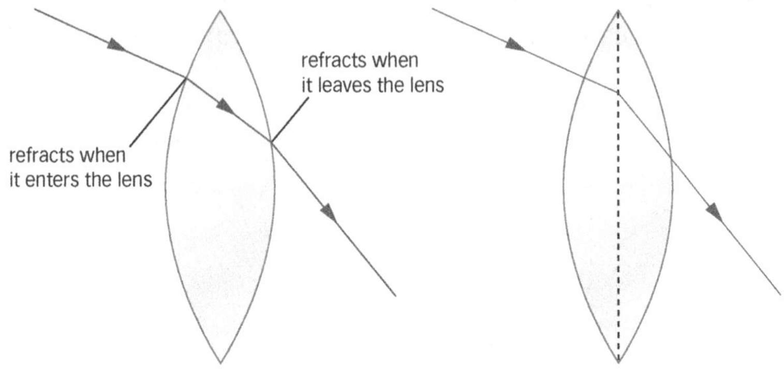

▲ Ray diagrams of lenses often show the refraction taking place halfway through the lens. This makes the diagrams simpler to draw.

Converging lens

A **converging** lens takes rays that are parallel to the **principal axis** of the lens and refracts them so that they all pass through the **principal focus**. The distance from the centre of the lens to the principal focus is called the **focal length**.

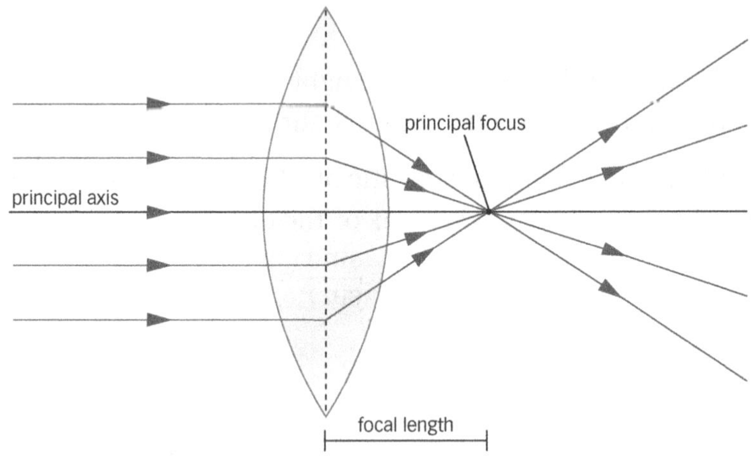

▲ Action of a converging lens.

Diverging lens

A **diverging** lens takes rays that are parallel to the principal axis and refracts them so that they appear to come from the **virtual focus**. This means that the rays spread out after passing through the lens instead of coming together.

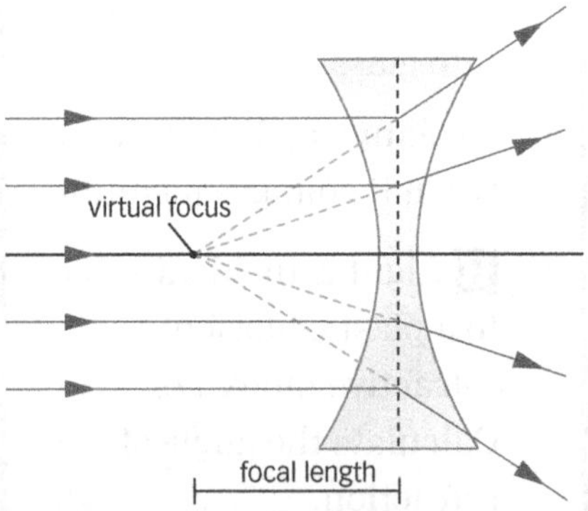

▲ Action of a diverging lens.

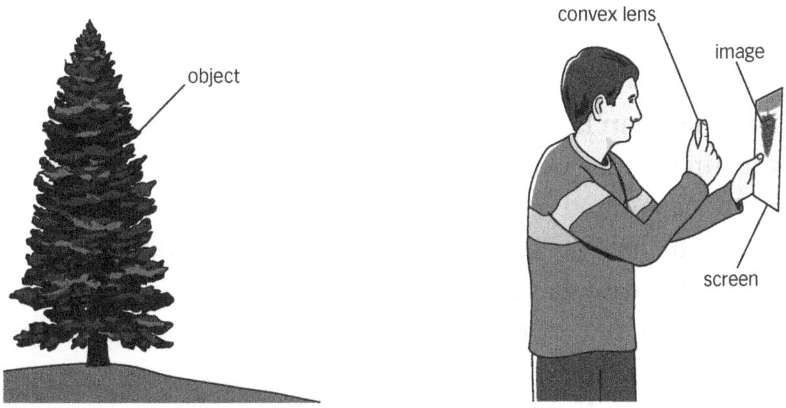

▲ The image of the tree is real, diminished, and inverted.

Key words

image, converging, principal axis, principal focus, focal length, diverging, virtual focus, inverted, upright, magnified, diminished, real, virtual

Images

A lens takes light from an object and uses it to make an image. The image is a copy of the object, but may be different from it in a number of ways. A number of different terms describe these differences:

- **inverted** means upside down compared with the object
- **upright** means the same way up as the object
- **magnified** means bigger than the object
- **diminished** means smaller than the object
- **real** means that the image can be seen on a screen
- **virtual** means that the image can't be seen on a screen

The image will be formed at a particular distance away from the centre of the lens.

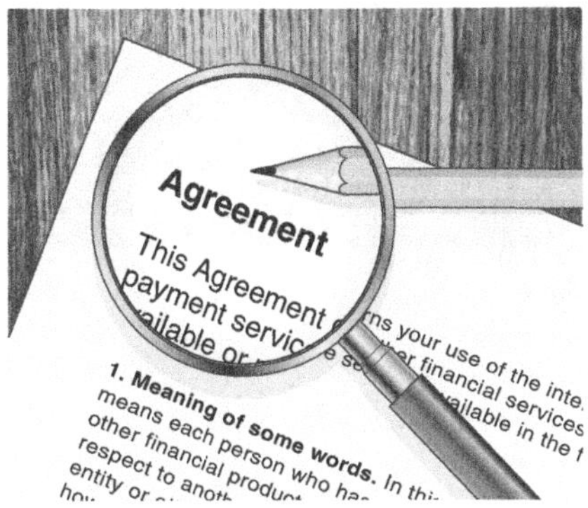

▲ The image formed by this magnifying glass is virtual, magnified, and upright.

Questions

1 Draw pictures of converging and diverging lenses.

2 Draw a labelled ray diagram for light passing through a converging lens.

3 **H** Describe the image formed in this picture.

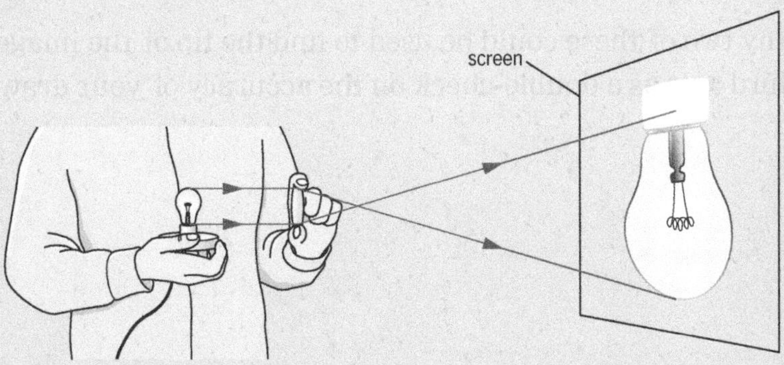

Exam tip AQA

Remember you need to state four things when you describe an image.

Revision objectives

- construct ray diagrams to show how images are formed by lenses
- describe the images formed by lenses

Student book references

3.8 Converging lenses
3.9 Diverging lenses

Specification key

- P3.1.3 g and h

Drawing rays

A **ray diagram** is a scale drawing that can be used to determine the properties of an object formed by a lens. You draw it on squared paper as follows:

- draw the lens at right angles to the principal **axis**
- draw the **object** as an upright arrow on the principal axis
- draw rays that leave the tip of the object and pass through the lens
- the tip of the **image** is where the rays are focussed by the lens.

Each ray should have an arrow to show its direction. You will need to select suitable scales for the diagram. The vertical and horizontal scales do not have to be the same.

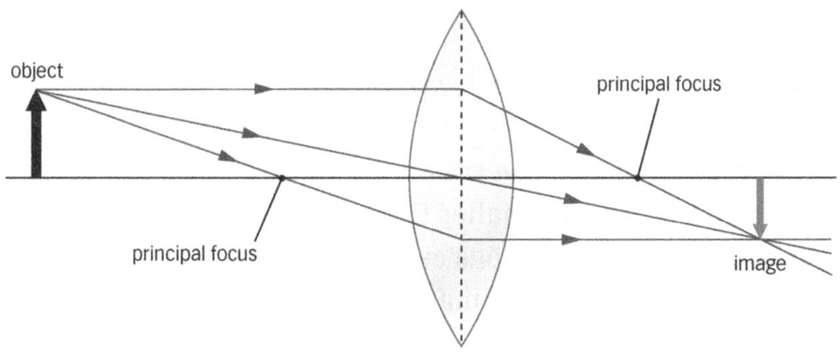

▲ A ray diagram for a converging lens.

Converging lens

Rays leave the tip of the object in all directions. All rays that enter a converging lens will be focussed at the tip of the image. Three rays in particular can be used to find that focus:

- The ray that enters the lens at its centre goes straight through without any change of direction.
- The ray that approaches the lens parallel to the axis passes through the **principal focus** when it leaves the lens.
- The ray that passes through the principal focus before entering the lens is parallel to the axis when it leaves the lens.

Any two of these could be used to find the tip of the image. The third acts as a double-check on the accuracy of your drawing.

Diverging lens

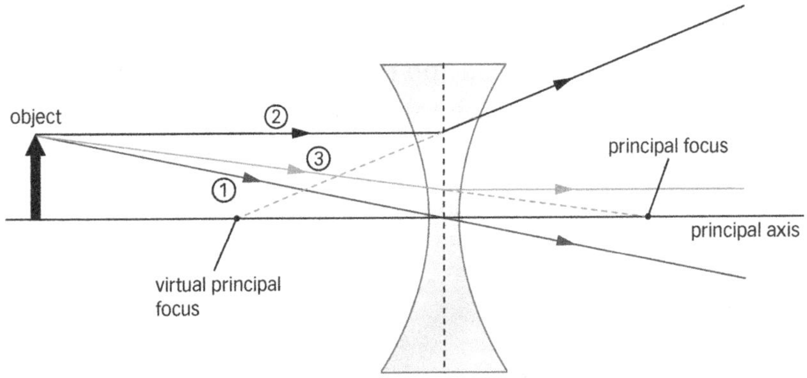

▲ Three special rays for working out images from diverging lenses.

These three rays can be used to find the position of the tip of the image formed by a diverging lens.

- The ray that enters the lens at its centre goes straight through without any change of direction.
- The ray that approaches the lens parallel to the axis appears to come from the virtual principal focus when it leaves the lens.
- The ray that is heading towards the principal focus when it meets the lens travels parallel to the axis when it leaves the lens.

The result is three rays coming out of the lens, spreading apart from each other. When these rays enter your eye, your brain works out where the rays appear to come from and places the tip of the image there. This is always somewhere behind the lens, where a screen would block out the light, so it is always a **virtual** image.

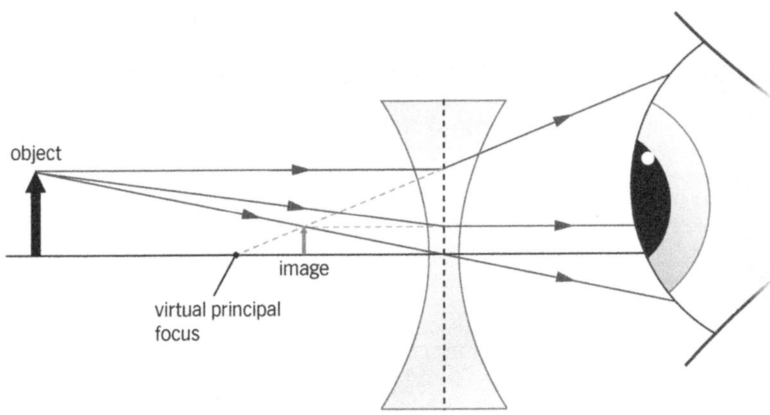

▲ The image is where the rays appear to come from.

Key words

ray diagram, axis, object, image, principal focus, virtual

Exam tip AQA

Always use a ruler when drawing ray diagrams.
Draw all three of the special rays to find the image.
Use the correct symbols for the lenses.

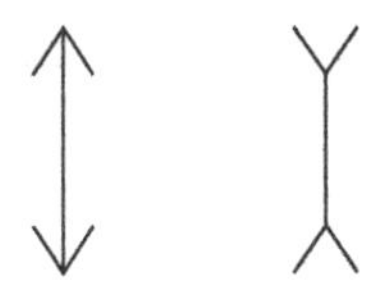

▲ These symbols will represent lenses in the exam.

Questions

1 What happens to light that enters the centre of a lens?

2 Draw diagrams to show the effect of converging and diverging lenses on light rays parallel to the axis.

3 **H** A converging lens has a focal length of 5 cm. Describe the image formed by the lens of a 2-cm-high object placed 10 cm away from the lens.

6: Magnification and power

Revision objectives

- calculate the magnification of an object
- calculate the power of a lens
- describe the factors affecting the power of a lens
- use refraction to explain the factors affecting the power of a lens

Student book references

3.10 Magnification

3.14 Lens power

Specification key

- P3.1.3 e, f and i
- P3.1.4 e – g

Magnification

The image formed by a lens and the object itself usually have different heights. You calculate the **magnification** produced by the lens with this equation:

$$\text{magnification} = \frac{\text{height of image}}{\text{height of object}}$$

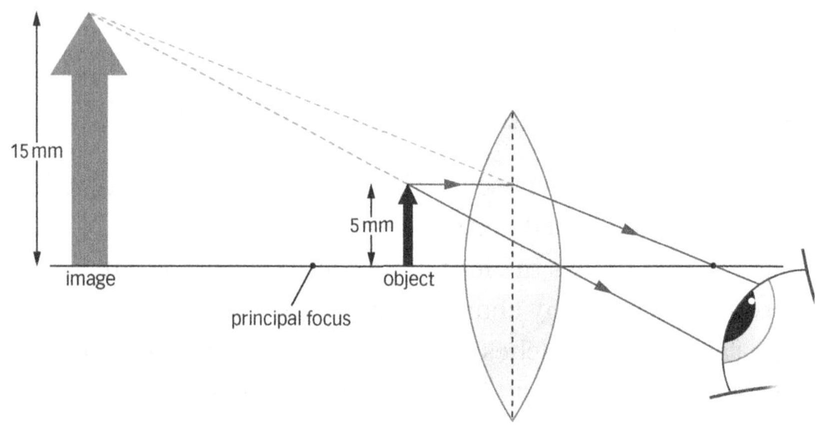

▲ Using a convex lens to give a magnification of 3.

Suppose you look at a 5 mm object with a magnifying glass. If the image is 15 mm high, what is the magnification?

$$\text{magnification} = \frac{\text{height of image}}{\text{height of object}} = \frac{15\,\text{mm}}{5\,\text{mm}} = 3$$

The magnification is often smaller than 1. This means that the image is diminished. For example, suppose that a convex lens produces an image that has a magnification of 0.7. What is the size of the image if the object is 5 cm high?

$$\text{magnification} = \frac{\text{height of image}}{\text{height of object}}$$

so magnification × height of object = height of image

$$\text{height of image} = 0.7 \times 5\,\text{cm} = 3.5\,\text{cm}$$

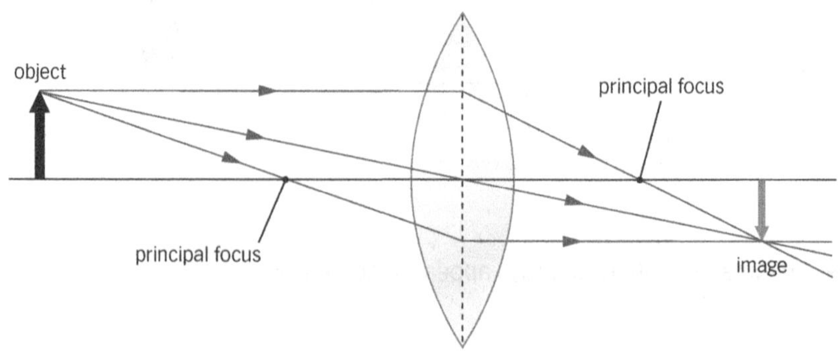

▲ This lens is providing a magnification of only 0.7.

Power

The **power** of a lens tells you how good it is at converging or diverging light. You calculate it from this equation:

$$P = \frac{1}{f}$$

P is the power of the lens in **dioptres** (D)
f is the **focal length** of the lens in metres (m)

So if a converging lens has a focal length of 20 cm, what is its power?

$$P = \frac{1}{f} = \frac{1}{0.20\,\text{m}} = +5\,\text{D}$$

The power of a converging lens is always positive. Diverging lenses have negative powers.

Increasing power

To increase the power of a lens you have to reduce its focal length. There are two ways of doing this:

- increase the **refractive index**
- increase the curvature (how fat the lens is).

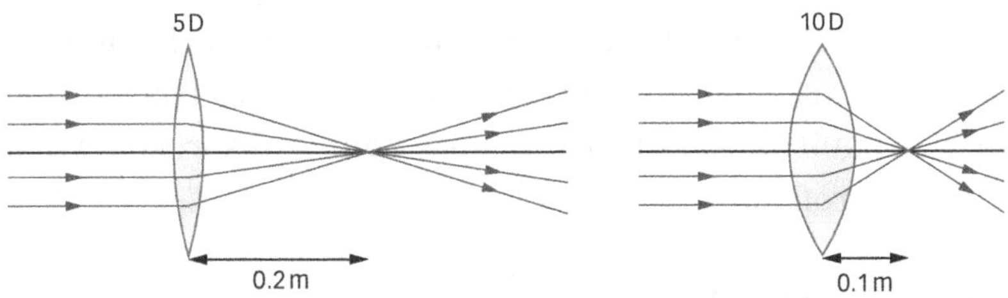

▲ Both of these lenses have the same refractive index, but different curvatures.

H A high-power lens changes the direction of light more than a low-power one. The refractive index of the material used affects how much the light changes direction on its way through the lens. So increasing the refractive index of the material is a useful alternative to increasing the curvature of the lens when you need to increase its power.

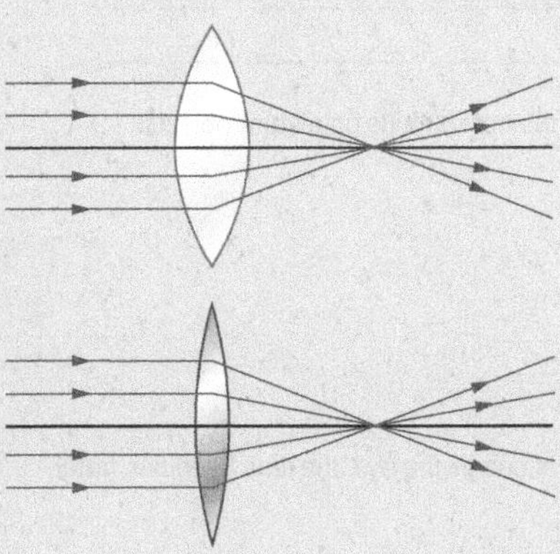

◀ Both lenses have the same power but different values of refractive index.

Key words

magnification, power, dioptre, focal length, refractive index

Exam tip AQA

Always remember to convert the focal length to metres before calculating power.

Questions

1. State the factors that affect the power of a lens.
2. A converging lens has a focal length of 0.05 m. Calculate its power.
3. **H** A lens has a power of –10 D. State the type of lens and calculate its focal length.

Revision objectives

- describe the structure and function of parts of the eye
- state the range of vision of the human eye
- understand the reasons for long- and short-sight
- understand the use of corrective lenses

Student book references

3.11 The human eye
3.12 Problems with eyesight

Specification key

- P3.1.4 a – c

Structure

The human eye contains several important structures:

- Light enters through the transparent **cornea**.
- The **pupil** controls how much light reaches the lens.
- The **lens** focuses the light onto the retina.
- Cells in the **retina** detect the intensity and colour of the light.
- The **optic nerve** carries electrical signals from the retina to the brain.

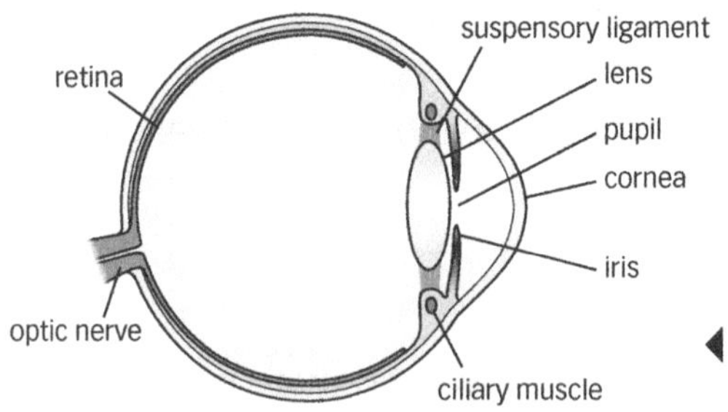

A cross-section through the human eye.

Brightness control

The cells on the surface of the retina can be damaged if they absorb too much light. The pupil automatically gets smaller in bright light to prevent this happening. The size of the pupil is altered by muscles in the **iris**. This is the coloured part of the eye. The pupil appears black because light is absorbed by the retina, not reflected.

Focus control

Light is refracted by both the cornea and the lens. The lens is held in place by **suspensory ligaments**. The lens is soft, so the **ciliary muscles** can be used to make it fatter or thinner. This happens automatically to keep the image correctly focussed on the retina. This allows the eye to focus on objects from 25 cm (the **near point**) to infinity (the **far point**).

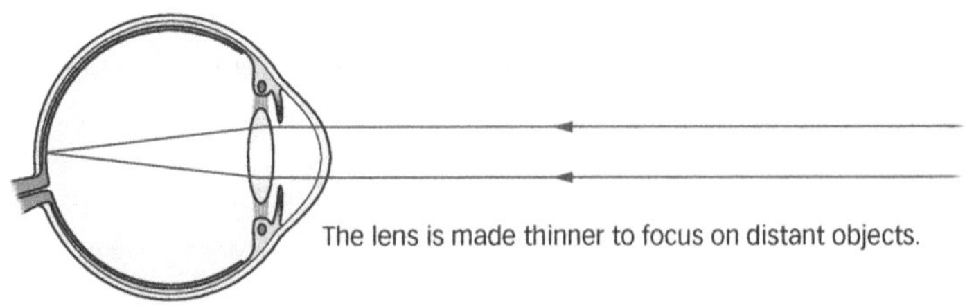

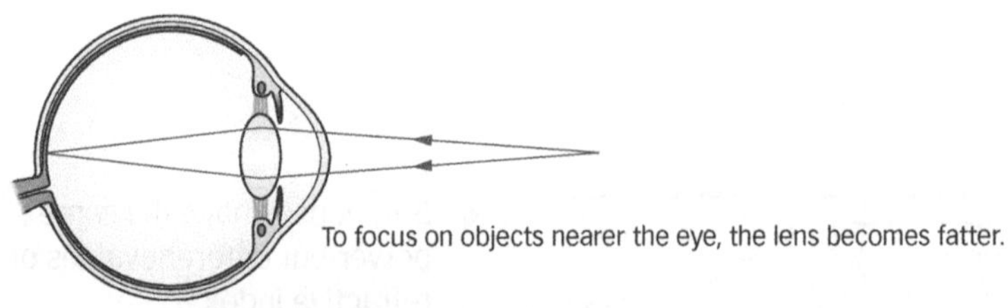

The ciliary muscles control the focal length of the lens.

Short-sight

Many people have **short-sight**. Their far point is much less than infinity – perhaps less than a metre. The image created by the lens is focussed in front of the retina. This means that distant objects appear blurred. It can be caused:

- by an eyeball that is too large
- when the lens cannot be made thin enough.

The condition can be corrected by placing a diverging (**concave**) lens in front of the eye – either as spectacles or as contact lenses.

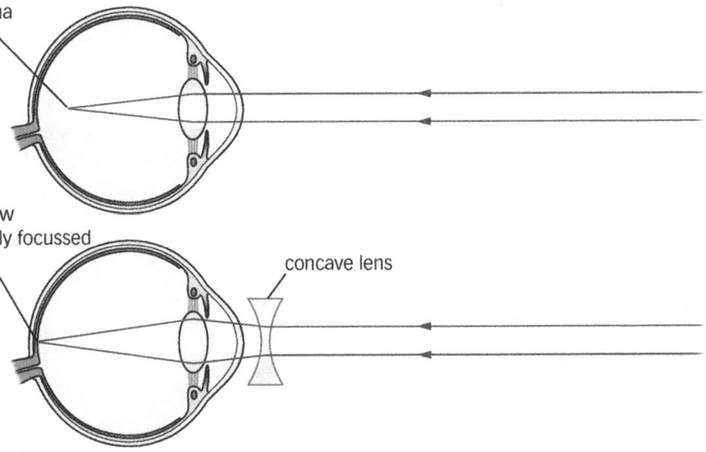

▲ A concave lens corrects short-sight.

Long-sight

People who have **long-sight** have a near point that is much larger than normal. It can be caused:

- by an eyeball that is too small
- when a lens cannot be made fat enough.

The condition can be corrected by placing a converging (**convex**) lens in front of the eye – either as spectacles or as contact lenses.

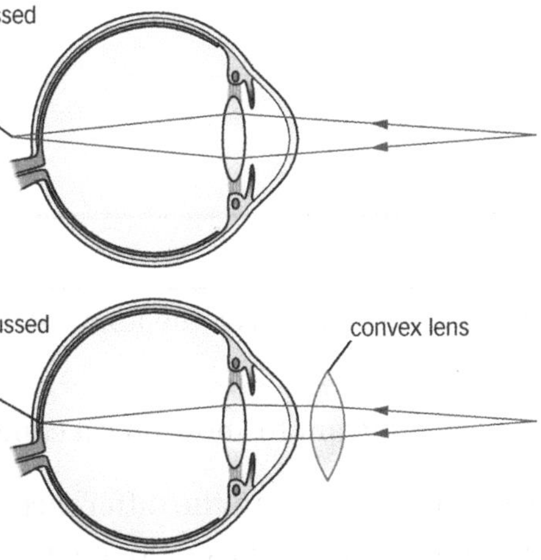

▲ A convex lens corrects long-sight.

Key words

retina, cornea, pupil, lens, optic nerve, iris, suspensory ligaments, ciliary muscles, near point, far point, short-sight, concave, long-sight, convex

Exam tip — AQA

Remember that the eye contains *two* lenses: a fixed cornea and an adjustable lens.

Questions

1 Draw a labelled diagram of the human eye.

2 Describe and explain the changes in the pupil when a bright light is shone into the eye.

3 **H** Describe and explain how short-sight can be corrected.

Revision objectives

- describe how a camera forms an image
- compare the structures of a camera and an eye

Student book references

3.13 The camera

Specification key

✔ P3.1.4 d

Common features

Many features of a camera match similar features in your eyes:

- a **convex lens** to catch light from an object and make an image
- an adjustable **iris** to control the amount of light in the image
- a **charge-coupled device (CCD)** or **film** to detect light in the image.

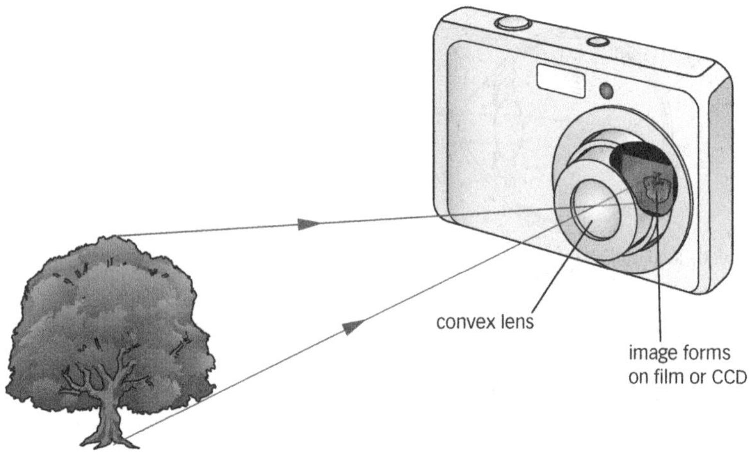

▲ The convex lens of the camera produces a real image of the object on the CCD.

Camera focus

Both eyes and cameras have to produce focussed images of objects at a range of distances. The eye does this by altering the shape of the lens, making it fatter or thinner. The lens in a camera is hard, so has a constant shape. It therefore has to be moved towards or away from the CCD to bring images into focus on the CCD. As the object gets nearer to the camera, the lens has to be moved away from the CCD to keep the image in focus.

Key words

convex lens, iris, charge-coupled device (CCD), film

Exam tip

AQA

Make sure that you can explain the differences between a camera and an eye.

Questions

1 What are the functions of the lens and the CCD in a camera?

2 Draw a ray diagram to show how a camera forms an image.

3 **H** Describe and explain the differences in how an eye and a camera adapt to an object moving towards them.

Questions
The power of lenses

Working to Grade E

1 Draw a diagram to show the refraction of light passing from glass into air.

2 Draw diagrams to show the effect of convex and concave lenses on parallel rays of light.

3 What is the difference between an object and an image?

4 A data projector produces an image that is **magnified** and **inverted**. What does this mean?

5 Some images are real. Others are virtual. What is the difference?

6 A magnifying glass has a magnification of 6. What does this mean?

7 Describe how the focal length of the human eye can be adjusted.

Working to Grade C

8 A ray of light has angles of incidence and refraction of 35° and 25°, respectively, when it goes into plastic. Calculate the refractive index of the plastic.

9 Draw a ray diagram to show how a convex lens can form an inverted and diminished image of an object.

10 Draw a ray diagram to show how a convex lens can form a magnified, upright, and virtual image of an object.

11 Explain the adjustment required of a camera lens when a close object moves away from the camera.

12 A magnifying glass produces an image with a magnification of 5. If the object is 2 mm high, how high is the image?

13 Explain the function of the iris of a human eye.

14 With the help of a ray diagram, explain the type of lens required to correct long-sight.

15 Calculate the power of a convex lens with a focal length of 15 cm.

16 Add labels to this diagram of the human eye.

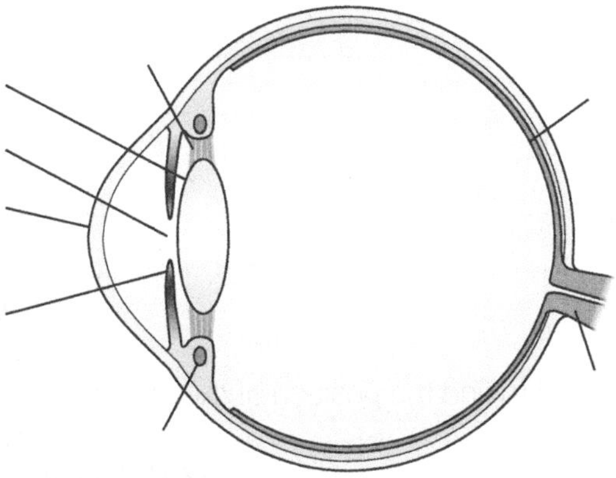

Working to Grade A*

17 A convex lens has a power of +10 D. It is used to form an image of an object that is 5 cm from the lens. Use a ray diagram to calculate the magnification of the image.

18 Explain the different ways that eyes and cameras produce focussed images of objects at various distances away.

1 The ray diagram shows a lens being used to project an image of an object.

The diagram has been drawn to scale.

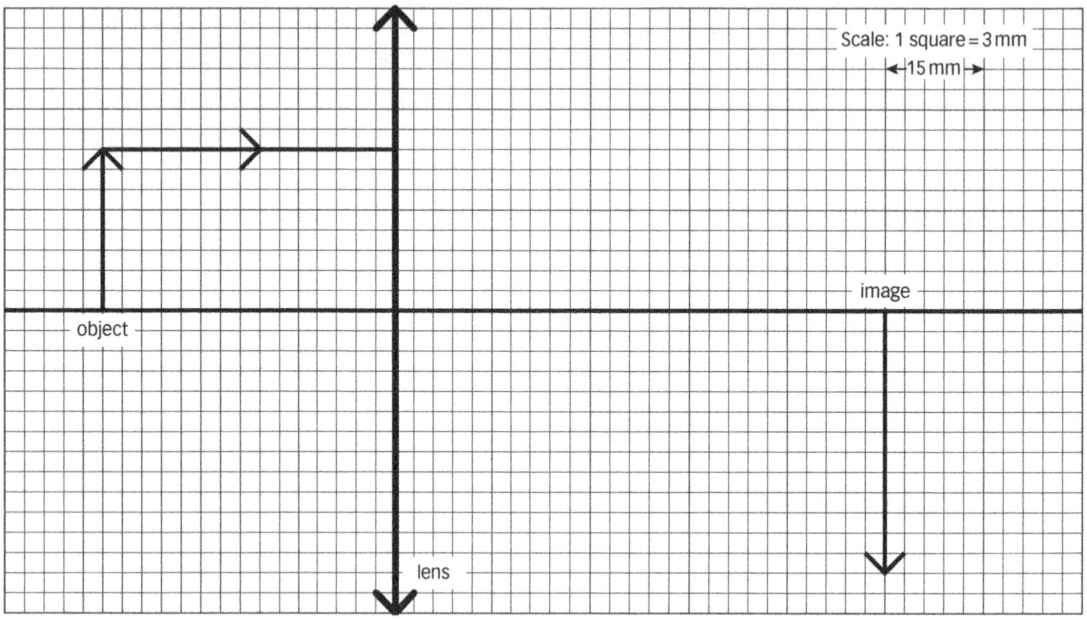

a Use **three** words from the box to complete the sentence that describes the image.

diminished	**inverted**	**magnified**	**real**	**upright**	**virtual**

The image is ...., ... and ....

(3 marks)

b **i** The ray diagram shows one ray leaving the top of the object. Draw the ray after it has left the lens.

(2 marks)

ii Use the ray diagram to calculate the power of the lens.

Write down the equation you use and then show clearly how you work out your answer.

....

....

....

....

....

....

power = ... D

(3 marks)

c Draw **two** more rays from the top of the object that can be used to find the position of the image.

(2 marks)

(Total marks: 10)

2 a The diagram shows the cross-section of a camera.

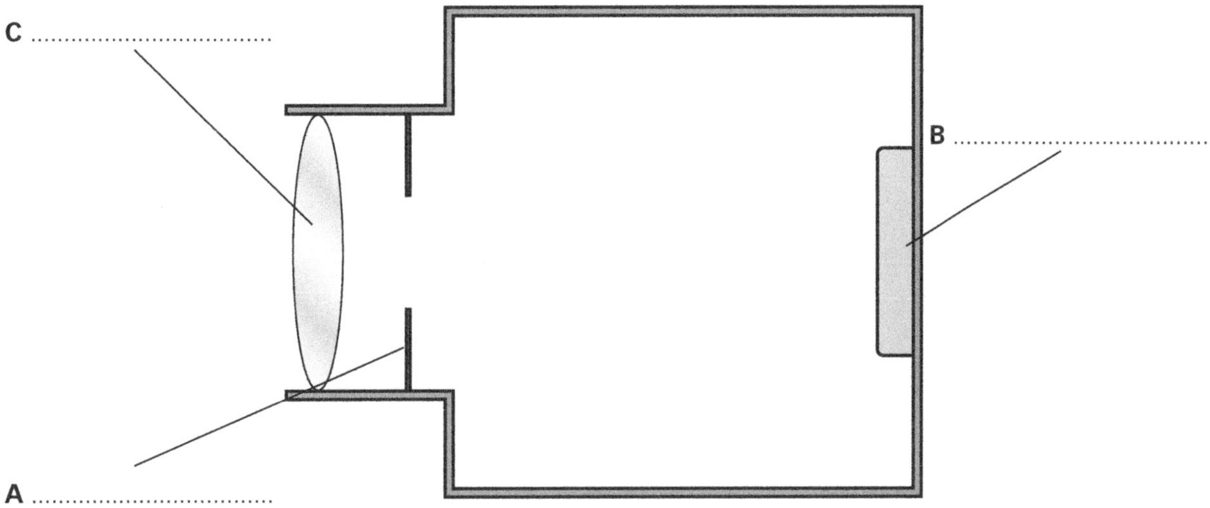

Use words from the box to label the parts **A**, **B**, and **C**.

CCD	**iris**	**lens**	**pupil**	**retina**

(3 marks)

b Cameras and human eyes have many things in common.

Which one of these things is **not** common to both eyes and cameras?

Tick (✓) **one** box.

The shape of the lens can be altered. ☐

The image is focussed on a light detector. ☐

The amount of light in the image can be altered. ☐

(1 mark)

c The ray diagram shows the lens of a human eye. The principal focus is marked F.

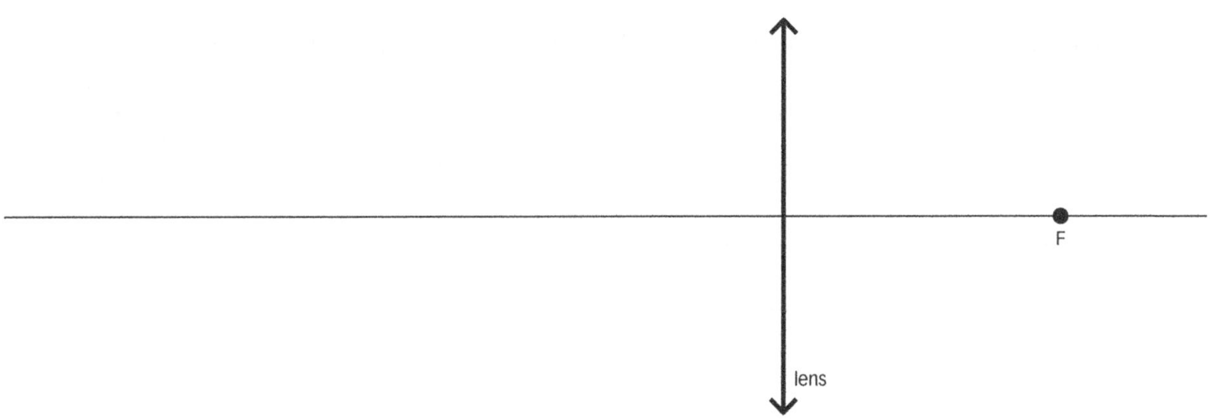

Draw **two** rays of light that come from a distant object at infinity to form an image.

(3 marks)

(Total marks: 7)

3 The diagram shows a ray of light passing from air into glass.

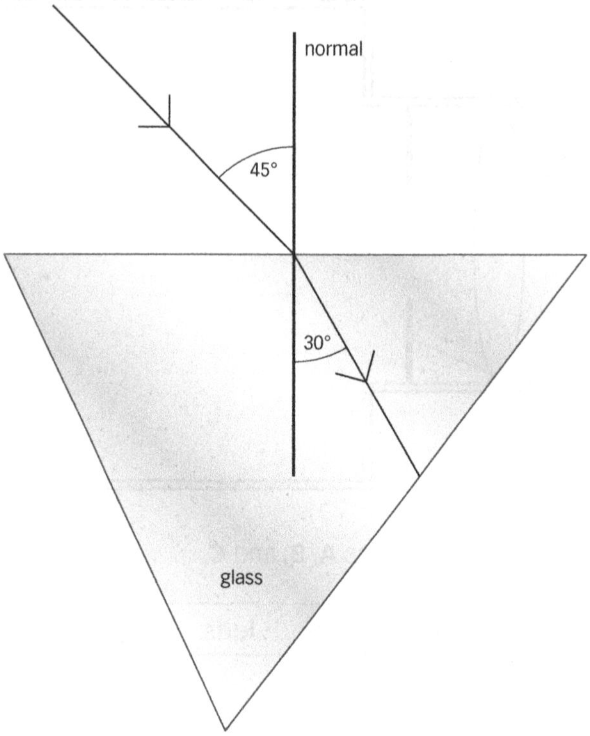

a Explain why the light changes direction where it enters the glass.

....

....

....

....

(3 marks)

b Calculate the refractive index of the glass.

Write down the equation you use and then show clearly how you work out your answer.

....

....

....

....

....

refractive index = ...

(2 marks)

c Continue the ray to show what it does when it passes out of the glass and back into the air.

You do not need to do any calculations.

(2 marks)

(Total marks: 7)

4 The ray diagram shows the position of the virtual principal focus P of a concave lens.

The diagram is drawn to scale.

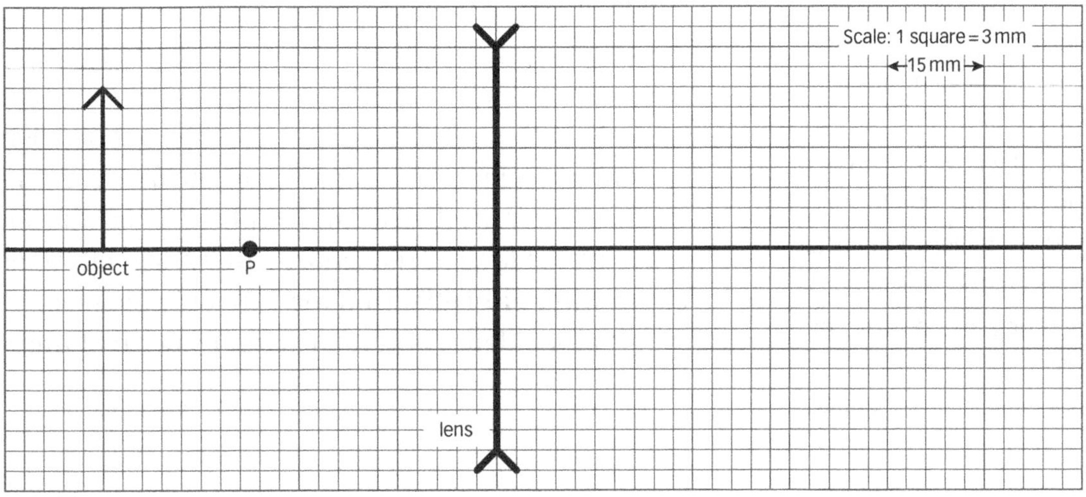

a Calculate the power of the lens.

Write down the equation you use and then show clearly how you work out your answer.

....

....

....

....

....

lens power = ...D

(3 marks)

b Draw **two** rays from the tip of the object to show how the image is formed.

Label the tip of the image with the word **image**.

(3 marks)

c Calculate the magnification of the image.

Write down the equation you use and then show clearly how you work out your answer.

....

....

....

....

....

magnification = ...

(3 marks)

(Total marks: 9)

Revision objectives

- describe the conditions needed for total internal reflection
- describe how light passes along optical fibres
- give examples of the use of total internal reflection
- describe medical uses of lasers
- calculate the critical angle

Student book references

3.15 Total internal reflection

3.16 Optical fibres and lasers

Specification key

✔ P3.1.5

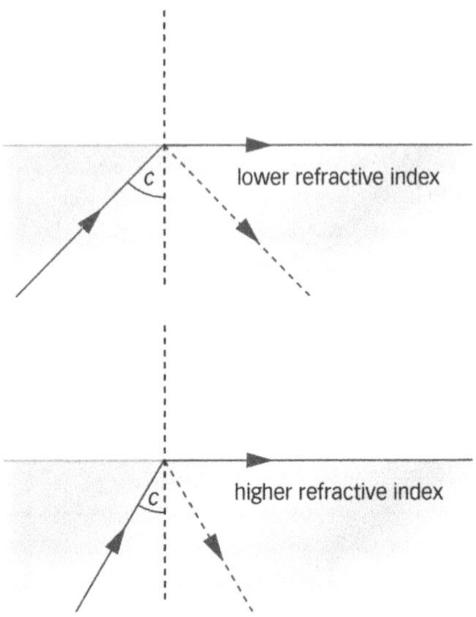

▲ The size of the critical angle depends on the refractive index.

Internal reflection

When light passes from one medium to another there is always some internal reflection as well as refraction. Some of the light reflects off the boundary, the rest changes direction as it passes through. If the light is travelling out of a denser medium at a large enough angle of incidence, then the light will only be reflected. All of it will reflect off the boundary, obeying the laws of reflection, with no loss of intensity. This **total internal reflection** (or **TIR**) only happens when the angle of incidence is greater than the **critical angle**.

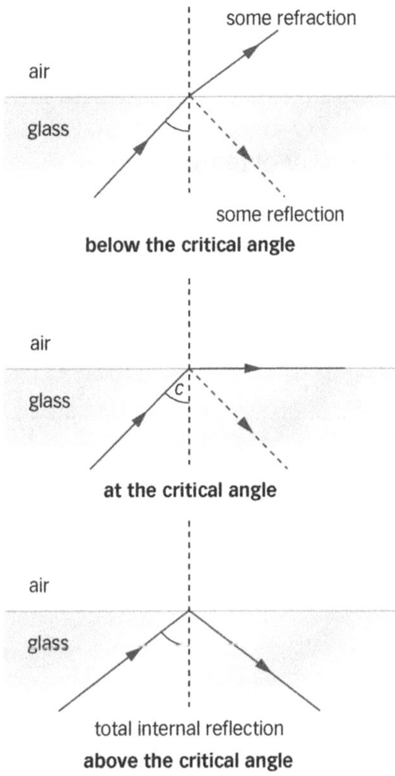

▲ Increasing the angle of incidence can lead to total internal reflection.

H Critical angle

When the angle of incidence equals the critical angle *c*, the angle of refraction is 90°. This means that you can calculate it with this equation:

$$\text{refractive index} = \frac{1}{\sin c}$$

So what is the critical angle for glass of refractive index 1.6?

$$\text{refractive index} = \frac{1}{\sin c}$$

$$\text{so } \sin c = \frac{1}{\text{refractive index}} = \frac{1}{1.6} = 0.625$$

$$\text{so } c = \sin^{-1} 0.625 = 39°$$

Optical fibres

An **optical fibre** is a narrow thread of very transparent glass or plastic. Light that enters one end at a shallow enough angle is unable to refract out into the air until it reaches the other end. The light totally internally reflects off the sides with no loss of energy. This happens even if the fibre is bent – the light has to follow the fibre.

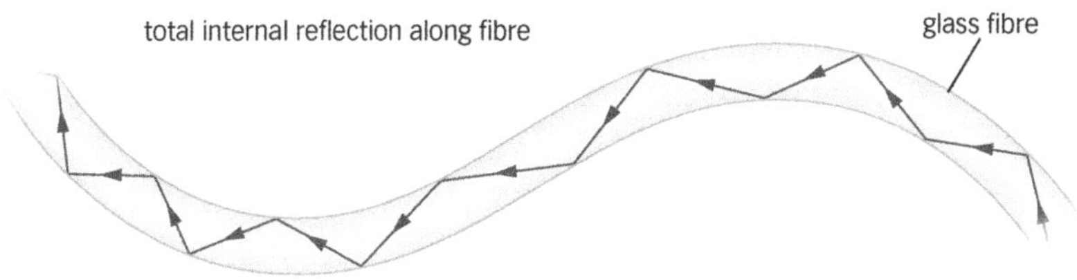

▲ Total internal reflection of light in an optical fibre.

Optical fibres have two main uses:

- They carry pulses of infrared over long distances, rapidly transferring large amounts of information in code for the internet and telephone communications.
- They allow photos to be taken deep inside the body with an **endoscope**. A bundle of fibres carries light into the body, usually through the mouth or anus. A lens collects reflected light and sends it back along another bundle of fibres, allowing the image to be viewed.

Lasers

Optical fibres often use light from a **laser** as the source of their pulses. Laser light forms a very narrow beam that does not spread very much as it travels. Some lasers can produce very intense light that is useful for burning and cutting materials. Medical uses of lasers include:

- precision cutting out of unwanted growths, such as tumours and scar tissue
- sealing off blood vessels by cauterising them
- correcting eyesight by changing the shape of the cornea.

Questions

1	Describe **two** applications of TIR.
2	What are the **two** conditions necessary for TIR to occur?
3	**H** Calculate the critical angle for a glass of refractive index 1.4.

Key words

total internal reflection (TIR), critical angle, optical fibre, endoscope, laser

Exam tip

AQA

Remember that, although there is always some reflection at a boundary, TIR only takes place when the conditions are right:

- light is moving into a less dense material, **and**
- the angle of incidence is greater than the critical angle.

Questions
Total internal reflection, optical fibres, and lasers

Working to Grade E

1 State **two** applications of lasers.

2 Describe an optical fibre and give **one** use for it.

Working to Grade C

3 Complete this diagram to show TIR in an optical fibre.

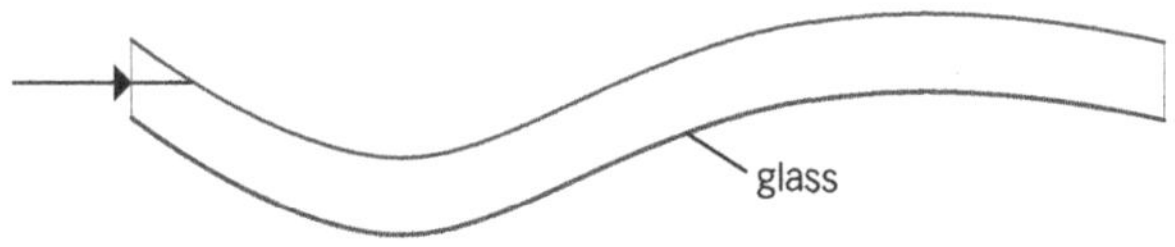

4 Why is it better to send pulses of laser light down an optical fibre instead of through the air for Internet communications?

5 A clear piece of plastic has a critical angle of 42°. Calculate its refractive index.

6 Explain the conditions required for TIR to take place.

7 Explain **one** use of lasers in surgery.

Working to Grade A*

8 A clear piece of plastic has a refractive index of 1.3. Calculate the critical angle for the plastic.

Examination questions
Total internal reflection, optical fibres, and lasers

1 The diagram shows how a glass prism can be used to see over the top of a wall.

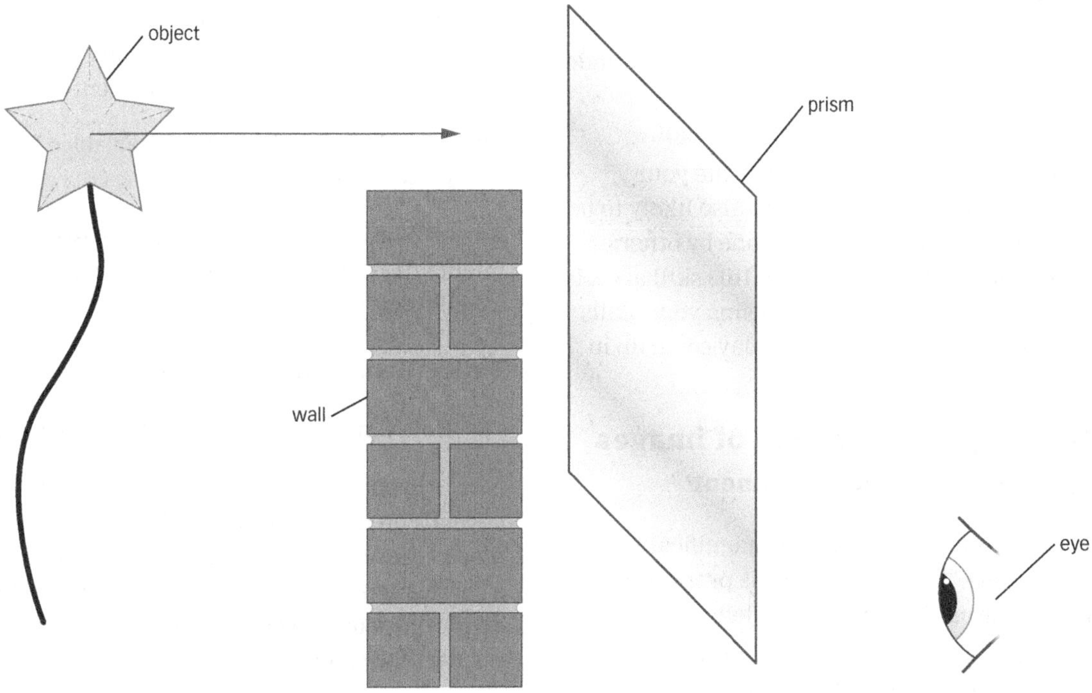

a The glass has a refractive index of 1.6. Calculate the critical angle for the glass.

Write down the equation you use and then show clearly how you work out your answer.

....

....

....

....

critical angle = ... degrees

(2 marks)

b The diagram shows a light ray leaving the object. Continue the ray on the diagram to show how it reaches the eye.

(3 marks)

c Draw a ring around the correct answer to complete the following sentence.

	inverted		false	
The image seen by the eye is	rotated	and	real	.
	upright		virtual	

(2 marks)

(Total marks: 7)

How Science Works
Lens magnification

Designing an investigation and making measurements

In this module there are some opportunities to design investigations and make measurements. These include measurements of sizes and positions of images produced by lenses, through refraction of light.

Although you may be asked to demonstrate your investigative skills practically, you are also likely to be asked to comment on investigations done by others. The example below offers guidance in this skill area. It also gives you the chance to practise using your skills to answer the sorts of questions that may come up in exams.

Investigating magnification of images

Skill – Understanding the experiment

Nina tested the hypothesis that the magnification of an image produced by a convex lens is proportional to its distance from the centre of the lens.

She drew a line of length 25 mm on a piece of tracing paper and placed it in front of a lamp. She placed a white card screen some distance away and moved a convex lens until it produced a focussed image of the line on the screen. Nina used a ruler to measure the height of the image and the distance of the screen from the centre of the lens. She repeated the experiment four times for different placements of the screen.

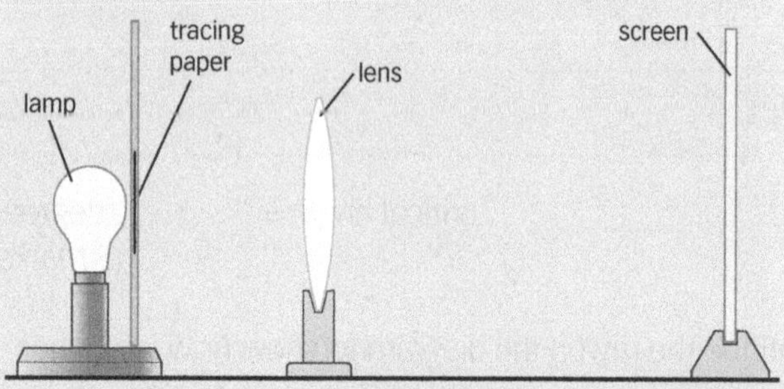

Nina's results are in the table.

Height of object in mm	Distance from paper to screen in cm	Height of image in mm	Distance from lens to screen in cm
25	120	9	34
25	135	98	109
25	103	54	69
25	92	31	49

1 Identify the independent and dependent variables.

In an investigation:

- The independent variables are the ones that are changed by the scientist.
- The dependent variable is the one that is measured for each change of the independent variables.

2 Suggest important control variables for the investigation.

A control variable is one that the investigator thinks might affect the outcome, so they try to keep this variable the same all the way through.

Skill – Using data to draw conclusions

3 How can Nina use the data to test her hypothesis?

Nina's hypothesis concerns how the image height depends on its distance from the lens. So she should plot a scatter graph of these two quantities and look for a correlation between them. Alternatively she could divide one variable by the other and look to see if the result is the same every time.

4 What should Nina do if her results don't support her hypothesis?

If the data does not support the hypothesis, then:

- the data needs to be checked by repeating the experiment, or
- the control variables need to be thought about more carefully – perhaps one has been overlooked, or
- the model used to make the hypothesis needs to be examined more carefully – Nina probably used ray diagrams to make her prediction.

Skill – Evaluating the experiment

5 Give reasons why Nina might get different results when she repeats the experiment.

There are several reasons why results of an experiment are different when it is repeated.

- Human error may change values in a random way, giving a spread of results.
- The limited resolution of the measuring instruments makes it impossible to set up the apparatus exactly the same, every time.
- A zero-error in the measuring instrument may give rise to a systematic error.

AQA Upgrade

Answering an extended writing question

In this question you will be assessed on using good English, organising information clearly, and using specialist terms where appropriate.

1 Explain the advantages and disadvantages of using X-rays for the diagnosis and treatment of cancer tumours. *(6 marks)*

QUESTION

G–E

Well, X-rays aren't much good for finding tumours as they aren't made of bone, only bone shows up in an X-ray, so you wouldn't see the tumour, it would look just like the rest of the skin and mussel. But X-rays are good at killing stuff, so once you kno where the tumour is you can focuss the X-rays onto it and fry it so that it is all killed and not dangerous any more.

Examiner: This answer is typical of a grade-G candidate. It is worth just 1 mark.

The candidate has mentioned only two correct facts about X-rays and has completely ignored the use of CT scans. There is no attempt to explain either fact. X-rays cannot be focussed. The sentences are rather long, with poor spelling and repetition.

D–C

X-rays stops doctors from having to open the patient up, as they can be used to make images of slices through the body. A CT scan sends a thin beam of X-rays through the body to a CCD detector on the other side. A computer puts together the information from sending the X-rays at lots of different angles, making an image on the screen. So doctors can see the tumour even if it is deep inside. However, X-rays are dangerous and can give you cancer if you don't already have it, so this is only worth doing if you know that you already have it.

Examiner: This answer is typical of a grade-D candidate. It is worth just 3 marks.

There is a good description of the CT scan process, but no reference to the variable absorption of X-rays by different tissues. The advantages for diagnosis are explained, as are the disadvantages of using X-rays. However, there is no mention of the use of X-rays for treatment, nor is there any mention of their ionising effect. The quality of English and spelling is good.

B–A*

X-rays are high energy electromagnetic waves with enough energy to ionise atoms in their path. This means that they can pass deep into the body before being absorbed. High density materials absorb better than low density ones, so the intensity of an X-ray beam which passes through part of the body depends on the organs in its path – including a tumour. So if the X-rays are fired through the same part of the body at lots of different angles a computer can create an image of that part. This allows doctors to detect tumours without having to cut open the body (which carries an infection risk). Beams of X-rays from lots of different directions can then be used to kill the cells of the tumour, provided it is where the beams cross. One problem is that other cells may have their DNA damaged by the ionisation, making them into cancer.

Examiner: This answer is typical of a grade-A candidate. It is worth 5 marks.

The information is well ordered, starting with the properties of X-rays, which can be used to explain the techniques described in the rest of the response. Both diagnosis and treatment have been discussed. There is no mention of how X-rays are detected, and the risk–benefit analysis of treatment is a little shallow. The use of English is excellent.

Part 1 Course catch-up
Physics in medicine

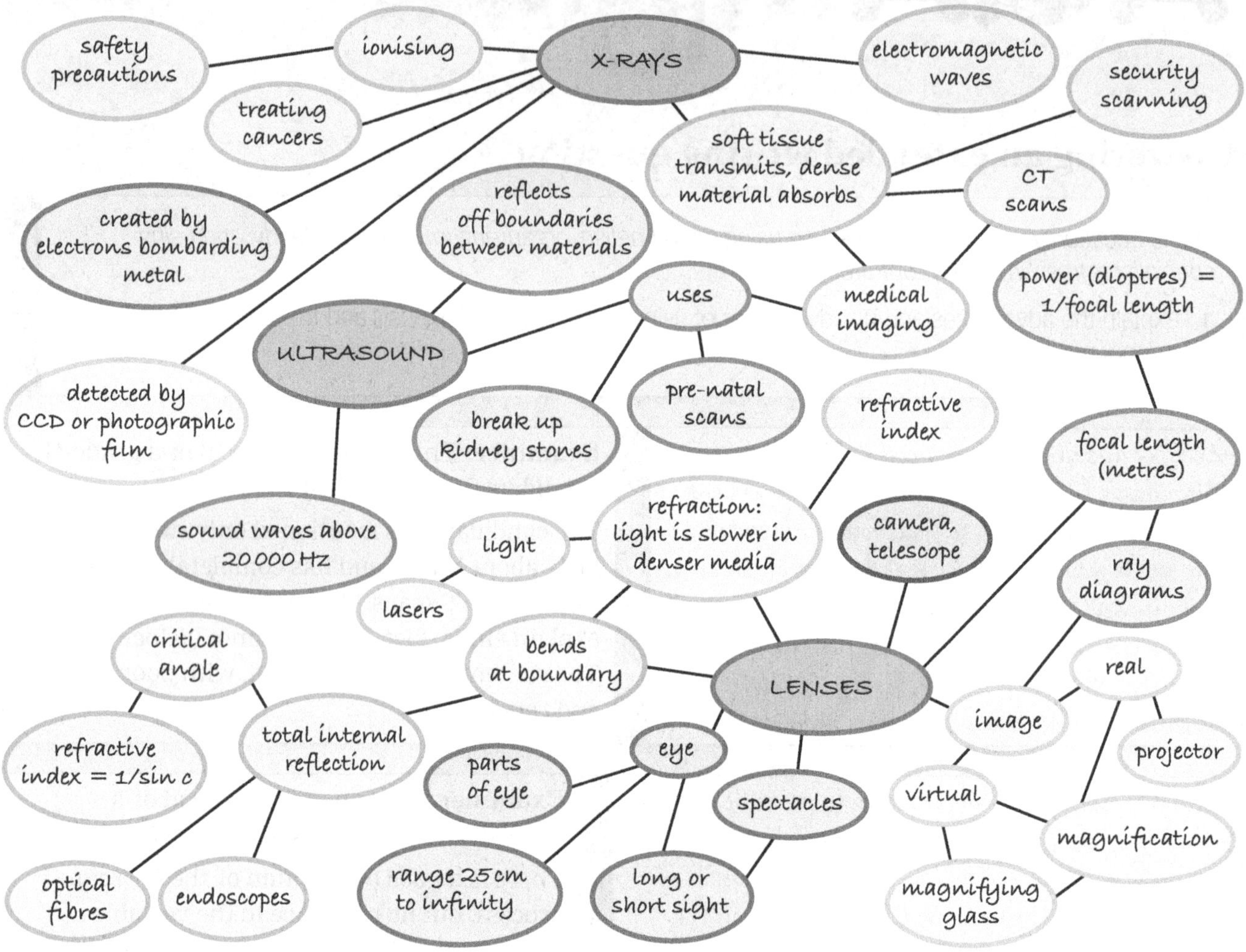

Revision checklist

- X-rays are electromagnetic waves with a short wavelength. They are ionising, so potentially dangerous.
- Ultrasound waves are sound waves with a frequency above 20 000 Hz. Ultrasound reflects off boundaries between materials.
- Refraction is the bending of light when it moves from one medium to another. Lenses use refraction to form an image.
- Refractive index is a measure of the speed of light through a material compared with the speed of light in a vacuum.
- The nature of an image is determined by its distance from the lens, its size, its orientation, and whether it is real or virtual.
- The image produced by converging lenses is real and inverted, or virtual, upright, and magnified.
- The image produced by diverging lenses is virtual, upright, and diminished.
- Magnification = image height/object height.
- The human eye has a range of vision from 25 cm to infinity. Features of the eye: retina; cornea; iris; pupil; ciliary muscles; suspensory ligaments.
- Short-sight is inability to focus on far away objects, corrected by diverging lenses.
- Long-sight is inability to focus on near objects, corrected by converging lenses.
- In a camera a converging lens focuses light onto photographic film or a charge-coupled device (CCD) to produce a real image.
- More powerful lenses have shorter focal lengths. Lens power is measured in dioptres. Power = 1/focal length.
- If the angle of light travelling from a denser medium towards a less dense medium exceeds the critical angle, total internal reflection (TIR) occurs.
- Optical fibres channel light through total internal reflection, and are used for communication and in endoscopes.
- Laser beams remain very narrow even over long distances. Their intensity means they can be used to cut, etch, or cauterise objects (including in laser eye surgery).

Stability

The **stability** of an object tells you how far it can be tilted before it falls over. So a pencil standing on its end is less stable than a traffic cone. This is because the cone has a much wider base than the pencil.

▲ The pencil is much easier to topple than the traffic cone.

Centre of mass

The stability of an object can be increased by:

- increasing the width of its base
- lowering its centre of mass.

The **centre of mass** of an object is the point at which all of its **weight** appears to act. You can find this point by suspending the object from two different points: the object always settles with the centre of mass directly below the suspension point.

▲ His centre of mass is directly below his right hand.

Revision objectives

- understand the meaning of the term 'centre of mass'
- describe how to find the centre of mass of an object
- state the factors that affect the stability of an object
- explain the conditions for an object to topple

Student book references

3.17 Centre of mass

3.22 Toppling objects

Specification key

- P3.2.1 a – c
- P3.2.2 f

Key words

stability, centre of mass, weight, symmetry, line of action, moment

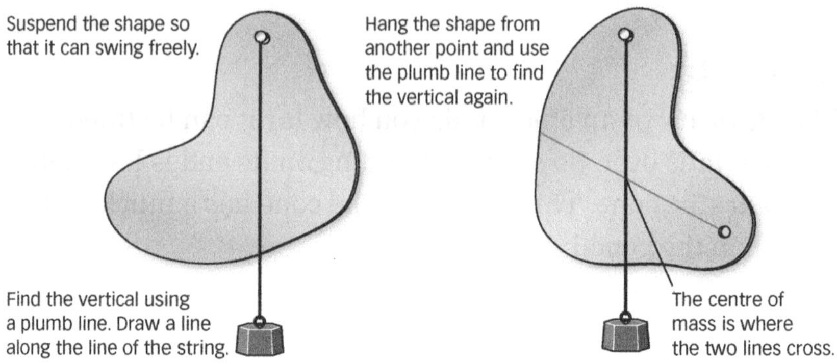

▲ Finding the centre of mass of an object.

Symmetry

When the mass is evenly spread over a symmetrical object, then the centre of mass is somewhere on the axis of **symmetry**.

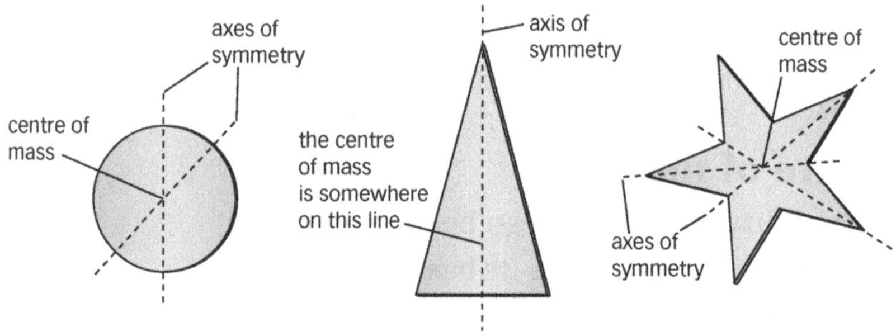

▲ Using symmetry to find centres of mass.

Exam tip AQA

The centre of mass of an object does not have to be at its centre if the mass is unevenly spread.

Questions

1 Where is the centre of mass of a solid cube?

2 State **two** ways of increasing the stability of an object.

3 **H** Explain why a pencil always topples over when it is placed on a table point down.

H Explaining stability

An object always settles with the **line of action** of its weight acting through the base. A slight tilt leaves the centre of mass above the base, so there is a **moment** returning it to its previous position. A large tilt puts the centre of mass outside the base, giving a moment that increases the tilt even more – so the object falls over.

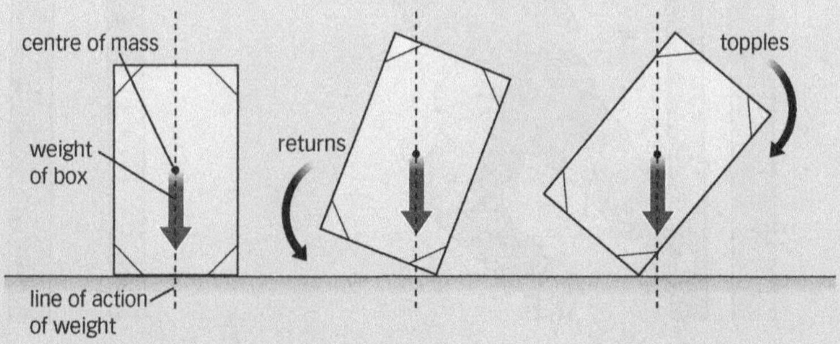

Pendulums

You can make a **pendulum** by suspending a heavy object on the end of a light, flexible support. So it could be a conker on the end of a string, or a child on a swing. You can always spot a pendulum by its behaviour – the suspended object swings backwards and forwards when you give it a brief push.

Period

Pendulums have been used in clocks for hundreds of years. This is because the time that the object takes to make one complete swing (the **period**) mostly depends on the length of its suspension. Changing the mass of the object or the size of its swing makes hardly any difference to its period. So the **frequency** of the pendulum remains steady – the number of oscillations per second does not change.

$$T = \frac{1}{f}$$

T is the time period in seconds (s)
f is the frequency in hertz (Hz)

So if a pendulum has a period of 0.25 s, what is its frequency?

$$T = \frac{1}{f} \text{ so } f = \frac{1}{T} = \frac{1}{0.25\,\text{s}} = 4.0\,\text{Hz}$$

Revision objectives

- describe the motion of a pendulum
- explain how the time period of a pendulum is related to its length

Student book references

3.18 Pendulums

Specification key

- P3.2.1 d – e

Key words

pendulum, period, frequency

Questions

1 What is the period of a pendulum?

2 Which of these variables has the most effect on the period of a pendulum: length, mass, or size of swing?

3 **H** A clock pendulum makes 15 complete swings in one minute. What is its frequency?

Exam tip

AQA

Remember that the period is the time for the pendulum to swing there and back again.

Revision objectives

- understand that the turning effect of a force is a moment
- calculate the size of a moment
- explain the principle of moments
- calculate forces and distance for objects balanced on a pivot

Student book references

3.19 Moments
3.20 Principles of moments

Specification key

- P3.2.2 a – d

Turning forces

Forces are often used to make things turn. The effect of a turning force depends on three things:

- the size of the force
- the direction of the force
- how far it acts from the pivot.

The **pivot** is the point on the object that does not move when it rotates.

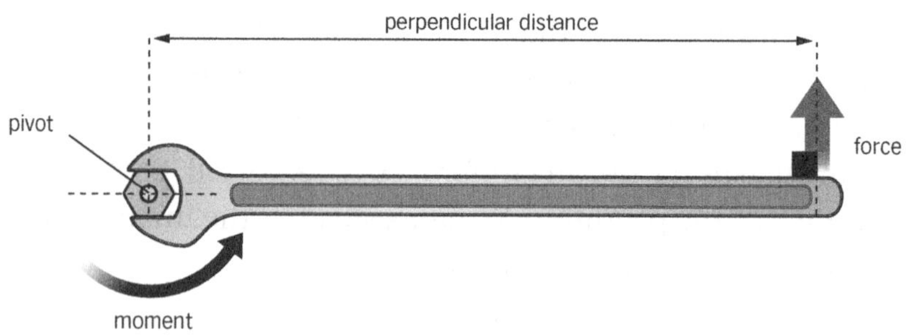

▲ A force on the spanner handle provides a moment about the nut. These factors are put together in the idea of a moment.

Calculating moments

You calculate the size of a **moment** with this equation:

$$M = F \times d$$

M is the moment of the force in netwon-metres (Nm)
F is the force in newtons (N)
d is the perpendicular distance in metres (m)

The **perpendicular distance** takes account of the direction of the force. It is the distance from the **line of action** of the force from the pivot. So what is the moment applied to this spanner?

$$M = F \times d = 60\,\text{N} \times 0.2\,\text{m} = 12\,\text{Nm}$$

Moments have direction as well as a size. The moment on the spanner is **anticlockwise**. Reversing the direction of the force would give a **clockwise** moment.

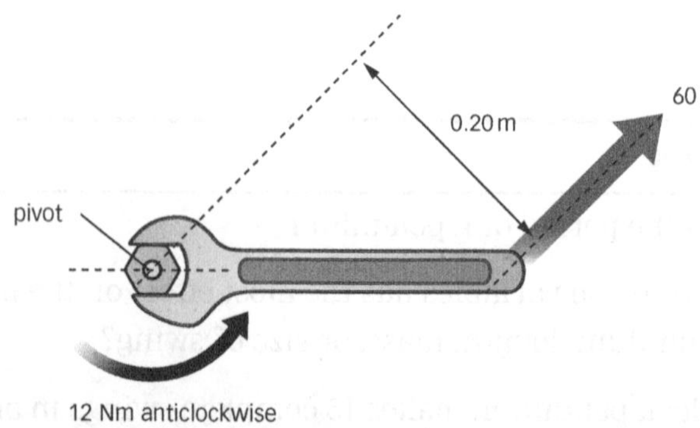

▲ The perpendicular distance is how far the force's line of action is from the pivot.

Principle of moments

The **principle of moments** says that an object balances when the moments acting on it cancel each other out.

The wheelbarrow on the right is balanced. The clockwise moment from the man is 150 N × 1.2 m = 180 Nm. The anticlockwise moment from the weight of the wheelbarrow is 600 N × 0.3 m = 180 Nm. They cancel out.

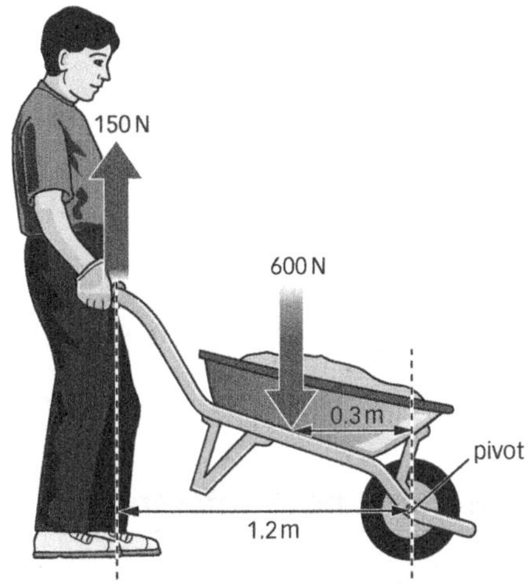

▲ The wheelbarrow is balanced.

H Calculating with moments

Sam and Jo sit on a seesaw. The seesaw balances when they sit as shown. If Sam has a weight of 600 N, what is Jo's weight?

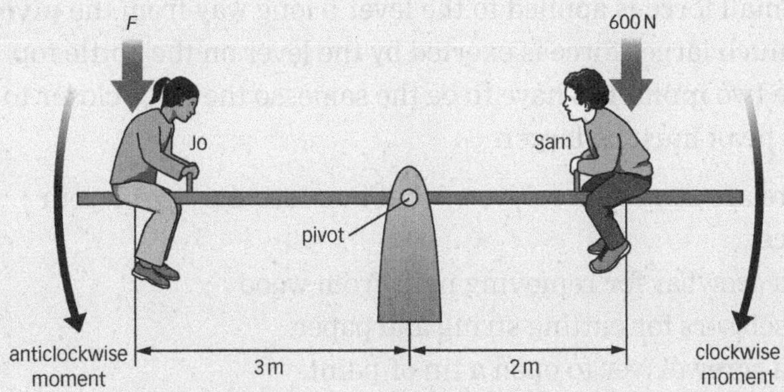

anticlockwise moment = clockwise moment

$F \times 3\,\text{m} = 600\,\text{N} \times 2\,\text{m} = 1200\,\text{Nm}$

$F \times 3\,\text{m} = 1200\,\text{N}$ so $F = \dfrac{1200\,\text{Nm}}{3\,\text{m}} = 400\,\text{N}$

Questions

1 What is the direction of the moment applied to the door?

2 How big is the moment applied to the door?

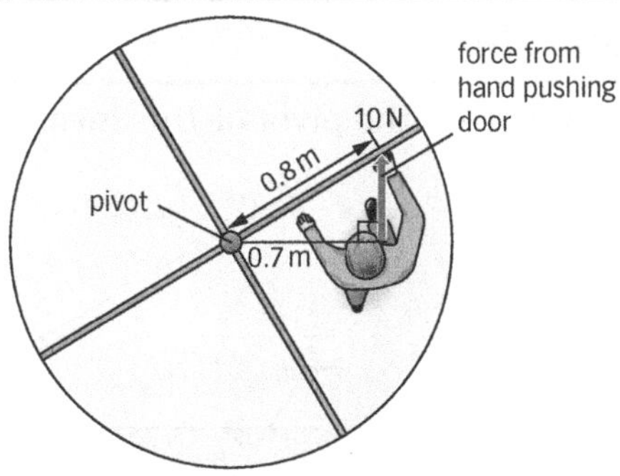

▲ Turning force on a revolving door.

3 **H** Bill and Ted sit on a balanced seesaw. Bill has a weight of 600 N and sits 2.4 m to the left of the pivot. Ted has a weight of 800 N. Where does he sit?

Key words

pivot, moment, perpendicular distance, line of action, anticlockwise, clockwise, principle of moments

Exam tip AQA

Always state the direction of a moment as well as its size.

Revision objectives

- state some examples of levers
- explain how a lever multiplies a force

Student book references

3.21 Levers

Specification key

✔ P3.2.2 e

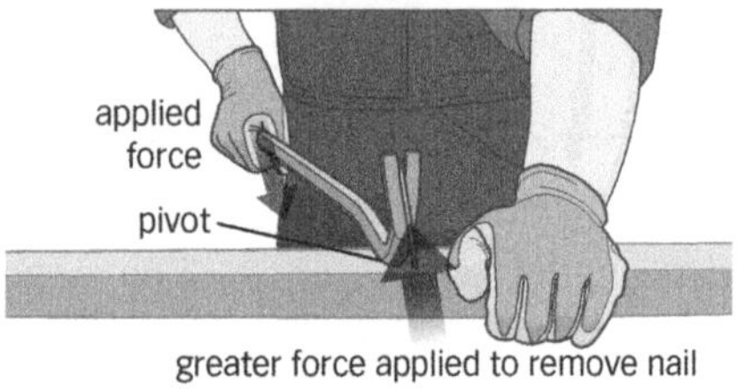

▲ A crowbar.

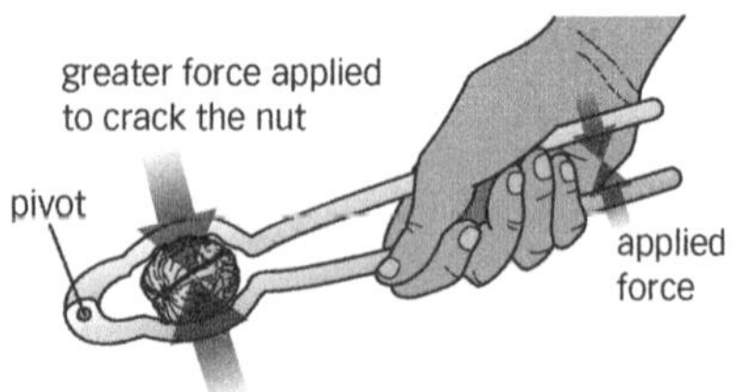

▲ A nutcracker.

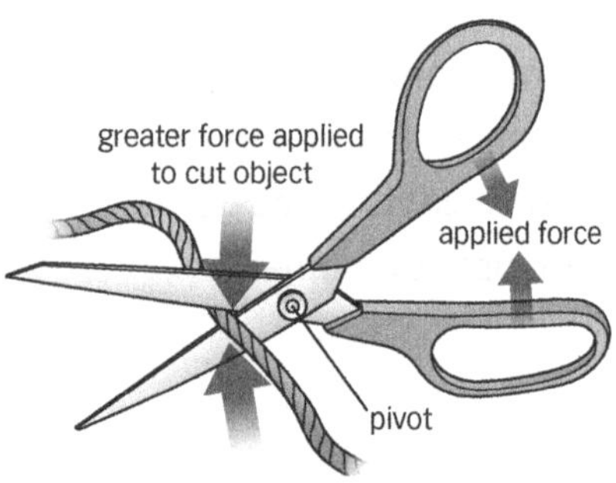

▲ A pair of scissors.

Key words

lever, force multiplier, pivot, moment

Force multiplier

This bottle opener uses a **lever** as a **force multiplier**.

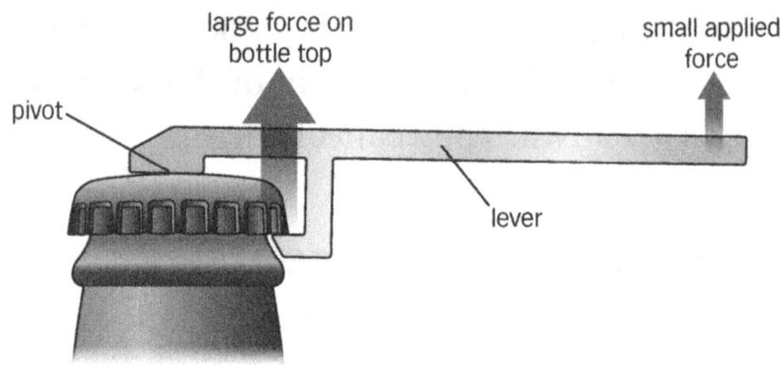

▲ A bottle opener in action.

A small force is applied to the lever a long way from the **pivot**. A much larger force is exerted by the lever on the bottle top. The two **moments** have to be the same, so the force closer to the pivot must be larger.

Here are some other devices that increase the size of your force:

- a crowbar for removing nails from wood
- scissors for cutting string and paper
- a screwdriver to open a tin of paint.

They all work in the same way. The lever is pivoted near one end and your force is applied to the other end. This allows a much larger force at some point close to the pivot.

Exam tip

AQA

Always start analysing a lever by identifying the pivot.

Questions

1 Where is the pivot of this lever?

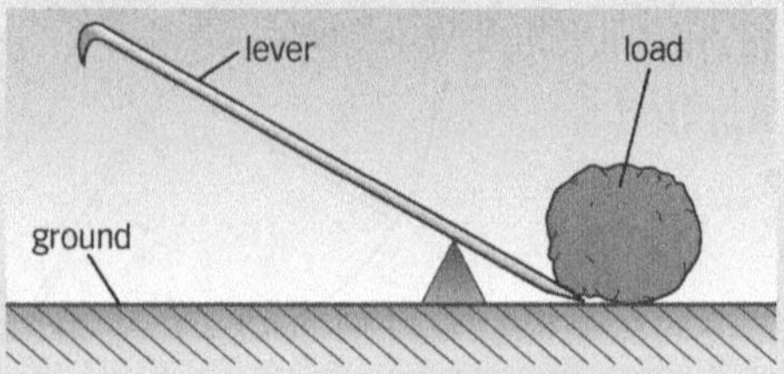

2 Label the force applied to the lever and the force from the lever on the load.

3 **H** Explain how increasing the length of the lever makes it easier to raise the load.

Pressure

The weight of the liquid in this cylinder exerts a downwards **pressure** on its base. You can calculate pressure with this equation:

$$P = \frac{F}{A}$$

P is the pressure on a surface in pascals (Pa)
F is the force acting on the surface in newtons (N)
A is the area of the surface in metres squared (m^2)

So if the base has an area of $0.01\,m^2$ and holds up water of weight 50 N, what is its pressure?

$$P = \frac{F}{A} = \frac{50\,N}{0.01\,m^2} = 5000\,Pa$$

A liquid always exerts a pressure at right angles to the surface in contact with it. So the side walls at the base of the cylinder also have a pressure of 5000 Pa, but in a horizontal direction.

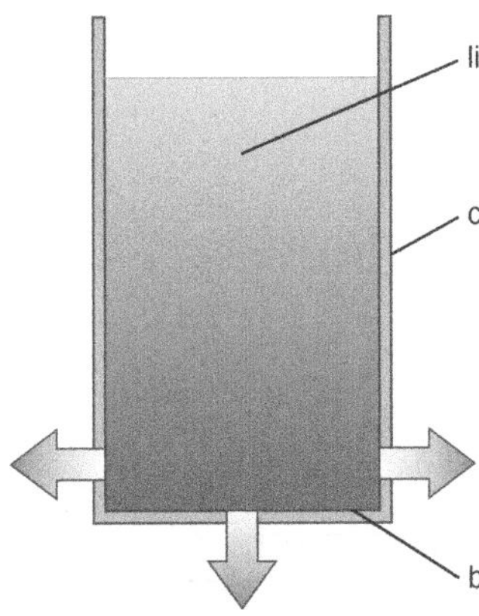

▲ The weight of the liquid pushes against the walls and base of the cylinder.

Hydraulic systems

Any extra pressure applied to a liquid raises the pressure at any surface in contact with it. This is exploited by **hydraulic systems**, where a force applied at one point is transmitted through liquid in a pipe to a different point. This is widely used for car brakes:

- A force is applied to the brake pedal.
- The pressure of the oil in the cylinder increases.
- The pressure of the oil in the pipes also increases.
- The oil applies a force on the brake pads.

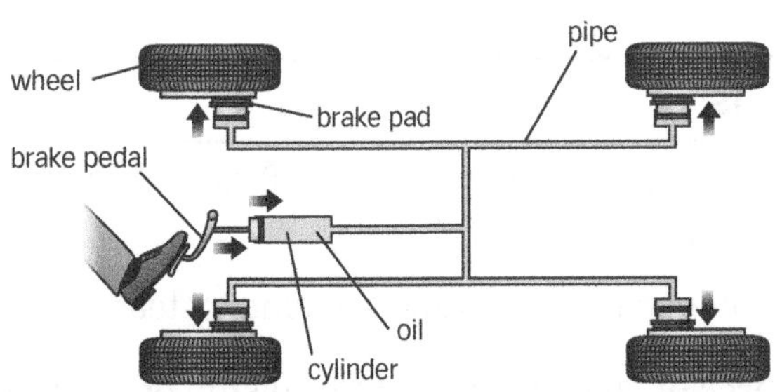

▲ Pressure from the brake pedal passes through the oil in the pipes to the brake pads.

Revision objectives

- recall that liquids are almost incompressible
- explain that pressure in liquids is transmitted equally in all directions
- use the equation linking pressure, force, and area
- explain how a hydraulic system multiplies a force

Student book references

3.23 Pressure in liquids
3.24 Hydraulics

Specification key

✔ P3.2.3

Key words

pressure, hydraulic systems, incompressible, force multiplier

Incompressible

Like all liquids, the oil used in a hydraulic system is **incompressible**. Its particles are already very close to each other, so when the pressure increases, its volume hardly changes. So any change of pressure rapidly spreads through the liquid.

Force multipliers

Hydraulic systems do more than allow a force applied at one point to be delivered to a different point some distance away. They also act as **force multipliers**, making that force bigger or smaller.

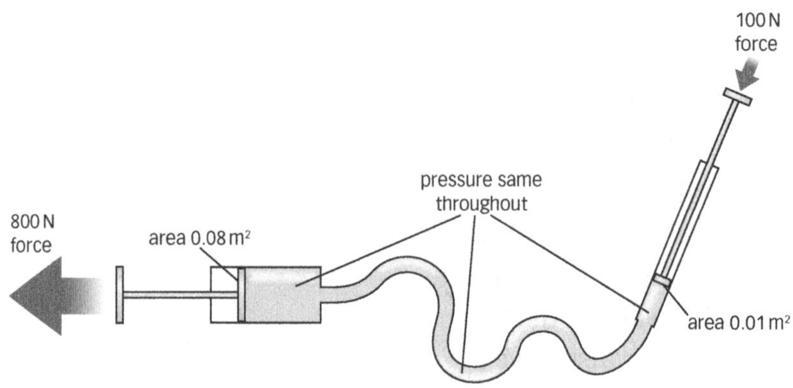

▲ A hydraulic system as a force multiplier.

This is how this hydraulic system works:

- A force of 100 N is applied to the oil over an area of $0.01\,m^2$ in the narrow cylinder.
- This raises the pressure of the oil by:

$$P = \frac{F}{A} = \frac{100\,N}{0.01\,m^2} = 10\,000\,Pa$$

- The pressure of the oil is the same in both cylinders.
- For the wider cylinder:

$$P = \frac{F}{A} = \text{so } F = P \times A = 10\,000\,Pa \times 0.08\,m^2 = 800\,N$$

So the force at the output of the system is eight times larger than the force applied at the input.

Exam tip AQA

The pressure is the same everywhere in a hydraulic system, always pushing outwards.

Questions

1 A force of 500 N acts on an area of $0.25\,m^2$. What pressure does it exert?

2 Why is oil used in hydraulic systems instead of air?

3 **H** A force of 600 N is applied to a piston of area $0.02\,m^2$. If that pressure is transmitted through a liquid to another piston of area $0.08\,m^2$, what force is exerted on it?

Moments, masses, hydraulics, and levers

Working to Grade E

1 Where is the centre of mass of a box that is an empty cube?

2 A pendulum has a frequency of 0.5 Hz. How long does it take for 10 complete swings?

3 Calculate the moment of a force of 45 N applied at a distance of 0.8 m from a pivot.

4 Identify the clockwise and anticlockwise moments.

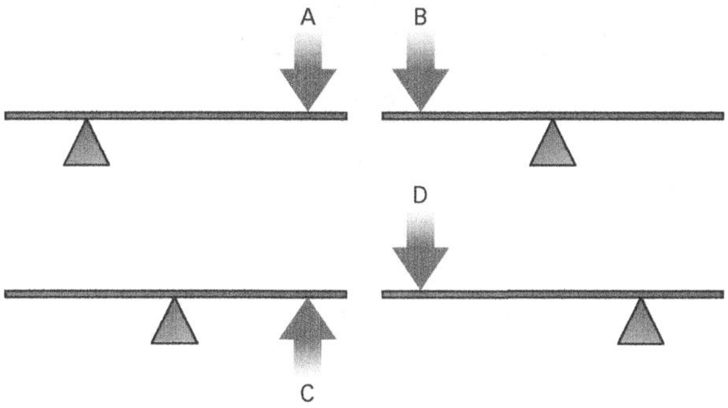

5 Give **two** examples of levers used at home.

6 Calculate the pressure when a force of 600 N is applied over an area of 0.3 m^2.

Working to Grade C

7 Explain how you would find the centre of mass of a tennis racket.

8 State **two** factors that do **not** have much effect on the period of a pendulum.

9 Explain why this system is balanced.

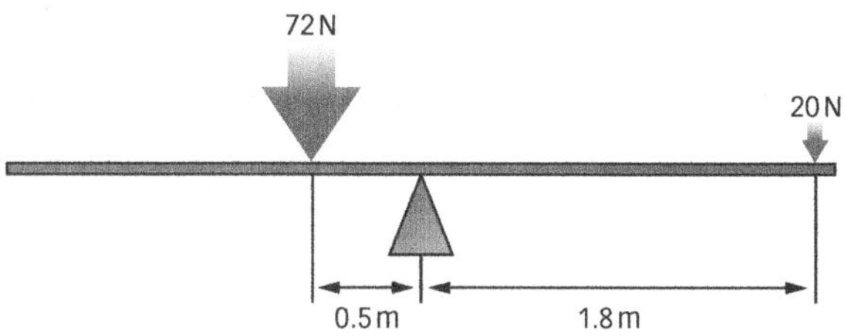

10 State **two** ways of increasing the stability of an object.

11 Why is there the same pressure on both pistons A and B?

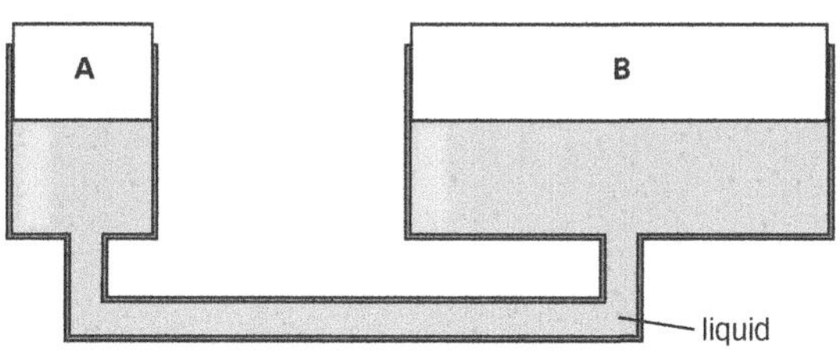

Working to Grade A*

12 Calculate the force on piston B.

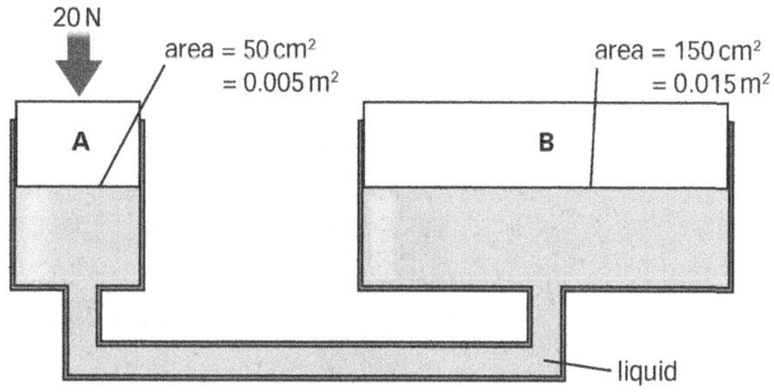

13 Calculate the value of *d* for the seesaw to balance.

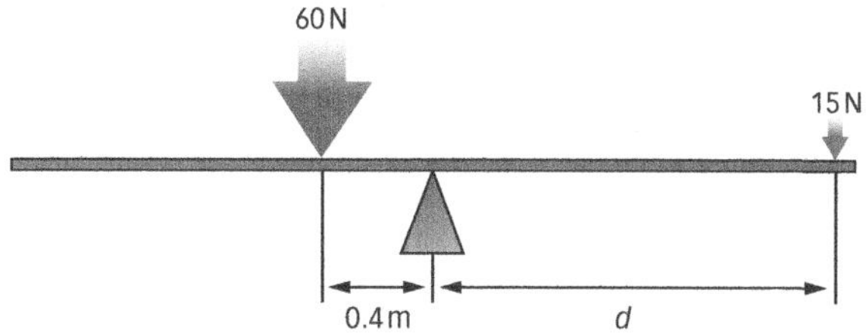

14 Explain why nutcrackers allow you to crack a nut that you couldn't crack with your bare hands.

Examination questions
Moments, masses, hydraulics, and levers

1 The diagram shows Jack and Jill balancing on a seesaw.

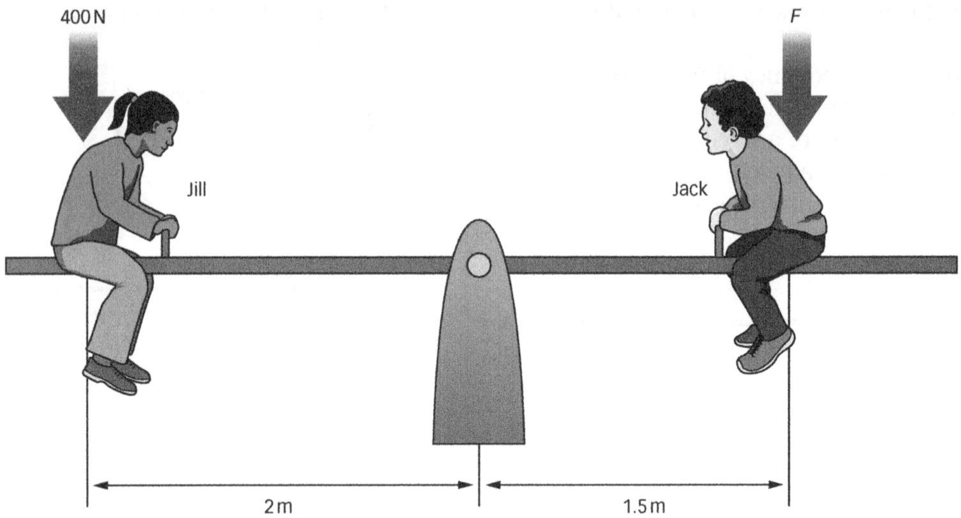

a Label the pivot of the seesaw.

(1 mark)

b Calculate the moment produced by Jill's weight.

Write down the equation you use and then show clearly how you work out your answer. Give the unit for your answer.

....

....

....

....

....

moment = ...

(4 marks)

c Draw a ring around the correct answer to complete the sentences.

Jill applies a moment in the [clockwise / downwards / anticlockwise] direction.

Jack's moment must be [the same as / smaller than / greater than] Jill's moment to balance the seesaw.

(2 marks)

d Calculate the force produced by Jack's weight.

Write down the equation you use and then show clearly how you work out your answer.

....

....

....

....

....

force = ...N

(3 marks)

e Jack owns a table tennis bat.

Describe how he could find the centre of mass of his table tennis bat.

....

....

....

....

....

....

....

(4 marks)

(Total marks: 14)

Revision objectives

- understand that objects moving in a circle are accelerating
- describe centripetal force
- explain the effect of mass, speed, and path radius on centripetal force

Student book references

3.25 Circular motion

3.26 Size of centripetal force

Specification key

✔ P3.2.4

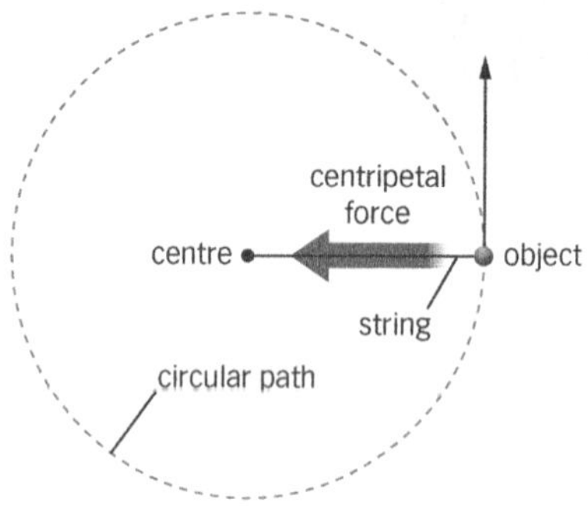

▲ As the object moves around the circle it keeps on changing direction.

Changing direction

The string attached to the object in the diagram below makes it follow a circular path as it moves. This means that the direction of the object's motion has to keep on changing. So even if it keeps a constant **speed**, its **velocity** (which is fixed by both speed and direction) is continually changing. A changing velocity means that the object is accelerating.

$$\text{acceleration} = \frac{\text{change of velocity}}{\text{time taken for change}}$$

Centripetal force

An object can only accelerate if there is a resultant force acting on it. The force that makes an object move in a circular path is called **centripetal force**, and it always has to act towards the centre of the circle. This is because the object is continually accelerating towards the centre of the circle. If there isn't a centripetal force on an object, it cannot move in a circle.

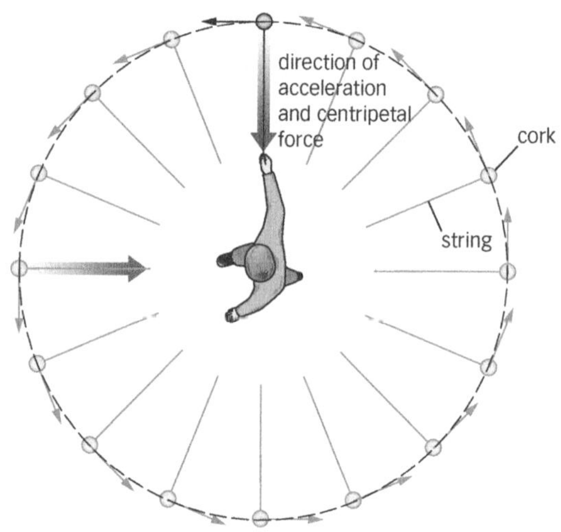

▲ The centripetal force on the cork is provided by the tension in the string.

▲ Friction between the tyres and the road provides the centripetal force for this car as it goes around the bend.

Changing centripetal force

The size of the centripetal force on an object can be increased by:

- increasing the **mass** of the object
- increasing the speed of the object
- decreasing the radius of the circular path.

The mass affects the centripetal force because force = mass × **acceleration**.

Making the object go faster means that its direction changes more in the same time, so it has a greater rate of change of velocity.

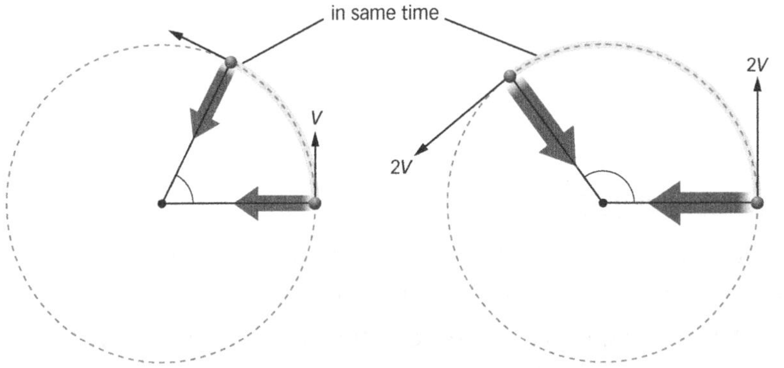

▲ Increasing the speed makes the direction change faster.

Making the circular path smaller also results in a greater change of direction in the same time. So there is a greater rate of change of velocity.

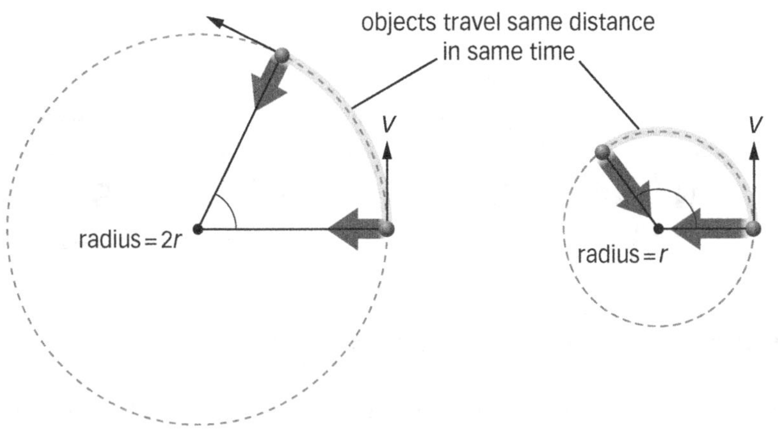

▲ Making the circle smaller makes the direction change faster.

Exam tip

AQA

Remember that if an object moves in a circle the resultant force **must** point to the centre of the circle.

Key words

speed, velocity, centripetal force, mass, acceleration

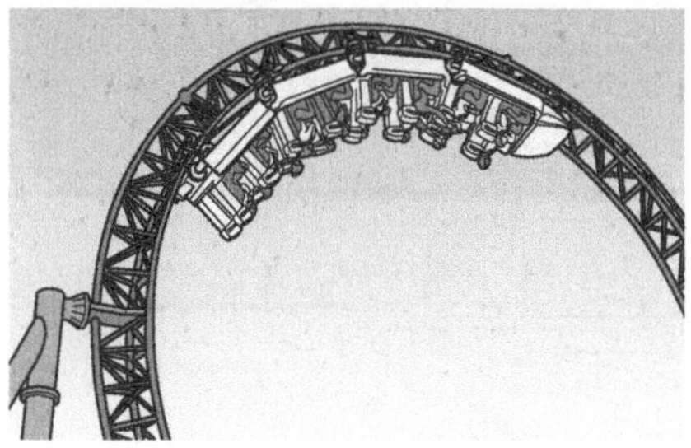

Questions

1 What is the direction of the resultant force on the first rollercoaster car in the picture?

2 Explain why an object moving in a circle must have a centripetal force.

3 **H** You are sitting in a moving car when it swerves to the right. Explain why you appear to be pushed to the left-hand side of the car.

Revision objectives

- understand that a current in a wire produces a magnetic field
- describe the force produced by the motor effect
- describe how to change the size and direction of this force
- describe and explain some applications of the motor effect

Student book references

3.27 Electromagnets and the motor effect

3.28 Using the motor effect

Specification key

✔ P3.3.1

Making magnetic fields

Whenever charge flows through a wire to make a **current**, a **magnetic field** appears around the wire. The shape of the field lines depends on the shape of the wire. The field lines are concentric circles for a straight wire, and like those of a bar magnet for a wire coiled into a **solenoid**.

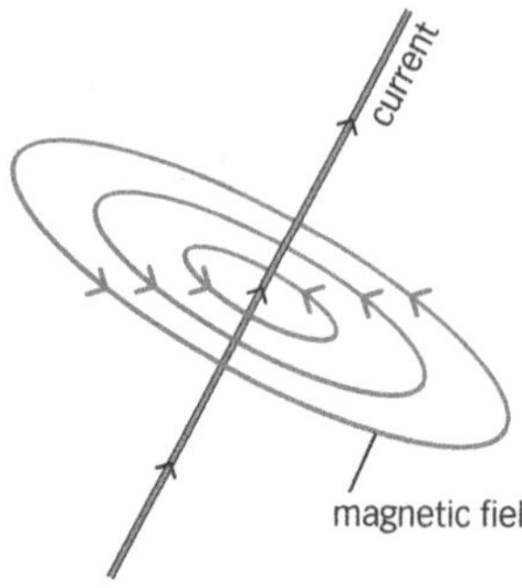

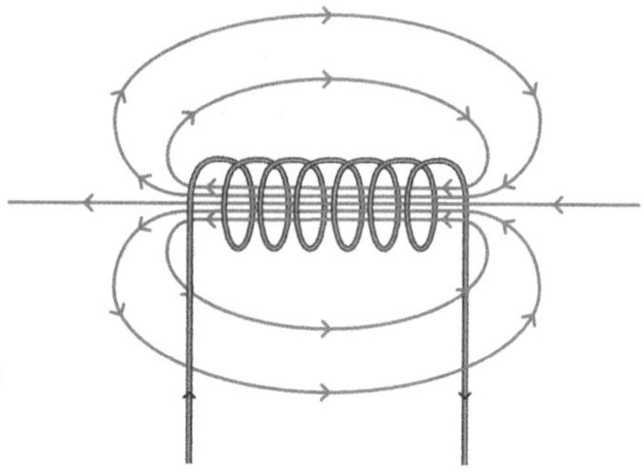

Motor effect

When magnets are placed close to each other, forces act between them. So when there is a current in a wire placed near to bar magnets, there is a **force** on the wire. This is called the **motor effect**. The size of the force can be changed by:

- increasing the size of the current
- increasing the strength of the bar magnets.

If the wire runs parallel to the magnetic field, it will not experience a force.

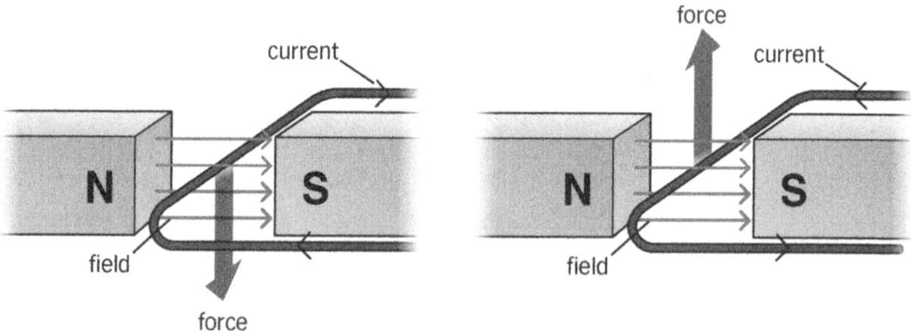

▲ There is a force on a current in a magnetic field.

The direction of the force is at right angles to both the current and the magnet's field, as shown by **Fleming's left-hand rule**. Changing the direction of either the current or the field changes the direction of the force – but changing the direction of both at the same time has no effect.

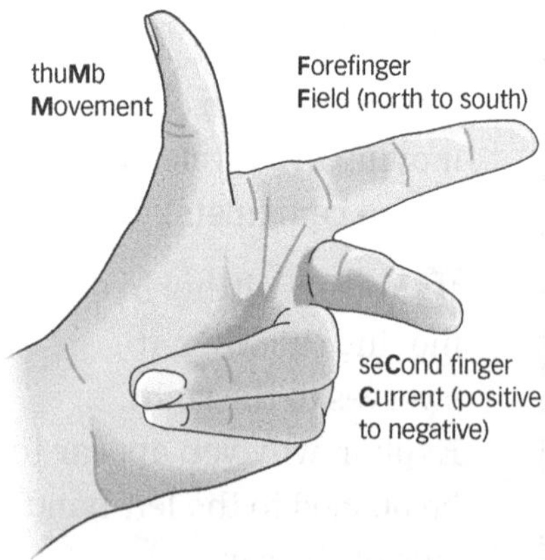

▲ Fleming's left-hand rule.

Electric motors

Electric motors are everywhere – from high-speed trains to vibrators in mobile phones. They use the motor effect to make a **coil** of wire spin round between a pair of magnets. Current from the power supply enters the coil via a pair of fixed **brushes** touching a **split-ring commutator**. The current in the coil interacts with the magnetic field to make a pair of equal forces which act in opposite directions. These forces are on different sides of the coil, so they make it turn. Each time the loop is vertical, the current is reversed. The side of the loop that was pushed up is now pushed down. The brushes and commutator act as a switch to keep the coil spinning in the same direction.

Key words

current, magnetic field, solenoid, force, motor effect, Fleming's left-hand rule, coil, brushes, split-ring commutator, loudspeaker

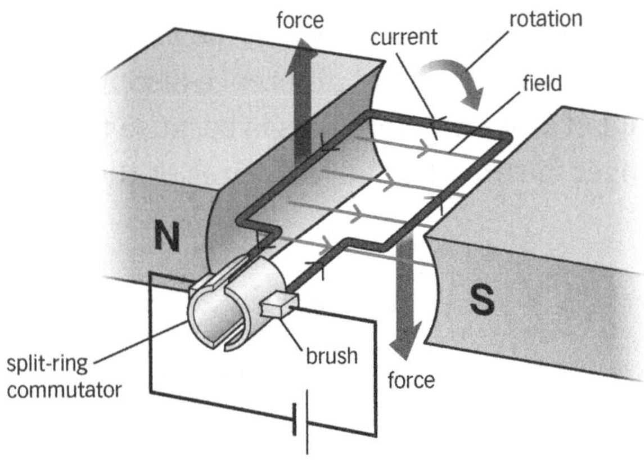

▲ A simple electric motor.

Meters and speakers

An analogue ammeter measures current by passing it through a coil between magnets. The arrangement is very similar to that of an electric motor, with a spring to keep the coil in position. Increasing the current increases the force on the coil, twisting it round more against the spring.

Loudspeakers use the motor effect to make a paper cone vibrate rapidly. Alternating current is fed into the coil fastened to the back of the cone. The direction of the force from the magnet in the coil depends on the direction of the current. So as the current changes direction, so does the force.

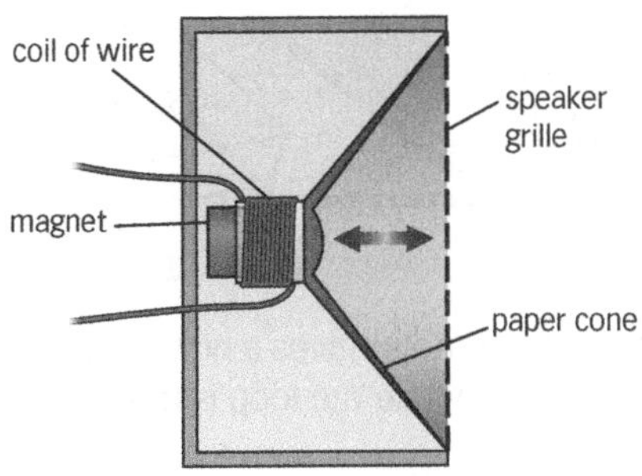

▲ Loudspeakers use the motor effect.

Questions

1 Describe the magnetic field around a straight wire that has a current in it.

2 Explain why a solenoid can be used to make a magnet that can be turned on and off.

3 **H** Explain **four** ways of making an electric motor spin round faster.

Exam tip AQA

Don't use your right hand when trying to apply Fleming's left-hand rule.

Revision objectives

- describe the conditions required for electromagnetic induction
- describe the construction of a transformer
- explain the operation of a transformer
- calculate the potential difference change for a transformer

Student book references

3.29 Transformers

3.30 Step-up and step-down transformers

Specification key

- P3.3.2 a – d and g

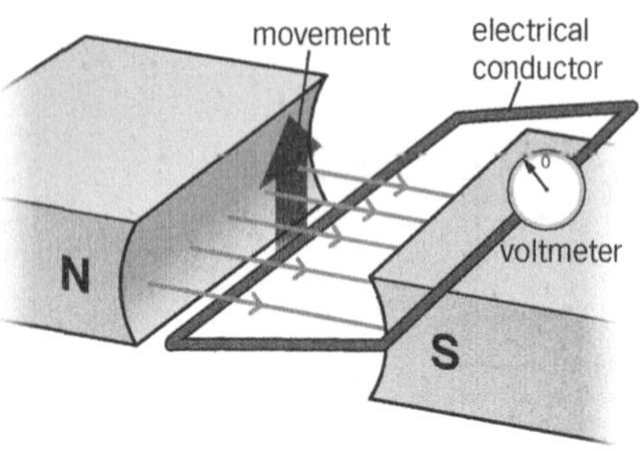

▲ The voltmeter gives a non-zero reading while the loop is moving.

Electromagnetic induction

Suppose a loop of wire sits in a **magnetic field**. Whenever the loop is moved so that part of it passes through the field lines, a **potential difference** is **induced** in the circuit.

The potential difference is only present during the movement of the loop, while it cuts the field lines. As soon as the movement stops, the potential difference disappears.

Magnets and coils

Moving a magnet towards and away from a coil of wire induces a potential difference across the ends of the coil. The sign of the potential difference is reversed when the motion of the magnet is reversed. The potential difference disappears as soon as the magnet stops moving. This is because the field lines are no longer cutting through the wires of the coil.

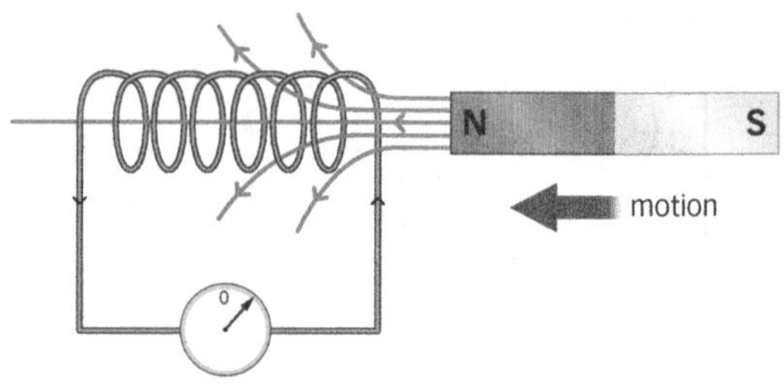

▲ Electromagnetic induction with a coil of wire and a magnet.

Transformers

A **transformer** has two coils of wire wound on a single **iron core**. The **primary coil** is connected to a supply of **alternating current**, so that it becomes an electromagnet. Current in the primary coil creates magnetic field lines that pass through the core. As the current changes direction, so does the direction of the magnetic field. Each change of magnetic field direction in the core induces a potential difference across the **secondary coil**.

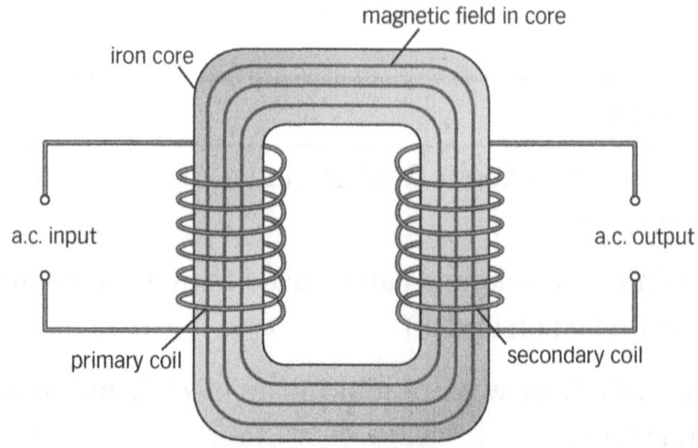

▲ A transformer.

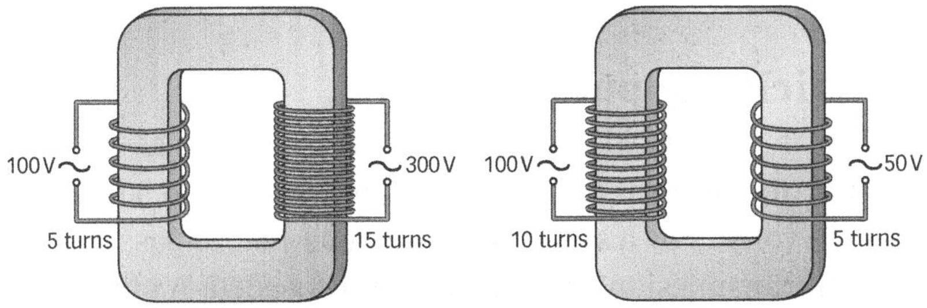

▲ Transformers make potential differences bigger or smaller.

Key words

magnetic field, potential difference, induced, transformer, iron core, primary coil, alternating current, secondary coil

Changing potential difference

Transformers are widely used to change the potential difference of an alternating current. You can calculate the change with this equation:

$$\frac{V_p}{V_s} = \frac{n_p}{n_s}$$

V_p is the potential difference across the primary coil in volts (V)
V_s is the potential difference across the secondary coil in volts (V)
n_p is the number of turns of wire on the primary coil
n_s is the number of turns of wire on the secondary coil

Suppose a transformer is used to reduce the 230 V mains supply to 12 V. How many turns of wire should the secondary coil have if the primary has 4600 turns?

$$\frac{V_p}{V_s} = \frac{n_p}{n_s} \text{ so } n_s \times \frac{V_p}{V_s} = n_p \text{ and } n_s \times V_p = n_p \times V_s$$

$$\text{therefore } n_s = n_p \times \frac{V_p}{V_s} = 4600 \times \frac{12\,\text{V}}{230\,\text{V}} = 240$$

Notice that the ratio of the turns of wire on the two coils is the also the ratio of the potential differences across them.

Questions

1 Describe the construction of a transformer.

2 There is a potential difference of +0.05 V across a coil while a magnet is being pushed into it. What is the potential difference while the magnet is being pulled out of the coil?

3 **H** A transformer has 9200 turns in its primary coil and 360 turns in its secondary coil. What is the potential difference across the primary when the secondary produces a.c. at 9 V?

Exam tip AQA

Remember that a potential difference is **only** induced across the ends of a coil while the magnetic field inside it is changing.

Revision objectives

- use the transformer power equation
- compare transformers used for different applications
- know that switch mode transformers operate at high frequency
- describe the advantages of using a switch mode transformer

Student book references

3.31 Transformer power equation

3.32 Switch mode transformers

Specification key

- P3.3.2 e – k

Electricity supply

Much of the electrical energy you use is generated as **alternating current** in power stations. This has to be raised to a high voltage by a **step-up** transformer before passing through transmission lines to where it is needed. A **step-down** transformer reduces the voltage of the alternating current to a safer value of 230 V before it arrives at your home. Both of these transformers can have a very high **efficiency**, so nearly all of the energy transferred into the **primary** coil is transferred out of the **secondary** coil. You can use this equation to calculate the rate of energy transfer:

$$P = V \times I$$

P is the rate of energy transfer for the coil in watts (W)
V is the potential difference across the coil in volts (V)
I is the alternating current in the coil in amperes (A)

A transformer that is 100% efficient will have the same **power** for both coils; all the energy transferred into the primary coil is transferred out of the secondary coil. You can therefore do calculations with this equation:

$$V_p \times I_p = V_s \times I_s$$

V_p is the potential difference across the primary coil in volts (V)
I_p is the alternating current in the primary coil in amperes (A)
V_s is the potential difference across the secondary coil in volts (V)
I_s is the alternating current in the secondary coil in amperes (A)

Suppose a step-down transformer reduces the potential difference from 11 kV to 430 V. If the current drawn from the secondary coil is 100 A, how much current enters the primary coil?

$$V_p \times I_p = V_s \times I_s \text{ so } I_p = \frac{V_s}{V_p} \times I_s = \frac{430\text{ V}}{11\,000\text{ V}} \times 100\text{ A} = 3.9\text{ A}$$

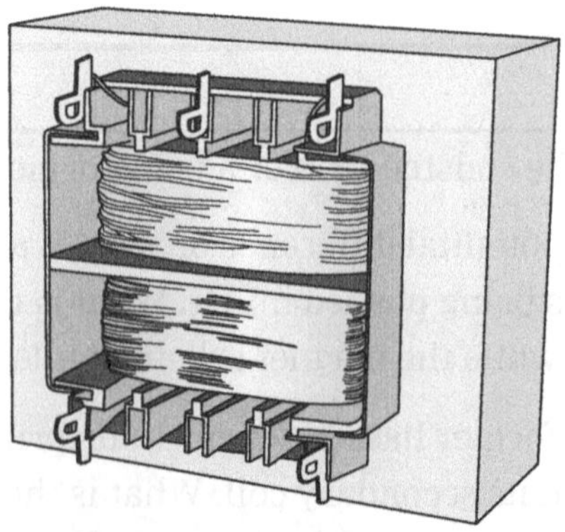

▲ Both coils transfer electrical energy at the same rate through the iron core. The low-voltage coil has to have thicker wire because it carries a larger current than the high-voltage coil.

Switch mode transformer

Many devices plug straight into the mains supply. These include cookers, heaters, washing machines, and lights. They are designed to use alternating current at 230 V. Some devices, such as phones, computers, and games can only work on **direct current** at a low potential difference, perhaps 6 V. These devices are usually connected to the mains supply through a **switch mode transformer**.

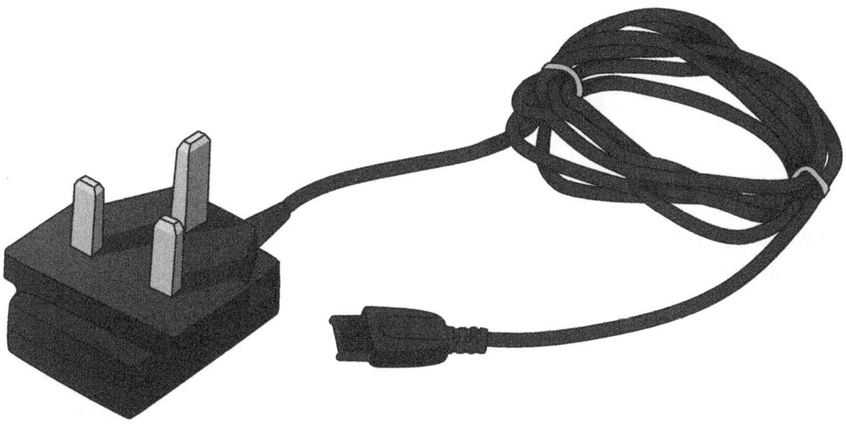

▲ The switch mode transformer is built into the mains plug of this mobile phone charger.

The switch mode transformer does two things:

- It uses a small transformer to reduce the potential difference of the mains supply.
- It converts alternating current from the mains supply into direct current.

The transformer operates at a very high **frequency**. This allows it to be much smaller and lighter than a transformer that deals with 50 Hz alternating current.

Efficiency

The electronic controls inside a switch mode transformer require their own power supply, so a switch mode transformer can never have an efficiency of 100%. However, the efficiency of a switch mode transformer can be as high as 95%. This means that it stays relatively cool as it transfers energy from the mains supply to the **load** to which it is connected. The current supplied by the switch mode transformer is determined by the potential difference across the load and its resistance. As soon as the load is removed from the switch mode transformer, this current drops to zero, so the only current drawn from the mains supply is the tiny amount for the control electronics.

Key words

alternating current, step-up, step-down, efficiency, primary, secondary, power, direct current, switch mode transformer, frequency, load

Exam tip AQA

Show all the steps in your working out when doing transformer calculations. This allows you to spot mistakes.

Questions

1 What does a switch mode transformer do?

2 What is the difference between a step-up and a step-down transformer?

3 **H** A step-up transformer has a primary coil of 500 turns and a secondary coil of 6 000 turns. If the current in the primary coil is 4 A, what is the current in the secondary coil?

Questions
Circular motion and power

Working to Grade E

1 The diagram shows a satellite in circular orbit around the Earth. Which arrow (A, B, C, or D) shows the direction of the resultant force on the satellite?

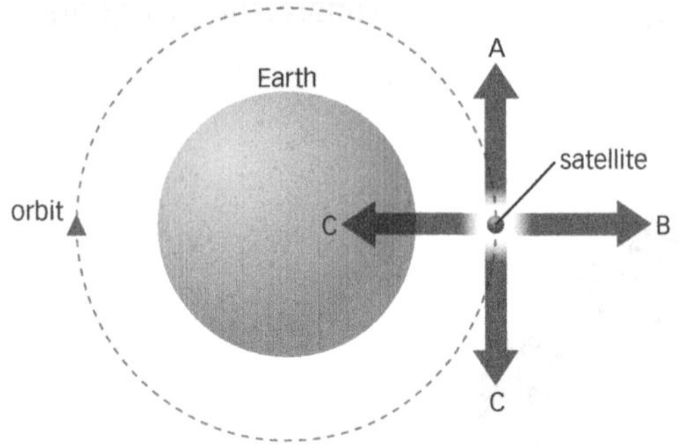

2 A wire in a magnetic field is pushed upwards by the current in it. State **two** different ways of making the push on the wire go downwards instead.

3 Give **two** examples of the use of the motor effect.

4 What does a transformer do?

5 A transformer has more turns on the secondary coil than the primary coil. What type of transformer is it?

6 Describe the magnetic field around a current-carrying straight wire.

Working to Grade C

7 A ball on a string is whirled around in a circle. How does the tension in the string change when:

a the mass of the ball is increased?

b the rate of rotation is reduced?

8 A wire carrying a current in the downwards direction passes through a magnetic field that points to the right. In what direction is the wire pushed?

9 Explain why an electric motor has a commutator.

10 Describe the construction of a loudspeaker.

11 A transformer has 1150 turns on its primary coil and 25 turns in the secondary coil. If the primary is connected to the 230 V mains supply, what is the potential difference across the secondary?

12 A current of 2 A at a potential difference of 12 V is drawn from the secondary coil of a transformer. What is the current drawn from the 230 V supply connected across the primary coil?

13 Explain the advantages of using a switch mode transformer to provide power for low-voltage devices.

Working to Grade A*

14 Explain why a transformer can only operate from an a.c. supply.

15 Explain why the coils in the secondary of a step-down transformer need to be of thicker wire than those in the primary.

16 Explain the operation of the brushes and commutator of an electric motor.

Examination questions
Circular motion and power

1 The picture shows a racing car going round a corner.

The diagram shows the position of the car, halfway round the corner, viewed from above.

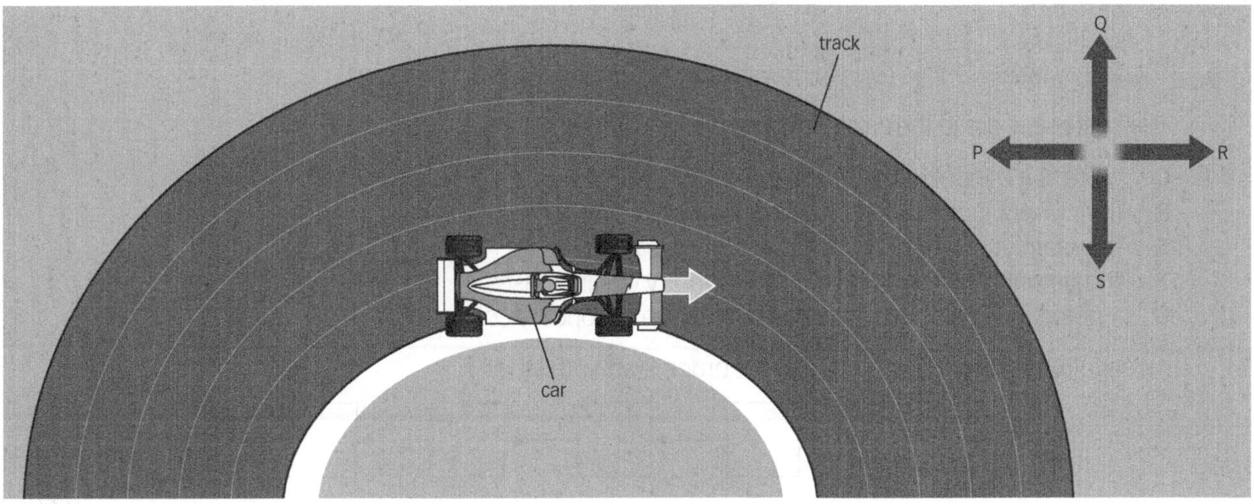

Draw a ring around the correct answer to complete the following sentences.

a The [braking / centripetal / gravitational] force on the car is needed for it to turn the corner.

(1 mark)

b The resultant force on the car is in the direction [P. / Q. / S.]

(1 mark)

c The resultant force on the car comes from [gravity. / friction. / speed.]

(1 mark)

(Total marks: 3)

2 The diagram shows a transformer designed to operate a 3V light bulb from the mains supply.

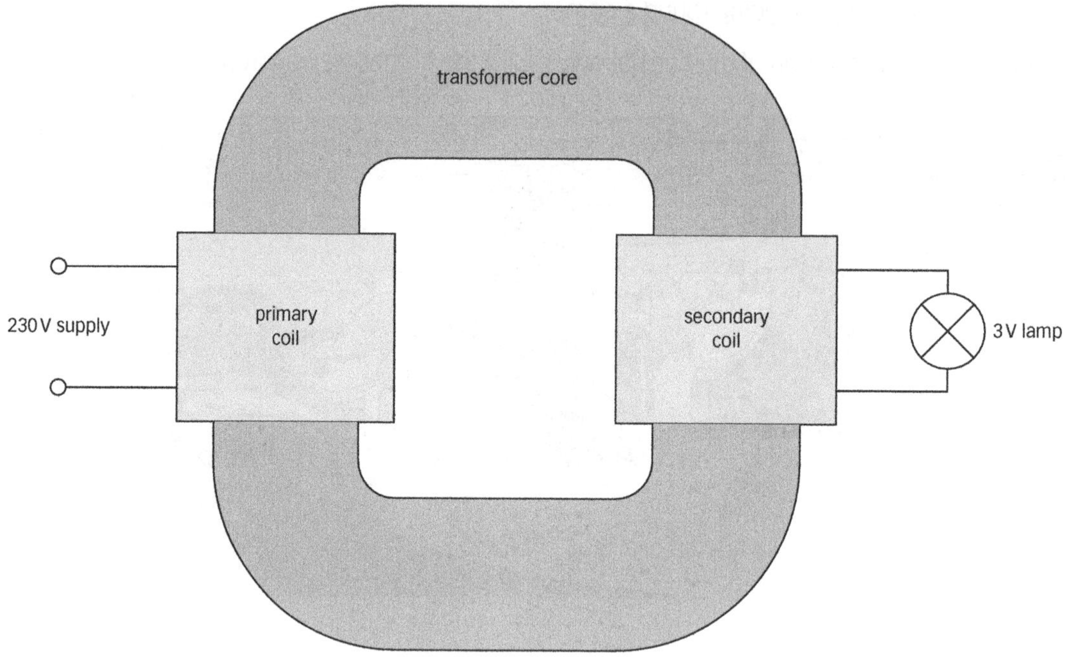

a The following sentences explain how the transformer operates.

The sentences are in the wrong order.

Q There is a current in the secondary coil.
R The current in the primary coil increases.
S The magnetic field in the core becomes stronger.
T The potential difference across the primary coil increases.
U A potential difference is induced across the secondary coil.

Arrange these sentences in the correct order. Start with letter **T**.

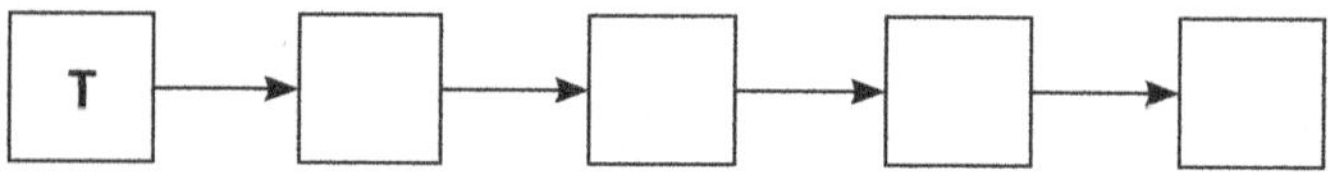

(3 marks)

b The secondary coil of the transformer has 90 turns of wire.

Calculate the number of turns of wire in the primary coil.

Write down the equation you use and then show clearly how you work out your answer.

....

....

....

....

....

turns of wire = ...

(3 marks)

c The current in the lamp is 0.5 A.

Calculate the current in the mains supply.

Write down the equation you use and then show clearly how you work out your answer.

....

....

....

....

....

current = ... A

(3 marks)

d A switch mode transformer could also be used to operate the 3 V lamp from the mains supply.

Explain the advantages of using the switch mode transformer.

....

....

....

....

....

....

(4 marks)

(Total marks: 13)

3 The diagram shows a simple electric motor.

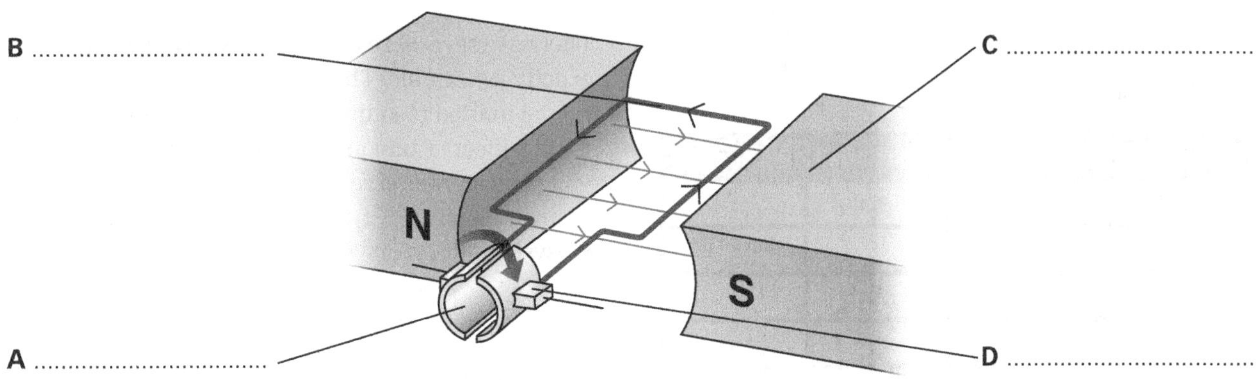

Use words from the box to label the parts A, B, C, and D.

battery	**brush**	**coil**	**commutator**	**magnet**

(4 marks)

(Total marks: 4)

Electromagnets

Designing an investigation and making measurements

In this module there are some opportunities to design investigations and make measurements. These include measurements of potential difference and current from transformers, strength of electromagnets, and output forces from electric motors.

Although you may be asked to demonstrate your investigative skills practically, you are also likely to be asked to comment on investigations done by others. The example below offers guidance in this skill area. It also gives you the chance to practise using your skills to answer the sorts of questions that may come up in exams.

Investigating the strength of electromagnets

Skill – Understanding the experiment

Sarah tested the hypothesis that the strength of an electromagnet is proportional to the product of the current and the turns of wire in the coil.

She made an electromagnet by coiling some insulated wire around a large iron nail, and connecting it in series with an ammeter to a variable d.c. power supply. For a given number of turns and current, she counted the maximum number of paper clips that the electromagnet could hold up.

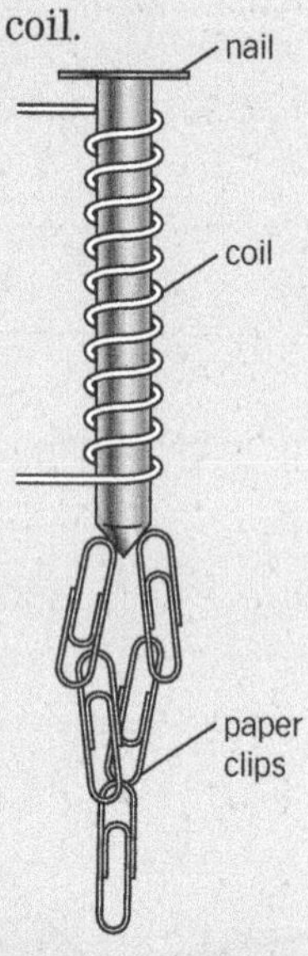

Sarah's results are in the table.

Coil current in amperes	Coil turns	Paper clips
2.2	27	6
1.3	15	2
1.7	22	4
0.7	45	3

1 Identify the **two** independent variables of the investigation.

In an investigation:

- The independent variables are the ones that are changed by the scientist.
- The dependent variable is the one that is measured for each change of the independent variables.

2 Suggest some important control variables for the investigation.

A control variable is one that the investigator thinks might affect the outcome, so they try to keep this variable the same all the way through.

Skill – Using data to draw conclusions

3 How can Sarah use the data to test her hypothesis?

Sarah needs to use the two independent variables to calculate the independent variable of her hypothesis. Looking for a straight line on a scatter graph of the independent and dependent variables is a good way of establishing proportionality. An alternative is to divide one variable by the other and look for a constant value.

4 Explain why Sarah should repeat her experiment more than just four times to get a valid conclusion.

By increasing the amount of data, scientists can spot outliers – data points that might be in error – and double check them. By increasing the range of the independent variable, the hypothesis can be tested more thoroughly. A hypothesis that survives tests over a wide range of variables is more likely to become an accepted theory than one that only predicts results over a narrow range.

Skill – Evaluating the experiment

5 Suggest reasons why Sarah might get different results when she repeats the experiment.

There are several reasons why experiments are not exactly repeatable. These include:

- the limited resolution of the measuring instruments
- the effect of uncontrolled variables
- experimenter error, such as misreading an instrument
- systematic errors, such as zero-errors in instruments.

Skill – Societal aspects of scientific evidence

6 Describe how Sarah could apply her results to the design of electromagnets for use in scrap yards.

When applying the results of their experiments to make useful devices, scientists need to take account of the effects of changing scale as well as economic factors. A number of prototypes are usually built, starting off at lab scale and getting increasingly larger.

AQA Upgrade

Answering an extended writing question

QUESTION

In this question you will be assessed on using good English, organising information clearly, and using specialist terms where appropriate.

1 Explain the operation of a step-up transformer. *(6 marks)*

G–E

Both coils have to be on a ring of metal. One coil is connected to the mains, this is the prime coil and it magnetises the metal so that electricity can be passed through it to the other coil. More electricity comes out of a step-up transformer than goes in, this is because their is more wire in one coil than in the other.

Examiner: This answer earns one mark and is typical of a grade-F candidate. There is very little use of specialist terms, with few details of the required physics. There is no mention of the need for changing magnetism in the core, electricity is used instead of current or potential difference, and length of wire is confused with turns.

D–C

The potential difference across the primary coil makes field lines which cut the secondary coil. As the field lines are cut, they make a current in the secondary coil. The potential difference has to keep on changing, as magnetoelectric induction can only happen when the magnetic field lines pass through the wires. The power going into the transformer is the same as the power coming out, so its coils of wire don't heat up.

Examiner: This answer only earns three marks, and is typical for a weak grade-D candidate. Although specialist terms are spelled correctly, they are often used incorrectly. There was no mention of the iron core, nor was there any discussion of the turns ratio. The last sentence is irrelevant to the question.

B–A*

A step-up transformer has two coils of insulated wire wound on a thick ring of iron. The primary coil has fewer turns of wire than the secondary coil. The primary coil is connected to a source of alternating current. This creates a magnetic field in the iron, with the field lines pointing along the length of the iron so that they form continuous loops through the secondary coil. Because the field changes direction each time the primary current changes, the magnetic field in the secondary coil keeps on changing. This induces a potential difference across the secondary coil.

Examiner: This is a high-quality answer, typical of an A* candidate, earning six marks. The answer is well organised, with a logical order for the explanation. Correct specialist terms have been used throughout.

Part 2 Course catch-up
Making things work

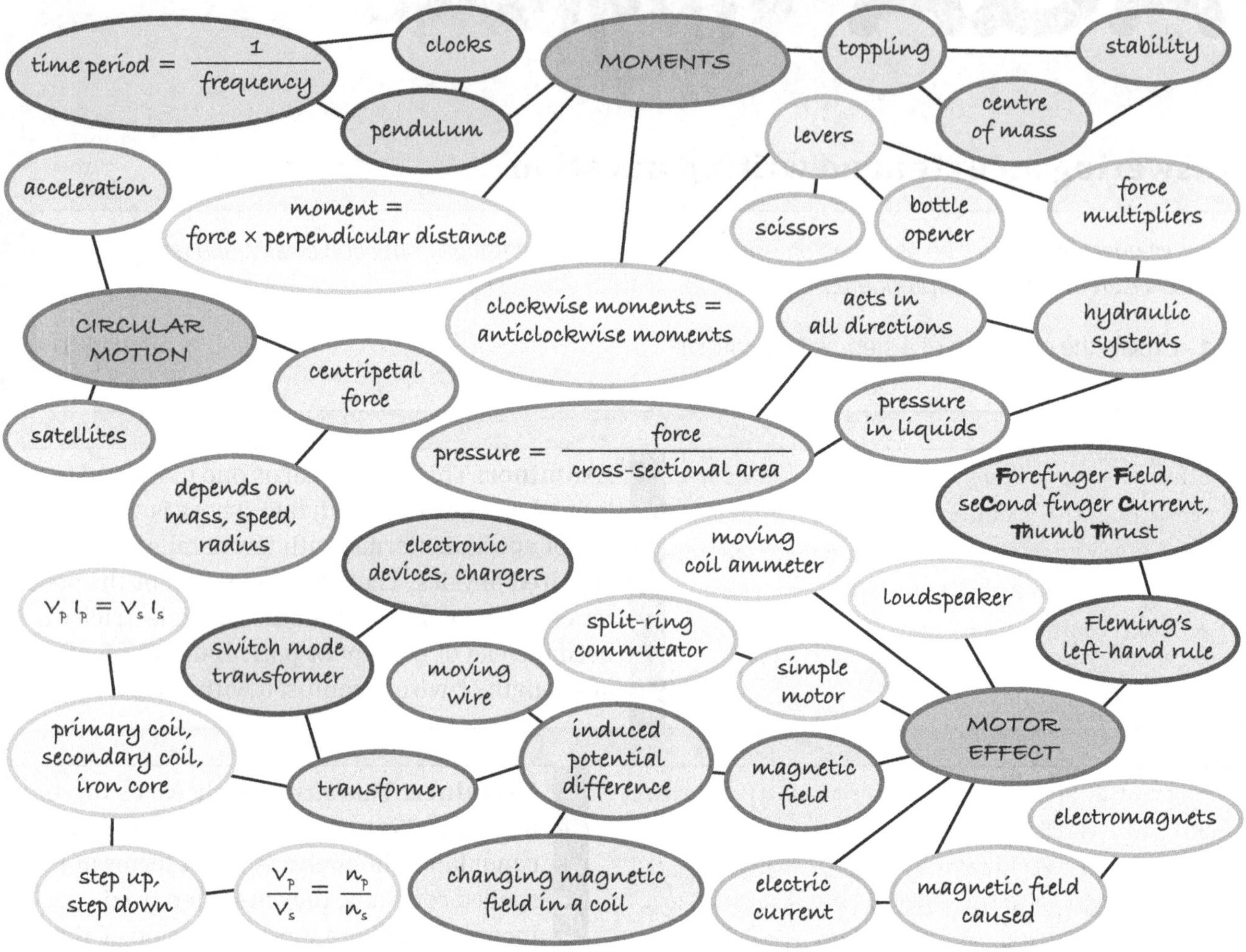

Revision checklist

- An object's centre of mass is the point at which all of the object's mass seems concentrated.
- The time period of a pendulum is the time taken to complete a full swing.
- Moment is the turning effect of a force.
- When an object is balanced, the total clockwise moment about the pivot is equal to the total anticlockwise moment. This is the principle of moments. Levers multiply forces using moments.
- An object will topple if the line of action of its weight falls outside the base of the object. Stability is increased by making the base wider and the centre of mass lower.
- Liquids are almost incompressible. Pressure in liquids is transmitted equally in all directions.
- Hydraulic systems multiply force.
- An object moving in a circle is constantly changing direction, so is constantly accelerating towards the centre of the circle.
- The force between an object in circular motion and the centre of the circle is a centripetal force.
- Flow of electric current through a wire produces a magnetic field around the wire.
- If a current-carrying wire is placed within another magnetic field, the magnetic fields interact, creating the motor effect.
- When a wire cuts across a magnetic field, a potential difference is induced across the ends of the wire.
- A transformer has an iron core with two coils of wire around it. If the primary coil is connected to an a.c. supply an alternating potential difference is induced in the secondary coil.
- In a step-up transformer, potential difference is higher across the secondary coil than the primary coil.
- In a step-down transformer, potential difference is lower across the secondary coil than the primary coil.
- Potential differences across the primary and secondary coils and the number of turns in the coils are related.
- In a transformer with 100% efficiency, the power input to the primary coil is equal to the output from the secondary coil.
- Most electronic devices use a lower potential difference than the 230 V mains supply. Step-down transformers are used.

Answers

P1 1: Infrared radiation

1 Darker/matt surfaces emit more infrared than light/shiny surfaces.
2 Black is a better absorber of infrared, so the pipes (and the water inside) heats up quicker.

P1 2: Kinetic theory

1

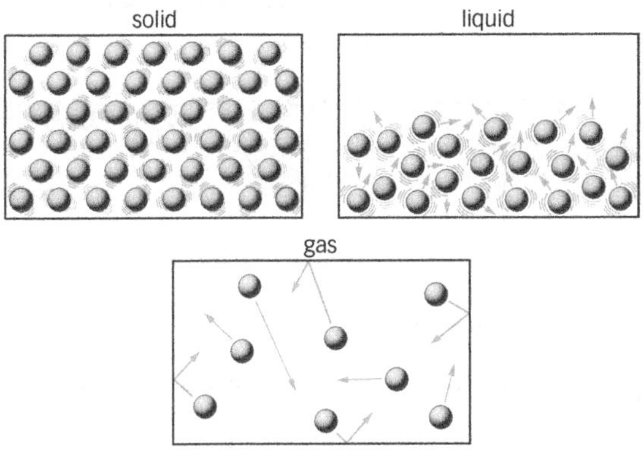

2 As the ice is heated, the particles gain energy and vibrate more. Eventually they have enough energy to move out of the regular arrangement and the block changes state to a liquid. The particles in the liquid gain energy and move faster. Eventually they move fast enough to break free from the liquid and so the liquid turns into a gas.

P1 3: Energy transfer by heating

1 They contain free electrons which can move through the metal, transferring the energy more quickly.
2 When the water is heated by the element in the base, the water particles gain energy and move faster. The hotter region expands and so becomes less dense. It rises through the cooler water. More water is drawn in to replace the water which has risen and the process repeats created a convection current.
3 Increase the surface area of the liquid; pass an air current over the liquid (e.g. blow on it); increase the temperature of the liquid.

P1 4: Comparing energy transfers

1

Factor	Effect
Temperature difference between object and surroundings	The greater the temperature difference, the greater the rate of energy transfer.
Surface area and volume	In general; the greater the surface area compared to the volume, the greater the rate of energy transfer.
Material	Some materials transfer energy more quickly than others (e.g. metals). The colour and finish of the material also affects the infrared radiation it emits (the darker and less shiny the material the more infrared radiation it emits).
Nature of the surface it is in contact with	Some materials transfer energy more quickly than others (e.g. metals).

2 Energy is unable to get into the flask to warm the liquid inside. The vacuum flask reduces the energy transfer into the flask.

Vacuum layer inside the glass vessel	Prevents conduction and convection.
Shiny silver on both the inside and outside of the glass vessel	Poor emitter of infrared radiation and good reflector.
Tight screw cap	Reduces convection and evaporation.

P1 5: Heating and insulating buildings

1

Cavity wall insulation	A material in between the walls (usually foam) traps air in pockets. Reducing conduction and preventing convection.
Loft insulation	Works in the same way as cavity wall insulation – a material in the loft (usually fibre glass) traps air. Reducing conduction and preventing convection.
Double glazing	Conduction is reduced by a layer of air trapped between two panes of glass.
Draft excluders	Energy loss through convection is reduced by making it more difficult to set up convection currents
Curtains	Reduces energy loss through radiation and conduction, by reducing the energy transfer to the windows.

2 The lower the U-value, the better the object is as an insulator.

3 Payback time $= \frac{\text{cost}}{\text{savings per year}}$

$= \frac{1200}{60}$

$= 20$ years

P1 6: Specific heat capacity

1 The energy required to increase the temperature of 1 kg of a substance by 1 °C.

2 $E = m \times c \times \theta$

$= 2.2 \times 4200 \times 70$

$= 646\,800\,J$

P1 1–6 Levelled questions: Energy transfer by heating

Working to Grade E

1 a True

b True

c Dark objects are good emitters of infrared radiation.

d The particles in a gas are very far apart and move very fast.

e True

f The lower the U-value, the better the material is as an insulator.

g The time taken for the saving made each year to pay for the purchase and installation of a type of insulation is called the payback time.

2 a reflectors

b gases

c decreases

d high

e bigger

3

Feature	Reduces energy transfer by...
vacuum	conduction and convection
silvered surface	radiation
tightly fitting lid	convection and evaporation

4 Three from:

Cavity wall insulation: A material in between the walls (usually foam) traps air in pockets. Reduces conduction and prevents convection.

Loft insulation: Works in the same way as cavity wall insulation – a material in the loft (usually fibre glass) traps air. Reduces conduction and prevents convection.

Double glazing: Conduction is reduced by a layer of air trapped between two panes of glass.

Draft excluders: Energy loss through convection is reduced by making it more difficult to set up convection currents.

Curtains: Reduces energy loss through radiation and conduction, by reducing the energy transfer to the windows.

5 Two from: Increase the surface area of the liquid; pass an air current over the surface (for example, blowing on a hot drink); increase the temperature of the liquid.

Working to Grade C

6

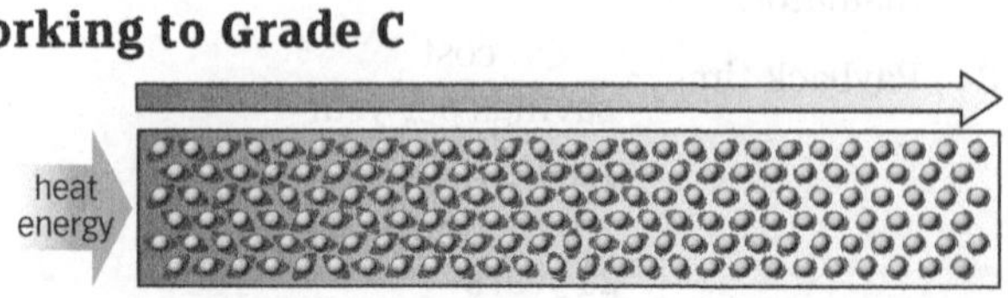

7 a cooler; volume; surface area; material; material

b larger; surface area; surroundings

8

Technique	Installation cost/£	Savings per year/£	Payback time/yr
A	300	50	6
B	2000	40	50
C	150	15	10

9 It can store a great deal of energy and then slowly transfer it to the surroundings.

10

Material	Specific heat capacity/J/kg °C	Energy required to heat it by 300 °C/J
A	900	540 000
B	450	270 000
C	3000	1 800 000
D	70	42 000

P1 1–6 Examination questions: Energy transfer

1 a You will gain 1 mark for each row.

Technique	Conduction	Convection	Radiation
Loft insulation	✓	✓	
Cavity wall insulation	✓	✓	
Double glazing	✓	✓	
Installing curtains		✓	✓

b Different U-values means the material is a better/worse insulator (1); The lower the U-value the better the material is an insulator (1).

c i You will gain 1 mark for correct calculations, 1 mark for identifying the correct technique to install first, and 1 mark for explaining why.

$$\textit{Payback time} = \frac{\textit{cost}}{\textit{savings per year}}$$

Cavity wall insulation $= \frac{200}{25} = 8$ years

Double glazing $= \frac{1500}{150} = 10$ years

Loft insulation 100 mm $= \frac{150}{10} = 15$ years

Loft insulation 350 mm $= \frac{300}{25} = 12$ years (1)

Cavity wall insulation should be installed first (1). It has the shortest payback time (1).

ii It is transferred to surroundings/atmosphere (1); increasing the temperature/warming the surroundings (1).

d Matt black is a good absorber of infrared radiation (1); so the pipes and the water inside them, heats up quicker (1).

2 a Particles gain energy and so vibrate more (1). The vibrations make their neighbouring particles vibrate more, and the energy is transferred through the material (1).

b energy; faster; less; rises (1 mark for each word in correct order).

c Evaporation.

d It increases.

3 a Energy required to increase the temperature of a substance. (You would gain 1 mark for this answer.)
Energy required to increase the temperature of 1 kg of a substance by 1 °C. (You would gain 2 marks for this more detailed answer.)

b Energy supplied $= m \times C \times \theta$
or $= 1.4 \times 4200 \times 80$ (1)
$= 470\,400$ J (1) for answer; (1) for units.

P1 7: Conservation of energy

1 Elastic potential energy (in the spring/clockwork) → kinetic energy → electrical energy (via a generator) → light and sound energy.

2

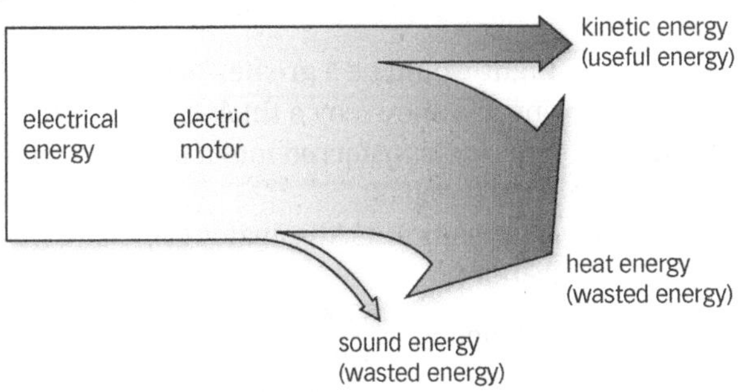

3 It spreads out (dissipates).

P1 8: Energy efficiency

1 a Efficiency $= \dfrac{\text{useful energy transferred}}{\text{total energy supplied}}$

efficiency $= \dfrac{1300\,\text{J}}{1500\,\text{J}}$

efficiency $= 0.65$ (or 65%)

b Efficiency $= \dfrac{\text{useful energy transferred}}{\text{total energy supplied}}$

efficiency $= \dfrac{600\,\text{J}}{1500\,\text{J}}$

efficiency $= 0.4$ (or 40%)

2 Efficiency $= \dfrac{\text{useful energy transferred}}{\text{total energy supplied}}$

efficiency $= \dfrac{300\,\text{J}}{1500\,\text{J}}$

efficiency $= 0.2$ (or 20%)

3

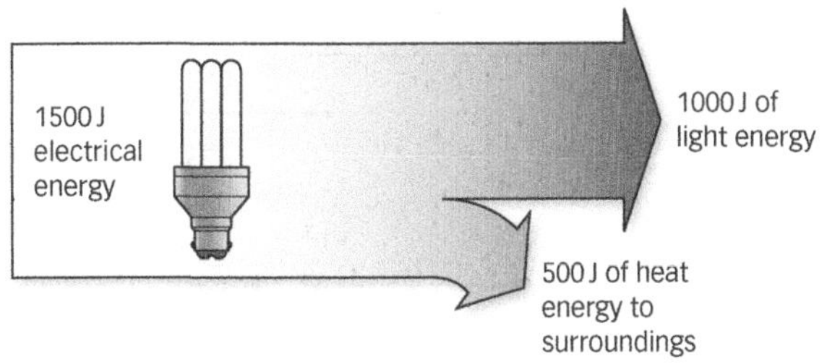

P1 7–8 Levelled questions: Energy conservation and efficiency

Working to Grade E

1 chemical; elastic potential; heat/thermal; nuclear; gravitational potential; light; sound; kinetic; electrical.

2 a energy; created; destroyed; transferred; dissipated.

b wasted; heat.

3

Device	Main energy transfers
Kettle	electrical → heat
Light bulb	electrical → heat and light
Wind-up radio	elastic potential → electrical → sound
A ball dropped from a height	gravitational potential → kinetic

4 a True

b Energy is measured in joules.

c When wasted energy is transferred to the surroundings, the surroundings get warmer.

d True

e True

Working to Grade C

5

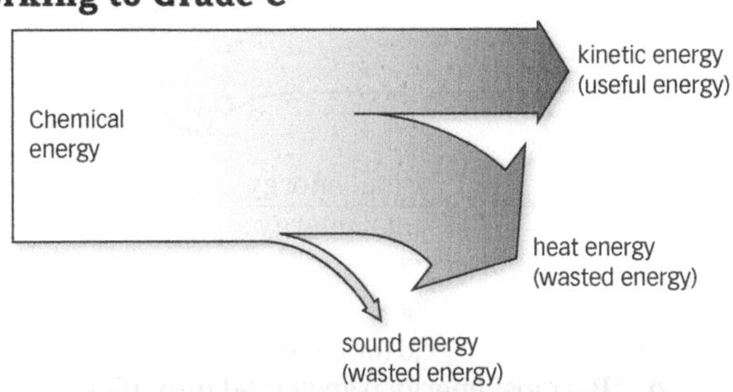

6 a

Bulb	Energy transferred into light/J	Energy transferred into heat/J
A	50	150
B	180	20
C	120	80
D	100	100
E	140	60

b

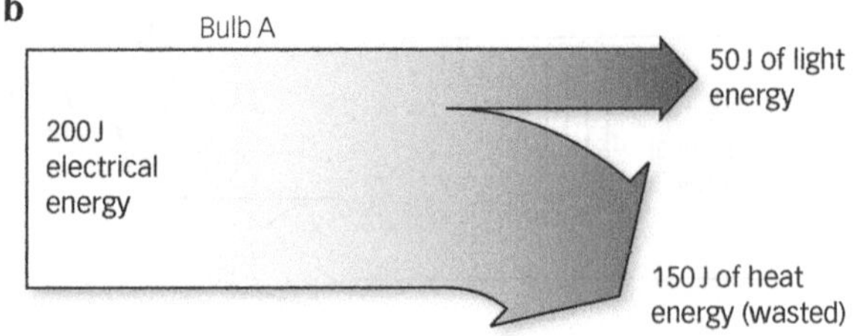

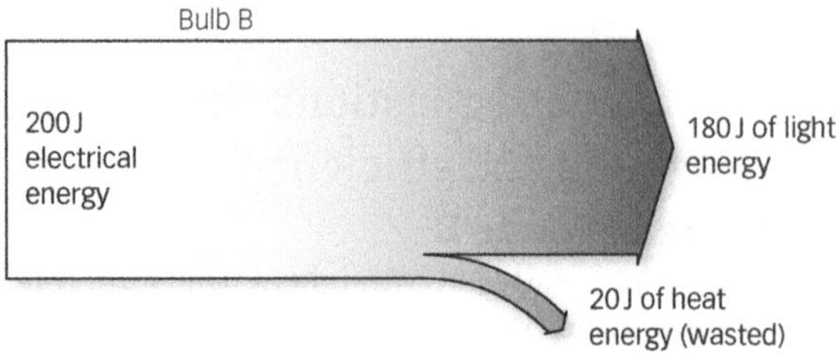

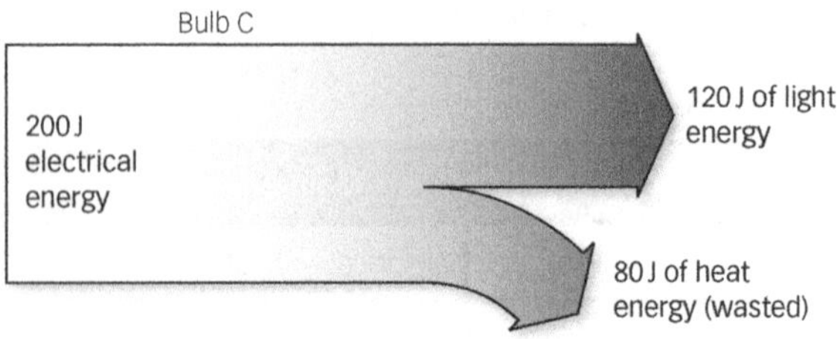

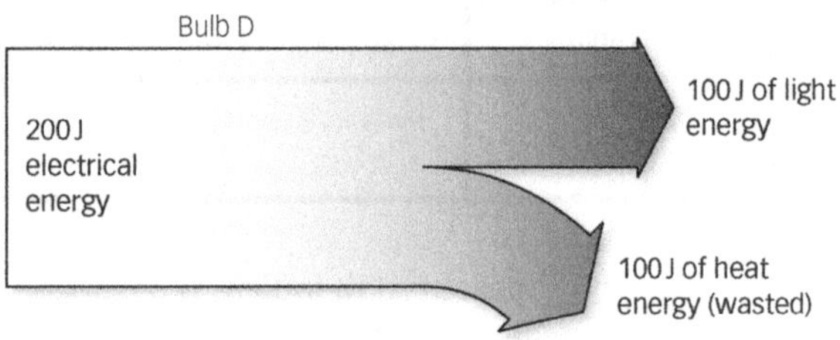

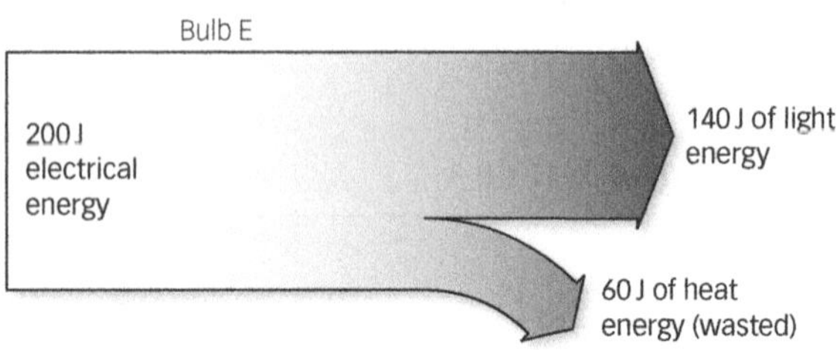

c Efficiency $= \frac{\text{useful energy}}{\text{total energy}}$

$= \frac{120}{200}$

$= 0.6$ (or 60%)

d B – most energy transferred into light (or least energy transferred into heat).

7 a Gravitational potential energy → kinetic energy → heat, sound and elastic potential (as it hit the ground) → kinetic energy → gravitational potential energy

b Some energy is lost (as heat and sound) when the ball hits the ground, so not all the kinetic energy is converted back into gravitational potential energy.

8 a 1500 J

b Transferred to surroundings (which get warmer).

c Efficiency $= \frac{\text{useful energy}}{\text{total energy}}$

$= \frac{1500}{5000}$

$= 0.3$ (or 30%)

9 a Efficiency cannot be more than 100%, as this would mean energy is being created.

b To ensure there is no bias in the results/presentation/analysis of the results.

P1 7–8 Examination questions: Energy conservation and efficiency

1 a Energy cannot be created or destroyed (1); but it can be transferred usefully, stored, and dissipated (1).

b Petrol engine: Chemical → kinetic (1)
TV: Electrical → light and sound (1)
Car battery: Chemical → electrical (1)

c i Your diagram must show electrical energy being transferred into heat and light (1). The heat arrow must be wider than the light arrow (1).

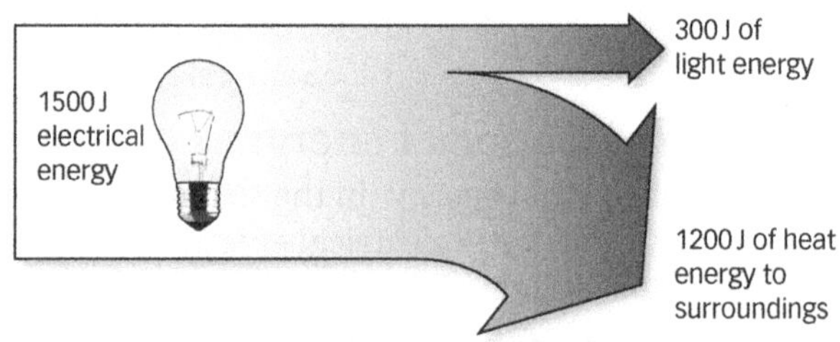

ii Light would be a greater proportion of the energy, shown by a thicker arrow (2).

2 a i Energy transferred into a form we do not want/need (2).

ii It spreads outs/dissipates (1).

b i 250 kJ (1)

ii Efficiency $= \frac{50\,000}{300\,000}$

$= 0.17$ (or 17%) (2)

P1 9: Using electrical devices

1 Any three of:

Appliance	Energy in	Main forms of energy out
Kettle	Electrical	Heat, kinetic
Toaster	Electrical	Heat, light
Electric motor	Electrical	Heat, sound, kinetic
Speaker	Electrical	Sound, kinetic
Computer	Electrical	Heat, light, sound, kinetic

2 a Energy = power × time = 20 × (10 × 60 × 60)
= 720 000 J

b Energy = power × time = 2200 × 250 = 550 000 J
So the light bulb transfers more energy.

3 Less energy is wasted as heat (therefore conserves resources and saves the owner money).

P1 10: Paying for electricity

1 a Energy = power × time = 3 × 6 = 18 kWh
 b Energy = power × time = 9.2 × 0.5 = 4.6 kWh
 c Energy = power × time 2 × 4 = 8 kWh

2 Cost = price × energy

$$= 11 \times \left(4 \times \frac{90}{60}\right)$$
$$= 11 \times 6$$
$$= 66\text{p}$$

P1 9–10 Levelled questions: The use and cost of electricity

Working to Grade E

1

Appliance	Energy in	Main forms of energy out
Kettle	Electrical	Heat, sound, kinetic
TV	Electrical	Heat, sound, light
Radio	Electrical	Heat, sound
Escalator	Electrical	Heat, sound, kinetic, gravitational potential energy

2 a increases
 b increases
 c decreases
 d increases

3 a watts
 b energy
 c more
 d reduces

4

Power of appliance/W	Power of appliance/kW
1000	1
5500	5.5
800	0.8
1200	1.2
500	0.5
20	0.02

Working to Grade C

5 Conserve natural resources (including fossil fuels as less electrical energy is needed); saves you money.

6 a Energy = power × time = 15 × (10 × 60 × 60)
 = 540 000 J
 b Energy = 540 000 × 1200
 = 648 000 000 J or 648 MJ

7 a Energy = 3000 × (30 × 60)
 = 540 000 J
 b Energy = 3 × 0.5
 = 1.5 kWh

8 a House 1 = 875 units; House 2 = 6309 units; House 3 = 4561 units.
 House 2 used the most units
 b House 1 = £105.00; House 2 = £757.08; House 3 = £547.32

9 a 7 hours.
 b Energy = power × time = 12 × 7 = 84 kWh
 c Cost = £9.24

10 Battery one is portable, but the batteries may run out.

P1 9–10 Examination questions: The use and cost of electricity

1 a Energy = power × time
 = 2200 × 120
 = 264 000 J (2 marks for answer; 1 mark for units)
 (An answer of 264 or 4400 (multiplying 2200 by 2 instead of 120) gives 1 mark.)
 b It would increase (1).

2 a 320 units (1).
 b Cost = 320 × 0.12 = £38.40 (2)
 Unit = kWh (1)

How Science Works: Energy and efficiency

1 **Experiment 1**

a

Material	Start temperature (°C)	End temperature (°C)	Change in temperature (°C)
A	70	62	8
B	70	50	20
C	70	34	36
D	70	64	6

b Type of insulating material.
c Starting temperature; volume of water; time; surface; material of beaker.
d Otherwise it would not be a fair test as one of the control variables may have an effect on the dependent variable, making the experiment invalid.

Experiment 2

a

Volume (cm^3)	Start temperature (°C)	End temperature (°C)	Change in temperature (°C)
100	70	38	32
200	70	50	20
300	70	55	15
400	70	62	8
500	70	65	5

b Volume of water.
c Starting temperature; time; surface; material of beaker.
d Otherwise it would not be a fair test as one of the control variables may have an effect on the dependent variable, making the experiment invalid.

2 **Experiment 1**

a Independent – type of insulating material – categoric.
Dependent – temperature change – continuous.

b Bar chart: axis labelled (including units for the temperature change), bars correct length.

c The results support the hypothesis. Different materials led to different temperature drops, so energy must be transferred to surroundings at different rates.

Experiment 2

a Independent – volume – continuous.
Dependent – temperature change – continuous.

b Line graph: axis labelled (including units), sensible scale and graph takes up at least 1/3 of the graph paper, points plotted in the correct place, line of best fit (curve) drawn.

c The results support the hypothesis. Different volumes led to different temperature drops, so energy must be transferred to surroundings at different rates. The greater the volume the lower the rate of energy transfer and so the lower the temperature drop.

P1 11: Generating electricity and matching supply with demand

1 Fuel is burnt (or a nuclear reaction takes place): chemical or nuclear energy → heat energy.
The heat is used to turn water to steam, the steam turns a turbine: heat energy → kinetic energy.
As the turbine turns, it turns a generator that generates electricity: kinetic energy → electrical energy.

2 How quickly it can increase the amount of electrical energy it is generating.

3 When there is a sudden increase in demand, gates are opened and water from the reservoir rushes through them. This water turns turbines, which turn generators and produce electricity. When demand reduces the gates are closed again.

P1 12: The National Grid

1 Electricity is generated in power stations. Transformers are used to step-up the voltage (this reduces the current and so less energy is lost in transmission). The electricity is transmitted via a series of pylons or underground cables. Another transformer is used to step down the voltage (to a safer level for homes). Cables run into every home.

2 The current can be lower, so the wires do not get as warm. Much less energy is wasted as heat.

3 Advantages: higher voltages can be used (less energy is wasted); generally cheaper to install and maintain.
Disadvantages: the pylons are ugly; pylons can be easily damaged in extreme weather.

P1 13: Fossil fuels

1 Advantages: large amounts of electricity can be generated; it is an established technology; fossil fuels are relatively cheap (per kW of power generated).
Disadvantages: the fuels have to be mined/extracted and transported; burning fuels releases atmospheric pollutants (such as CO_2 which contributes to man-made global warming); the power plants are often very ugly and noisy.

2

Fossil fuel	Substance heated	CO_2 production	Start-up time
Coal	Water	Very high	Long
Oil	Water	High	Long
Natural gas	Water or air	Medium	Short

3 The CO_2 released in burning the fuel is captured and prevented from entering the atmosphere. It is stored underground. This would reduce the amount of CO_2 released and so reduce man-made global warming.

P1 14: Nuclear power

1 A nuclear reaction (the splitting of a uranium or plutonium nucleus) releases heat. This heat turns water to steam. The steam turns a turbine, which turns a generator that generates electricity.

2 They do not produce CO_2 as no fuel is burnt.

3 The dismantling of a nuclear power station when it reaches the end of its useful life. This is costly because of the radioactive waste in the nuclear reactor. This needs to be handed very carefully.

P1 15: Renewables

1 Water is pumped into the ground in areas where there are hot rock close the surface (or in some cases steam rises naturally). The steam is used to turn turbines that turn a generator, which generates electricity.
Advantages: cheap to build; no fuel costs; will not run out.
Disadvantages: can only be built in certain areas; plants can be very ugly and noisy.

2 Solar and hydroelectric power.

3 The CO_2 released by burning biofuels is the same as the plants (used to make the biofuels) absorbed while they were growing. So there is no change in the amount of CO_2 in the atmosphere.

P1 11–15 Levelled questions: Generating power

Working to Grade E

1 a Nuclear power is a form of non-renewable energy.

b True

c Non-renewable energy resources use fuels which will run out.

d True

e A hydroelectric power station has a short start-up time.

f Natural gas produces less carbon dioxide than other fossil fuels.

2

Energy resource	Brief description
Wind	Wind is used to turn large turbines
Wave	The up-and-down motion of the sea is transferred into electrical energy
Tidal	This may include tidal lagoons or larger tidal barrages
Hydroelectric power (HEP)	Large dams are built across river valleys
Geothermal	Hot rocks turn water to steam – this is used to turn turbines
Biomass	Biofuels are burnt; the heat is used to turn water to steam
Solar (cells)	Energy from the Sun is transferred into electrical energy

3 Pylon or underground cables.

4 Coal, oil, natural gas or nuclear.

Working to Grade C

5 a increases; decreases

b decreases

c decreases.

d increases

6 nuclear – coal – natural gas – HEP

7 A nuclear reaction (the splitting of a uranium or plutonium nucleus) releases heat. This heat turns water to steam. The steam turns a turbine that turns a generator, which generates electricity.

8

	Advantages	Disadvantages
Wave	Renewable, no CO_2 released, no fuel costs.	Visual and noise pollution (can also be a danger to shipping). Unreliable/untested technology.
Tidal	Renewable, no CO_2 released, no fuel costs, and reliable and predictable electricity generation.	Affects marine habitats. Can be very expensive to build. Limited number of suitable sites.

9

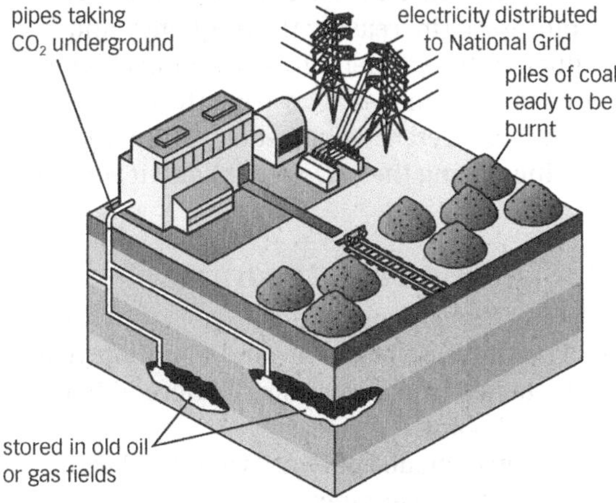

10 a In winter electricity is used for heating, so there is great demand.

b i People are waking up and having breakfast (using kettles, toasters, etc).

ii People are returning from work and starting to cook dinner.

P1 11–15 Examination questions: Generating power

1 a C – A – B – D (2 marks if all in correct order; 1 mark if two in correct order).

b i How quickly a power station can increase the amount of electricity it generates. (1)

ii Nuclear (1)

c When demand is high, the pump storage station can start to generate electricity very quickly by opening the lock gates so water from the reservoir drives the turbines (2). When demand is low, electricity from the National Grid is used to pump water back up to the reservoir (1).

2 a step-up; voltage; current; current; energy (1 mark for each word in correct order).

b Two from: voltage cannot be as high; expensive to install; difficult to maintain; more energy is wasted (2).

3 Your answer should be well-structured, with few spelling and grammatical errors. 6 points available. Answer might include:
Advantages: No fuel costs; no CO_2 released; renewable.
Disadvantages: Unreliable; ugly; noisy.

P1 16: Introduction to waves

1 In transverse waves the oscillations are at right angles to the direction of energy transfer. In longitudinal waves the oscillations are parallel to the direction of energy transfer.

Transverse	Longitudinal
Water waves, light (all electromagnetic waves: radio, microwaves, infra-red radiation, ultraviolet radiation, x-rays, gamma rays) and some mechanical waves on springs or strings.	Sound and some mechanical waves on springs.

2

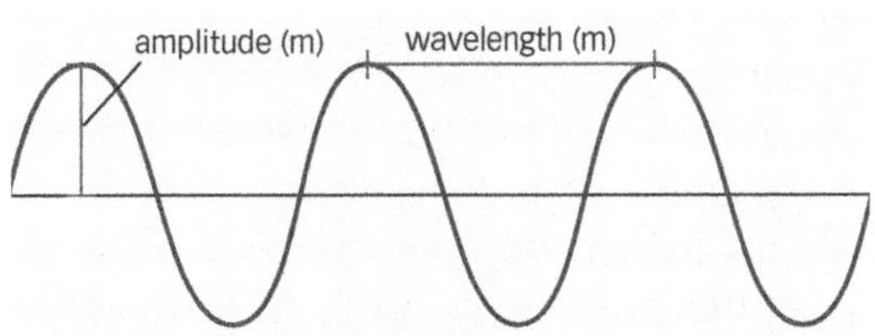

3 0.5 Hz (1 wave every 2 seconds).

P1 17: Wave experiments

1 The angle of incidence = the angle of reflection.

2 a

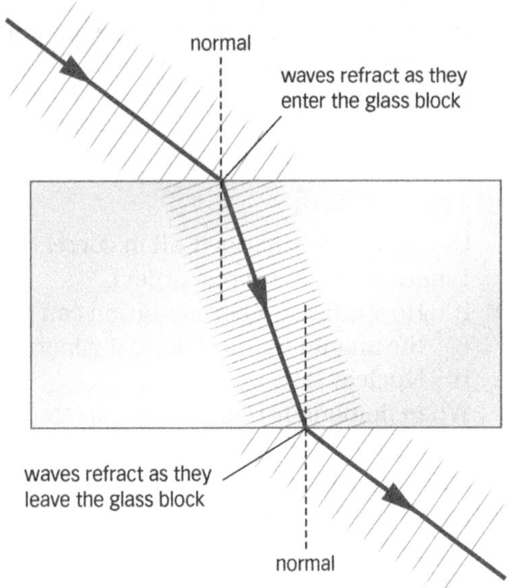

b The light will slow down, but it does not change direction. Instead it passes straight through the glass block.

3 When a wave spreads out as it passes through a gap or around an obstacle. The best diffraction occurs when the size of the gap is the same as the wavelength of the wave.

P1 18: The electromagnetic spectrum

1 Gamma – X-rays – Ultraviolet – Visible light – Infrared – Microwave – Radio waves

2 TV, radio, and wireless communications (like Bluetooth).

3 Research has shown they have a small heating effect on living tissue. Scientists are not sure whether this is a serious health risk and if it will cause any long term damage.

4 Radio up to 10 km/gamma 10^{-15} m

P1 19: The wave equation

1 Using the formula: $v = f \times \lambda$

a $v = 0.5\,\text{Hz} \times 4\,\text{m} = 2\,\text{m/s}$

b $v = 500\,\text{Hz} \times 0.60\,\text{m} = 300\,\text{m/s}$

c $v = 1200\,\text{Hz} \times 0.80\,\text{m} = 960\,\text{m/s}$

2 $v = f \times \lambda$

so $\lambda = \frac{v}{f}$,

$$\lambda = \frac{3 \times 10^8}{3 \times 10^{10}},$$

$$= 0.01\,\text{m}$$

P1 20: Images

1 When seen in a rear view mirror the image is laterally inverted and so appears normal.

2 Upright: The image is the right way up.
Laterally inverted: The image is flipped around horizontally.
Virtual: The image is not really there; it can't be projected onto a screen.

3

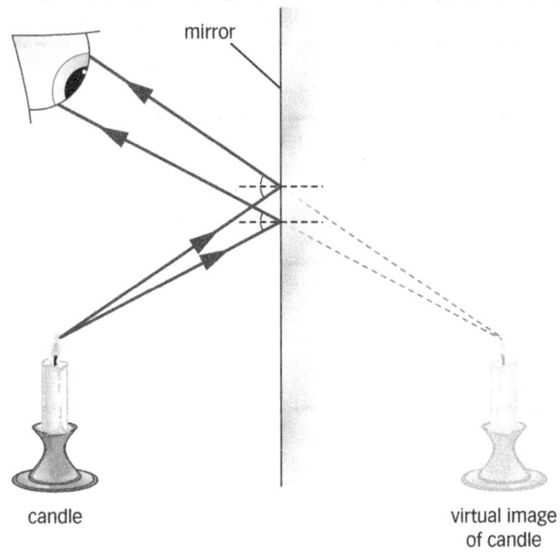

P1 21: Sound

1 Whenever an object vibrates (the air/medium around it vibrates and these vibrations travel through the medium).

2 Higher frequency = higher pitch;
lower frequency = lower pitch.

3

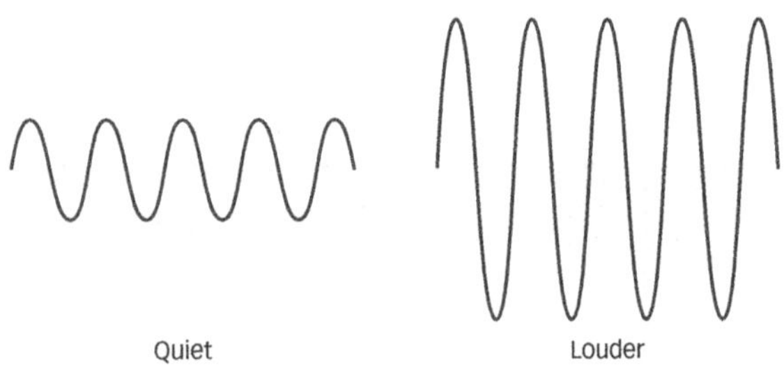

P1 22: Wave sources and the Doppler effect

1 Sound: Speaker, police siren, car engine
Light: Light bulb, galaxy
Microwaves: Satellite, microwave oven

2 As it approaches the observer the waves are compressed (increasing the frequency and reducing the wavelength) so it sounds higher pitched. As it moves away from the observer the waves are stretched out (reducing the frequency and increasing the wavelength) and it sounds lower pitched.

P1 23: The Big Bang theory

1 The Big Bang theory states:

- The Universe began around 14 billion years ago.
- It started from a very small, incredibly hot initial point.
- It then exploded outwards and has been expanding ever since.

2 Red shift shows most galaxies are moving away from us and the ones further away are moving faster. So the Universe must be expanding. In the past it must have been much smaller (as the Big Bang theory states).

3 Cosmic microwave background radiation is a form of radiation which fills the entire Universe. It is the 'heat' left over from the Big Bang. The Big Bang theory is currently the only theory that can explain the existence of the cosmic microwave background radiation.

P1 16–23 Levelled questions: Waves

Working to Grade E

1 a energy
  b transverse
  c reflection
  d longest
  e most
  f Infrared
  g higher
  h away

2 Gamma – X-rays – Ultraviolet – Visible light – Infrared – Microwaves – Radio waves

3

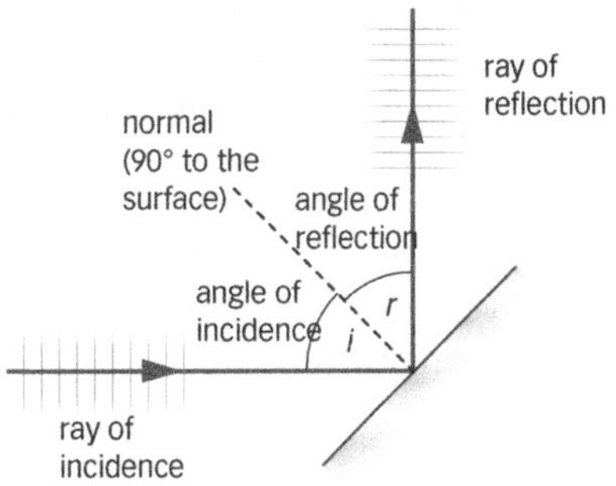

4 a Radio waves: TV, radio and wireless communications (like Bluetooth).
  b Microwaves: Mobile phones and satellite TV.
  c Infrared: Remote controls and some cable Internet connections.
  d Visible light: Photography and some cable Internet connections.

5 a True
  b All electromagnetic waves travel at the same speed through a vacuum.
  c When waves spread out as they pass through a gap this is called diffraction.
  d True
  e The amplitude of a wave is the height of the wave from the top of the peak to the middle of the wave.
  f Sound waves are examples of longitudinal waves.
  g True
  h A louder sound has a greater amplitude.
  i True
  j The light emitted by distant galaxies is stretched as they move away from us. This is called red-shift.

6

Wave speed	Frequency	Wavelength
2000 m/s	1000 Hz	2 m
1600 m/s	3.2 kHz	0.5 m
120 m/s	300 Hz	40 cm
108 m/s	0.9 kHz	12 cm

7 a Wavelength (in metres, m): The distance from one peak to the next.
  b Frequency (in hertz, Hz): The number of waves passing a point per second.
  c Amplitude (in metres, m): Maximum height of the wave, measured from the middle of the wave.

8

Upright	The image is the right way up.
Laterally inverted	The image is flipped around horizontally.
Virtual	The image cannot be projected onto a screen.

9 Red-shift (so the universe is expanding) and cosmic microwave background radiation.

Working to Grade C

10 a billion
  b small
  c exploded; expanding

11 Longitudinal: sound.
Transverse: radio waves, light, infrared, water waves, X-rays, microwaves, gamma waves.
Could be either: mechanical waves or springs.

12

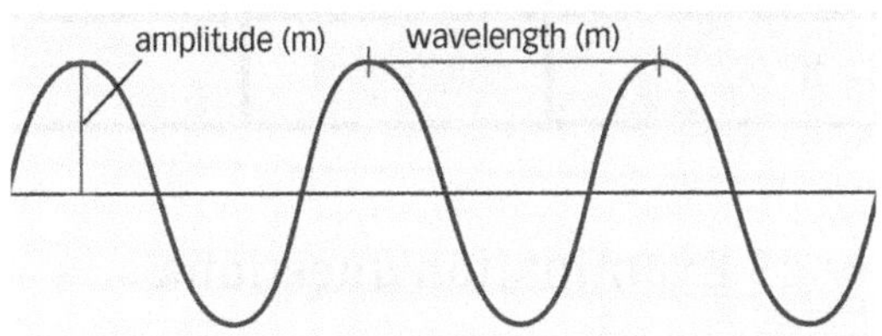

13

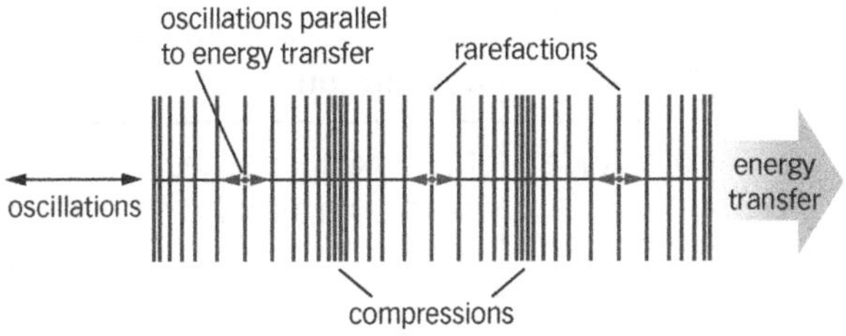

14 Light has a much smaller wavelength so does not diffract as much. Sound has a wavelength similar to the size of the gap (door frame) and so strong diffraction takes place.

15 a the wavelength decreases and the frequency increases.
  b the wavelength increases and the frequency decreases.

Working to Grade A*

16 When the car moves towards the observer the wavelength is compressed and so it sounds higher pitched. When it moves passed the observer the wavelength is stretched (increases) and so it sounds lower pitched.

17 First diagram – lower pitch, lower frequency, loud sound.
Second diagram – higher pitch, higher frequency, quiet sound.

18 Transverse: vibrations are perpendicular to the direction of energy transfer.
Longitudinal: vibrations are parallel to the direction of energy transfer.

19 a vibrates
b vibrations; vibrate
c longitudinal; vibrations; parallel

20
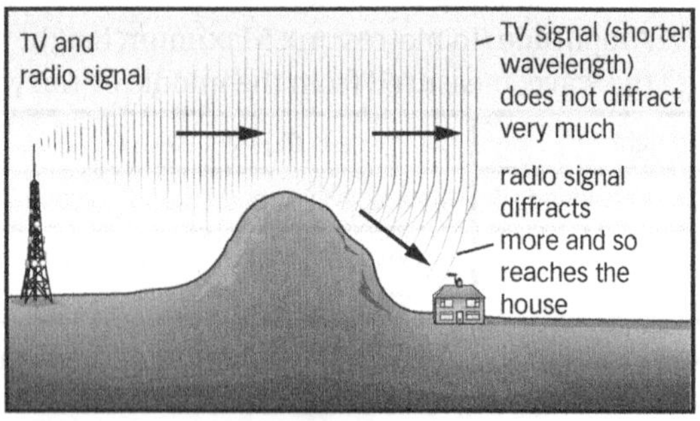

21

Wave speed (m/s)	Frequency (Hz)	Wavelength (m)
3500	75	47
340	1700	0.2
12000	200	60
3×10^8	150000000	2

P1 16–23 Examination questions: Waves

1 a Energy (1)
b

Term	Description	
amplitude	The maximum height of the wave, from the middle to the peak.	(1)
wavelength	The minimum distance from one peak to another.	(1)
frequency	The number of waves passing a point per second.	(1)

c i Perpendicular (1) to the direction of energy transfer/wave motion (1).
ii Any two from: water waves; radio waves; microwaves; infrared; visible light; ultraviolet; X-rays; gamma rays. (2)

2 a incidence (1); reflection (1); normal (1)
b i Both diagrams showing diffraction (waves spreading out) (1).
Wavelength (distance between the lines) stays approximately the same (1).
Stronger diffraction (waves spread out more) from the smaller gap (1).

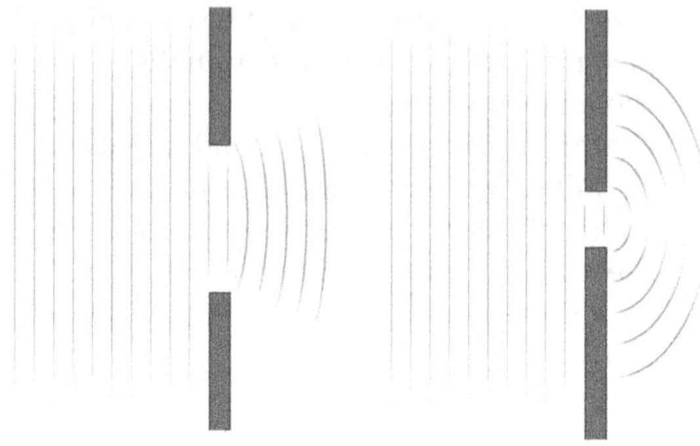

ii When the wavelength is the same size as the gap (1).

3 a wave speed = frequency × wavelength
= 1200 × 0.30
= 360 m/s (2 marks for answer; 1 mark for units)
(An answer of 36 000 or 0.36 only gains 1 mark.)
b Amplitude – no effect (1);
Wavelength – decreases (1).

4 Your answer should be well structured, with few spelling and grammatical errors. The answer might include:
Expanding universe (red shift): most galaxies are moving away from us; furthest galaxies are moving fastest; implies Universe is expanding; in the past was smaller.
Cosmic microwave background radiation: heat left over from the Big Bang; same everywhere in the universe; as the universe has expanded it has cooled; only the Big Bang theory can explain the origin of this heat (6).

How Science Works: Electrical energy and waves

1

Angle of incidence (°)	Angle of reflection (°)			
	1	2	3	Average
15	15	14	16	15
30	30	35	29	31 (or 30 if the 35 result is ignored)
45	45	45	45	45
60	62	65	62	63
75	69	75	76	73 (or 75 if the 69 result is ignored)

2 Line graph: axis labelled (including units); sensible scale and graph takes up at least 1/3 of the graph paper; points plotted in the correct place; line of best fit (curve) drawn.
The results generally support the hypothesis. However, there are some random errors which mean a few results do not show that the angle of incidence is equal to the angle of reflection.

3 a Most results are quite close to the true value and so they are quite accurate.
b In general there is very little spread from the mean value, except at 30° where there is one reading of 35° and at 75° where one reading was 69°.
c If repeated the experiment should produce similar results.
d If somebody else did the experiment, they should get a very similar set of results.
4 a Random.
b Human error in misreading the protractor; the mirror not being lined up perfectly.
5 A systematic error.
6 To ensure there is no bias in their findings/conclusions.

P2 1: Speed and velocity
1 5 m/s
2 a B
b C
3 3.25 m/s

P2 2: Acceleration
1 1.5 m/s^2
2 a 0.75 m/s^2
b The line is steeper.
3 48 m

P2 3: Force and acceleration
1 600 N upwards.
2 9 N to the left.
3 3.33 m/s^2

P2 4: Forces and braking
1 75 m
2 wet roads, poor car maintenance, inebriation, lack of attention
3 The resistive forces increase from zero at the start to 800 N at the top speed. This is because air resistance increases with increasing speed.

P2 5: Terminal velocity
1 241 N
2 On the edge the resultant force is zero as the reaction force from the ground balances out your downwards force from gravity. Over the edge, the only force is gravity, so you accelerate down.
3 From A to B the force of gravity accelerates the skydiver downwards. As the speed increases, so does the upwards air resistance, reducing the resultant force and the consequent acceleration. By point C the air resistance is big enough to cancel the force of gravity, so the speed doesn't change and the skydiver has reached terminal velocity. At D the parachute is opened, suddenly increasing the air resistance. The resultant force is now upwards, so the skydiver slows down rapidly until at E the air resistance is once more equal and opposite to the force of gravity.

P2 1–5 Levelled questions: Force and motion

Working to Grade E
1 a Speed increases.
b Speed decreases.
c Speed stays the same.
2 2700 N
3 50 m/s
4 zero, accelerates, steady, decelerates, steady
5 Any two from: poor car maintenance, wet road, inattention, inebriation
6 weight, air resistance, balanced, velocity

Working to Grade C
7 5 m/s^2 to the left
8 20 N downwards, balanced by the upwards reaction from the horizontal surface so that the resultant force in the vertical direction is zero.
9 –0.33 m/s^2
10 27.2 m/s, so slower than speed limit.
11 Speed is increasing with time.
12

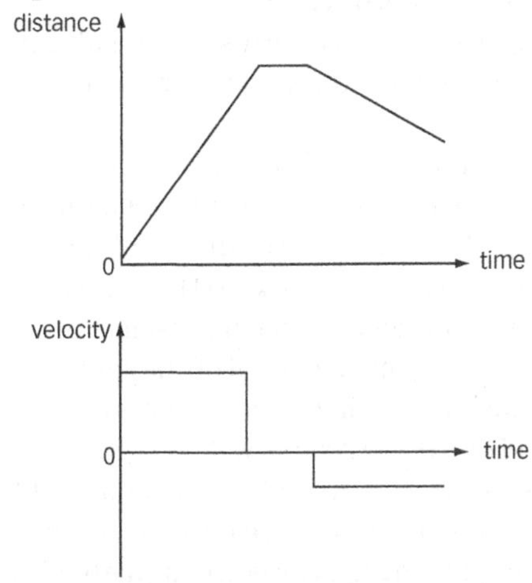

13 Braking distance: distance moved by a car while the brakes have been fully applied.
Stopping distance: total distance moved by the car as it is brought to a halt by the driver.
Thinking distance: distance moved by the car in the time between the driver deciding to stop and applying the brakes.

Working to Grade A*
14 +6 m/s, 0 m/s and –2 m/s
15 675 m

P2 1–5 Examination questions: Force and motion

1 One mark for each correct link.

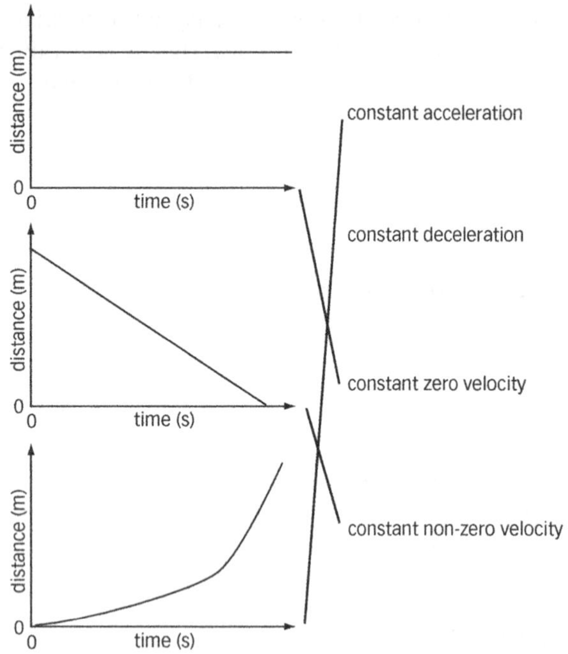

2 a The car has zero vertical acceleration (1) so the weight and reaction force from the ground must be equal and opposite to add up to zero (1).

b 1000 – 750 = 250 N (1) to the left (1).

c Mass = 8000 N/10 N/kg = 800 kg (1).
acceleration = force/mass (1) = 250/800 = 0.31 m/s^2 backwards (1).

d Velocity decreases (1) because the resultant force is against the direction of motion (1).

3 a 44 m (1)

b Time = distance/speed (1) = 6/10 = 0.6 s (1)

c i The brakes provide a steady decelerating force (1), so as the speed increases it takes longer to reduce it to zero (1). If the car is moving for longer, then it must move further; the higher speed of the car will also make it move further in the same time (1).

ii EITHER If the road is wet (1) then there is less friction between the road and the tyres (1) OR if the brakes are faulty (1) then the force slowing the car down is smaller (1) OR if you are going uphill (1) gravity helps to slow down the car (1).

P2 6: Work and energy

1 4800 J
2 240 000 J
3 333 N/m

P2 7: Energy transfer and power

1 120 W
2 4320 J
3 20 m/s

P2 8: Momentum and car safety

1 364 kg m/s
2 Increases the time needed to stop the car, so reducing the acceleration and force applied to the driver.
3 3 m/s

P2 6–8 Levelled questions: Work and energy

Working to Grade E

1 15 N
2 J, kg m/s, W and J (in order)
3 kinetic, heat, kinetic, gravitational
4 5000 W
5 Loses 1 000 000 J
6 Crumple zones, seat belts and airbags.
7 10 kg m/s

Working to Grade C

8 The seatbelt provides the force to slow down the driver over all the time that the car is slowing down. Without the seatbelt the driver would continue moving forwards until they hit the dashboard – slowing down in a shorter time by a much larger force.
9 5000 W
10 41 250 W
11 The total momentum of a set of objects remains constant, provided that they only interact with each other.
12 The extension of a spring is proportional to the force on it, providing that the spring has not been extended too far.
13 800 N/m
14 acceleration, force, momentum and velocity
15 The kinetic energy of the car is stored in a battery as the car slows down. This energy can be used to accelerate the car when it starts moving again, instead of transferring energy from fuel. So less fuel is used up by a car which slows down and accelerates as it goes along.

Working to Grade A*

16 0.6 m/s. Trolleys only interact with each other.
17 If all the GPE transfers to KE during the fall, then speed = 20 m/s.

P2 6–8 Examination questions: Work and energy

1 a

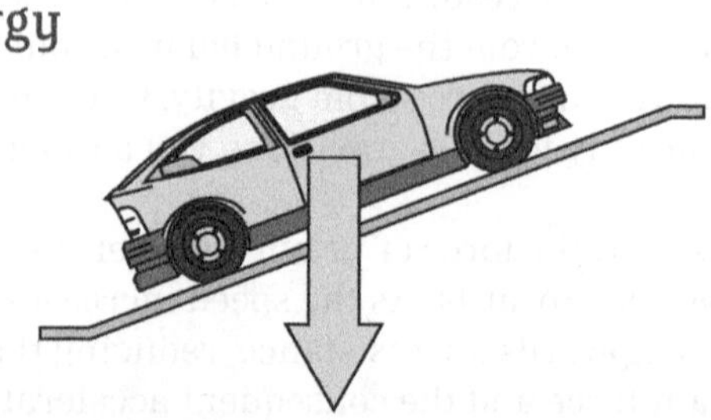

arrow pointing down from centre of car (1)

b $W = mg$ (1) = 1200 × 10 = 12 000 N (1)

c Work = force × distance (1) = 12 000 × 5 = 60 000 J (1)

d GPE (1)

2 a $KE = ½mv^2$ (1) = 0.5 × 900 × $(15)^2$ = 101 250 J (1)

b $P = \frac{E}{t}$ (1) = 101 250/5 = 20 250 W (1)

c When the car has a crash, a force must act on the driver to slow them down during the crash. If that force is too large, then it will damage the driver. The force can be reduced by reducing the acceleration required. This can be done by increasing the time taken to reduce the car from its initial speed to zero. The crumple zone between the front of the car and the driver does this by collapsing slowly, so that the car can keep moving for a short while after it has hit the obstacle instead of stopping instantly. (6 marks for a clear ordered answer with all steps clearly explained, no errors of physics and good use of spelling and grammar).

3 a $p = m \times v$ (1) = 0.025 × 400 = 10 kg m/s (1)

b i Total momentum (1)

ii $v = \frac{p}{m}$ (1) = 10/2.025 = 4.94 m/s (1)

How science works: Energy and distance

1 Independent variables are mass and initial speed, dependent variable is skid distance.

2 The surface that the cylinders skid on.

3 He needs to calculate kinetic energy from the mass and speed using $KE = ½mv^2$.

4 A scatter-graph of kinetic energy against skid distance.

5 He won't be able to repeat that trial exactly, so he just has to leave the result on the graph and get lots more results to put on it.

6 Yes, provided that his cylinders are made of rubber and the surface they slide on is made of tarmac.

P2 9: Static electricity

1 Electrons can move easily through a conductor but not an insulator.

2 The rod is negative, the cloth is positive.

3 Electrons transfer between the balloon and the hair. So all of the hairs have the same charge, repelling each other and standing on end. The hair and balloon have opposite charges, so they attract each other.

P2 10: Current electricity

1 3 A

2

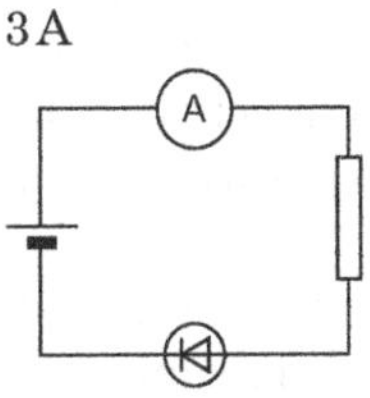

3 180 J

P2 11: Resistance

1 1.4 V

2

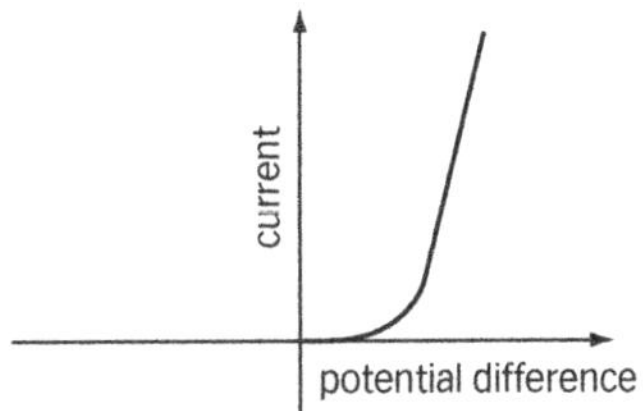

Small resistance in one direction of current, but a very large resistance for current in the other way.

3

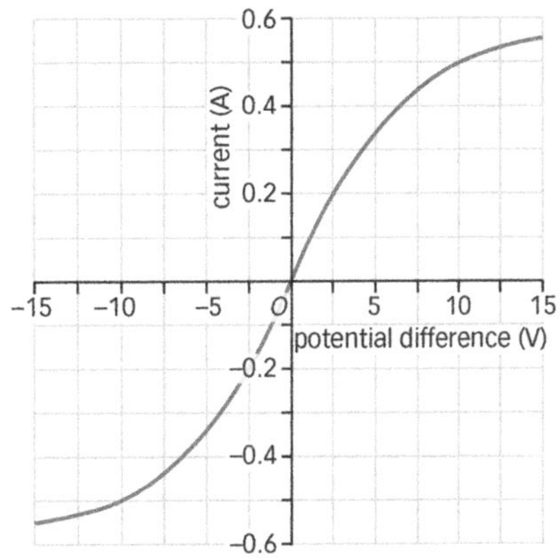

As electrons flowing through the wire hit the ions fixed in position, they give them vibrational energy, heating up the wire. As the temperature of the wire increases, the ions vibrate further from their position, making it more difficult for the electrons to get past them, increasing the resistance of the wire.

P2 12: Circuits in series and parallel

1

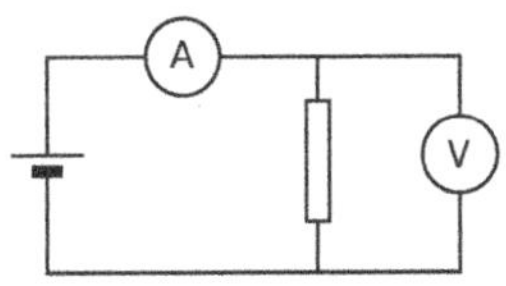

2 Total resistance = 9 Ω, 0.167 A for both, 1.0 V for 6 Ω and 0.5 V for 3 Ω.

3 For 6 Ω resistor, current = 0.25 A and for 3 Ω resistor, current = 0.5 A, so total resistance 2.0 Ω

P2 13: Mains electricity

1 The central cores are made from a bundle of copper threads to make it flexible and a good conductor. Each core is surrounded by a different coloured plastic to provide a flexible insulator which can be identified easily.

2 d.c. supplies make the current flow in one direction only, a.c. supplies make the current change direction all the time.

3 If the live wire touches the outer metal of a device, then there is a large current which escapes in the earth wire connected to the outer metal. This current heats up the fuse in the live part of the plug, causing it to melt and isolate the live part of the plug from the rest of the device.

P2 14: Electrical power

1 The 13 A cable has a larger diameter so that it has a smaller resistance and doesn't get too warm in use.
2 13 A
3 600 C

P2 9–14 Levelled questions: Electricity

Working to Grade E

1 The hair becomes negatively charged.
2 A flow of electrons along a wire.
3
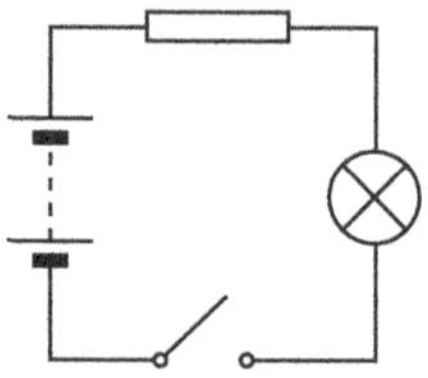
4 It shows an ammeter in series with a variable resistor and LED and cell.
5 180 V
6
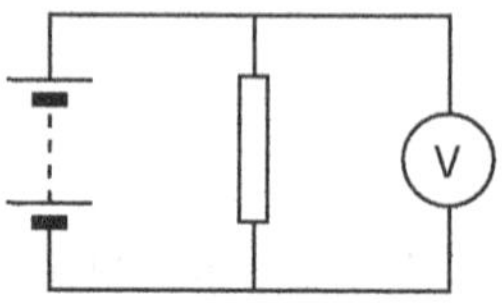

7 Light dependant resistor.
8 blue – neutral, brown – live, yellow and green – earth
9 690 W

Working to Grade C

10 Hair is negative, balloon is positive.
11 2 A
12
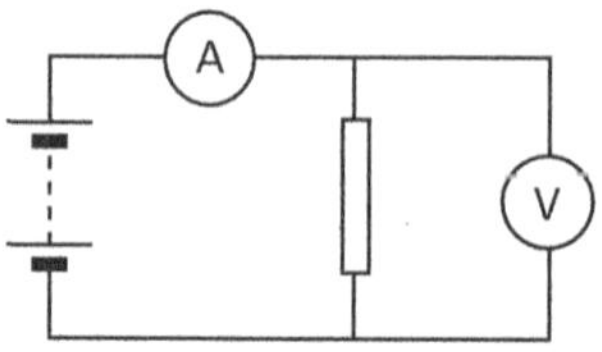

13 A is a diode, B is a lamp and C is a resistor.
14 8 A in the 6 Ω resistor and 12 A in the battery.
15 To switch off the supply automatically when the current is large enough e.g. when there is a fault. The current heats up the wire in the fuse enough to melt it and make a gap in the circuit.

Working to Grade A*

16 75 V and 25 Hz.

P2 9–14 Examination questions: Electricity

1 a A is battery (1), B is voltmeter (1) and C is switch (1).
b $V = I \times R$ (1) = 0.4 × 5 = 2.0 V (1)
c
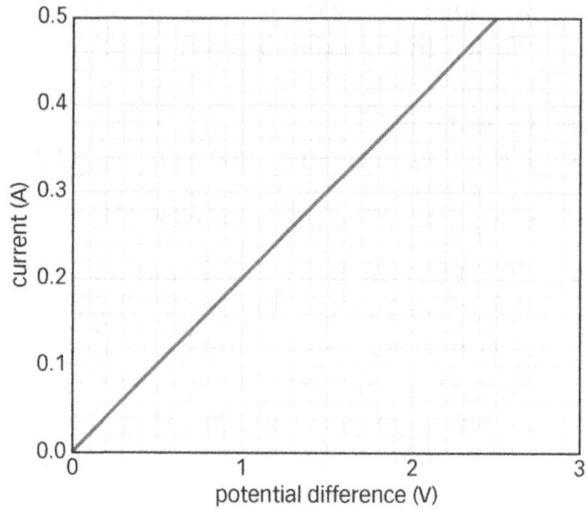

Straight line through the origin (1) passing through 0.40 A, 2.0 V (1).

2 a makes the kettle safe – green and yellow (1)
carries current at 230 V – brown (1)
carries low-voltage current – blue (1)
b $P = V \times I$ (1) = 230 (1) × 7 = 1610 W (1)
c 13 A (1)
d It acts as an automatic switch (1) which disconnects the supply (1) whenever the current in the plug exceeds a safe value (1).
e i Electrons (1) flow easily through a conductor but not through an insulator (1).
ii
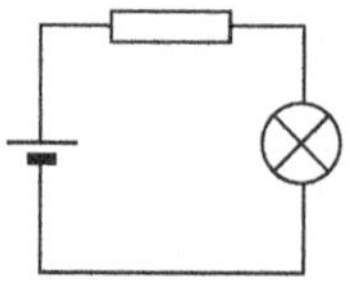
Correct symbols for components (1 mark each) drawn in a loop in any order (1).

P2 15: Atomic structure

1 Electron, proton, neutron.
2 38 electrons, 38 protons and 52 neutrons
3 5

P2 16: Radioactive decay

1 Wear protective clothing, don't handle directly, keep the exposure time short.
2 Not alpha because it goes through paper. Not gamma because it is stopped by aluminium, so must be beta.
3 One hour.

P2 17: Using radioactivity

1 Uranium and plutonium.
2 Only gamma rays escape from the body, carrying information about its interior. A short half-life ensures that the patient is not radioactive for long, reducing the danger from this exposure to people around them.
3 The number of beta particles getting through the paper decreases as the paper thickness increases. All gamma rays would go straight through and

none of the alpha particles would get through. A long half-life means that the number of betas getting through a given thickness of paper hardly changes with time.

P2 18: Star lives

1 nebula, protostar, red giant star, white dwarf
2 Gas in the nebula is pulled in by gravity to make a protostar. The work done by gravity heats the gas until it is hot enough for hydrogen to fuse into helium, making a stable star.
3 The main sequence is where hydrogen is fusing to make helium in the core. The energy released by fusion at the centre moves up through the rest of the star, counteracting the push of gravity that is trying to squash it smaller.

P2 15–18 Levelled questions: Radioactivity

Working to Grade E

1 Electron (0, –1)
Proton (1, 1)
Neutron (1, 0)
2 Neutron and proton.
3 Food, soil, space.
4 Alpha
5 Wear protective clothing, don't handle directly, keep the exposure time short.
6 Gamma ray with a half-life of a few hours or days.
7 uranium, neutron, fission
8 protostar, main sequence, super red giant, supernova, black hole

Working to Grade C

9 10 electrons, 10 protons and 12 neutrons.
10 Same number of protons and electrons but different numbers of neutrons.
11 250
12 Their radiation ionises cells, which can kill the cell or change its DNA so that it turns into cancer.
13 Wear protective clothing so that you don't ingest particles of the source. Don't handle directly but use tongs to keep your distance. Keep the exposure time short to reduce the changes of damaging your cells.
14 Beta and gamma.
15 Only gamma rays escape from the body, carrying information about its interior. A short half-life ensures that the patient is not radioactive for long, reducing the danger from this exposure to people around them.
16 Gas in a nebula is pulled in by gravity to make a protostar. The work done by gravity heats the gas until it is hot enough for hydrogen to fuse into helium, making a stable star. Once all the hydrogen in the core has been used the star swells to become a red giant and helium is fused instead. When the helium has been used the star starts to cool, collapsing to form a white dwarf. Eventually, as it gets cold enough, the dwarf stops glowing altogether.

Working to Grade A*

17 2 hours
18 $^{237}_{93}Np$
19 One of the neutrons becomes a proton and an electron. The electron carries away energy from the nucleus, so the change cannot be reversed.

P2 15–18 Examination questions: Radioactivity

1 a Any two of the following, for 1 mark each: food, soil, air, X-rays, cosmic rays, nuclear power stations, nuclear bomb tests.
b It damages cells by ionising them (1).
c Allowed dose from work = 20 – 2 = 18 mSv (1)
working hours = 18/0.02 (1) = 900 hours (1).
2 a $^{6}_{3}Li$ (1 mark for each correct number)
b

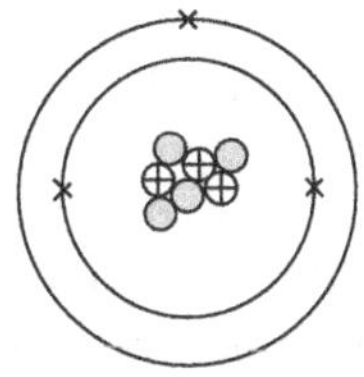

(two crosses in inner circle, one on the other for 1 mark)
(three crossed circles at the centre for 1 mark)
(four shaded circles at the centre for 1 mark)
c fission (1)
d The alpha particles ionise (1) the air in the detector allowing it to conduct electricity (1). A long-half life means that the detector keeps working for a long time (1).
e Wear protective clothing (1) to stop accidental ingestion (1).
f Beta – High speed electron (1), Alpha – Helium nucleus (1), Gamma – Electromagnetic waves (1)
3 a

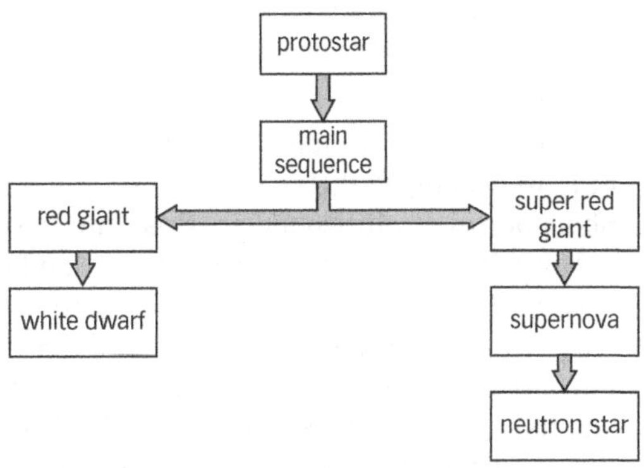

all correct (5)
one mistake (4)
two mistakes (3)
three mistakes (2)
four mistakes (1)
b Hydrogen nuclei (1) are fused together (1) to make helium nuclei (1).
c Some elements with atomic number below iron were made by fusion within stars (1). The rest were made by fusion when large stars exploded as supernovae (1). This happens when a star runs out of fuel for fusion and collapses (1).

How science works: Radioactivity

1 The independent variable is the sheet thickness. The dependent variable is the gamma ray count.
2 The distance between source and detector, the source itself.
3 Calculate the average of three trials for each sheet thickness.
4 Calculate the thickness of each sheet times the average rate of gamma rays getting through. If the answer is the same every time, then the hypothesis is true.
5 She should count the gamma rays for each thickness for a longer time.

P3 1: X-rays

1 No need for surgery, so no risk of infection from surgery.
2 Place a sheet of photographic film in black paper. Put the limb between the film and X-ray source. Briefly switch on the source. X-rays will pass through muscle and skin to ionise the film. Film under bone will not be ionised as the bone absorbs X-rays. When the film is developed, the ionised regions turn black, the rest goes white, creating the image.
3 A CT scan can be used to form an image of the tumour. A narrow beam of weak X-rays passes through the patient to be detected by a CCD on the other side. The X-ray source and detector rotate around the body, and a computer analyses the CCD signal to make an image of this slice of the body. To treat the tumour, an intense beam of X-rays is passed through the tumour from many different directions so that the tumour gets a much larger dose than the surrounding tissue – this should kill cells in the tumour without to much damage to healthy cells around it.

P3 2: Ultrasound

1 A sound wave of frequency above the range of human hearing (20 kHz).
2 Short pulses of ultrasound are fired into the mother towards the baby. As the pulses cross boundaries between tissues (skin, muscle or bone), they are partially reflected back towards their source where they are detected. The time delay between a pulse and its echo can be used to calculate the distance to the tissue boundary which caused the echo. A computer uses the information from the echoes to build up an image of the mother and baby as the ultrasound pulses are scanned across her.
3 133 μs

P3 1–2 Levelled questions: X-rays and ultrasound

Working to Grade E

1 atom
2 Ultrasound does not damage the baby's cells by ionisation, but X-rays do.
3 Wear a monitoring badge, have shielding between yourself and the source, keep the X-rays on for as short a time as possible.
4 100 kHz
5 The CT scan uses X-rays passing through a region of the body in many different directions, being detected by a CCD. The film uses X-rays coming from only one direction onto photographic film.

Working to Grade C

6 Place a sheet of photographic film in black paper. Put the limb between the film and X-ray source. Briefly switch on the source. X-rays will pass through muscle and skin to ionise the film. Film under bone will not be ionised as the bone absorbs X-rays. When the film is developed, the ionised regions turn black, the rest goes white, creating the image.
7 Three from: Wear a monitoring badge. Keep well away because X-rays spread out as they travel away from the source. Have shielding between yourself and the source to absorb the X-rays before they get to you. Keep the X-rays on for as short a time as possible – the longer you are exposed to X-rays, the more chance you have of developing a tumour.
8 A sound wave whose frequency is above 20 kHz, the upper limit of the range of human hearing.
9 A narrow beam of weak X-rays passes through the patient to be detected by a CCD on the other side. The amount of X-rays being absorbed before it reaches the CCD depends on the amount of bone, skin or muscle in the way, so the CCD signal is a measure of the organs between source and detector. The X-ray source and detector rotate around the body, and a computer analyses the CCD signal to make an image of this slice of the body.
10 Short pulses of ultrasound are fired into the mother towards the baby. As the pulses cross boundaries between tissues (skin, muscle or bone), they are partially reflected back towards their source where they are detected. The time delay between a pulse and its echo can be used to calculate the distance to the tissue boundary which caused the echo. A computer uses the information from the echoes to build up an image of the mother and baby as the direction of the ultrasound pulses is scanned across her.

Working to Grade A*

11 5×10^{-2} m or 5 cm

P3 1–2 Examination questions: X-rays and ultrasound

1 a T V R Q S U (4 marks if all correct, 3 marks for one or two mistakes, 2 marks for three mistakes, 1 mark for four mistakes in the order of steps)
b For their safety (1). The walls of the room will absorb some of the X-rays (1), causing less damage to her cells by ionisation (1).

2 a A sound wave (1) with a frequency above 20 kHz (1).
b X-rays ionise cells (1), damaging them, sometimes making them into cancer (1). Ultrasound does not ionise cells, so cannot harm the baby (1).
c Short pulses of ultrasound are fired into the mother towards the baby (1). As the pulses cross boundaries between tissues, they are partially reflected back towards their source where thay are detected (1). The time delay between a pulse and its echo can be used to calculate the distance to the tissue boundary which caused the echo (1). A computer uses the information from the echoes to build up an image of the mother and baby as the direction of the ultrasound pulses is scanned across her (1).

P3 3: Refraction

1

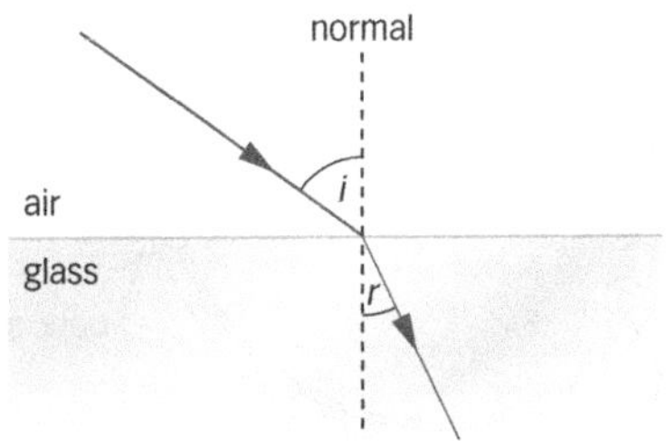

2 The speed of the light changes as it changes medium. In order to keep the frequency the same in both mediums, the wavelength must also change – this usually requires a change of direction.

3 26°

P3 4: Lenses

1

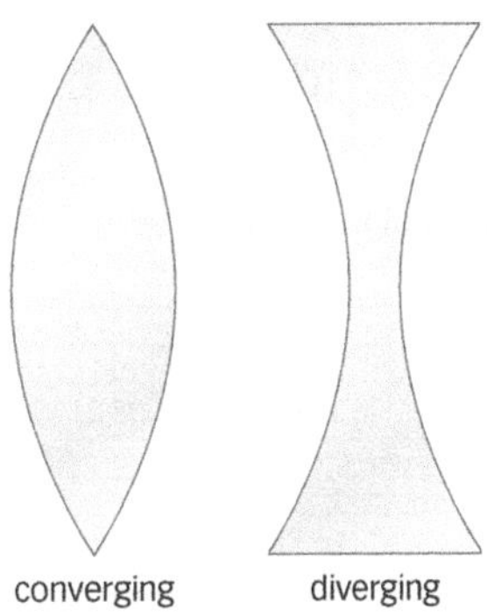

2

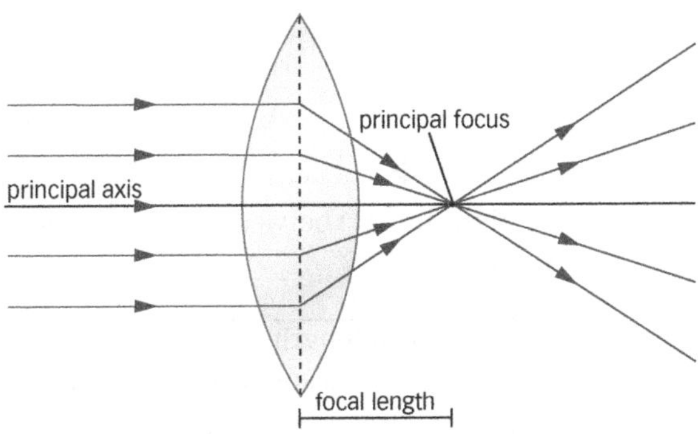

3 Inverted, real and magnified.

P3 5: Ray diagrams

1 It carries on in the same direction.

2

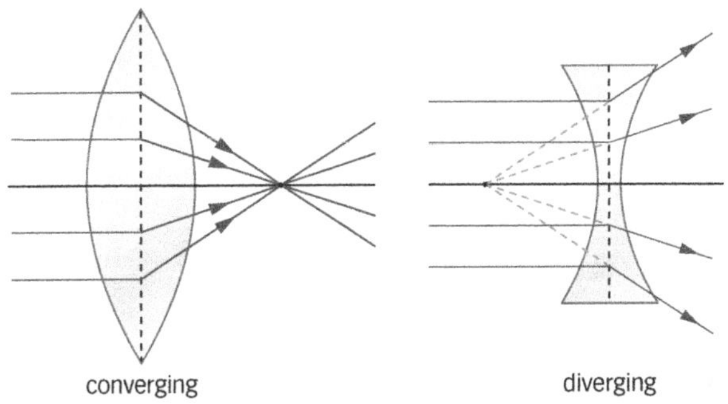

3 The image is 2 cm high, real, inverted and 10 cm in front of the lens.

P3 6: Magnification and power

1 The curvature of its surfaces and the refractive index of its material.

2 +20 D

3 Diverging with a focal length of 10 cm.

P3 7: Human eyes

1

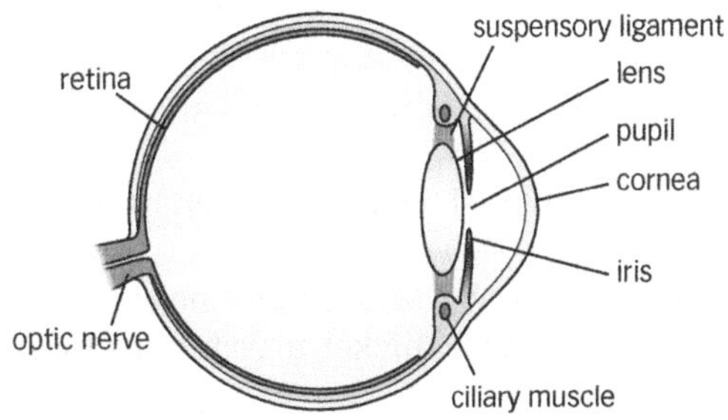

2 The pupil shrinks as the iris contracts to reduce the amount of light reaching the retina, preventing it from being damaged by too much light.

3 People with short-sight have eyes with too high a power. They focus images in front of the retina instead of on it, so a diverging lens placed in front of the cornea can reduce the overall power of their eyes to allow images to be focussed onto the retina.

P3 8: Cameras

1 The lens refracts light from the object to make a real image on the CCD which records it.

2

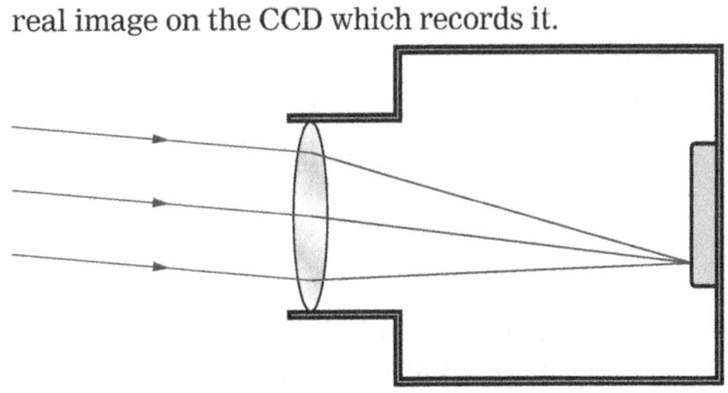

3 The eye lens is made fatter by the ciliary muscles, increasing the power of the lens so that the image is still in focus on the retina. The camera lens is moved away from the CCD to keep the image in focus on it.

P3 3–8 Levelled questions: The power of lenses

Working to Grade E

1

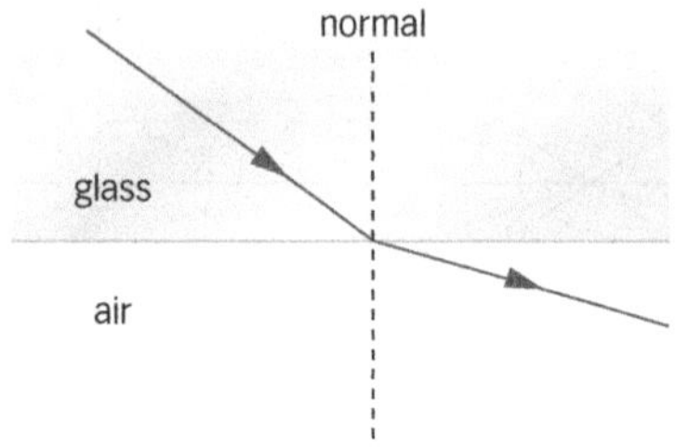

2

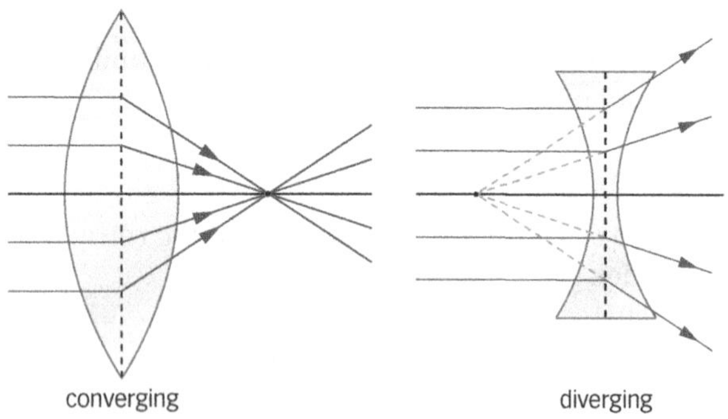

3 The object actually emits light, the image is where the light appears to come from after passing through the lens.

4 The image is bigger than the object and is upside down.

5 Real images can be shown on a screen, virtual images cannot.

6 The image is six times bigger than the object.

7 The lens can be made thicker to reduce its focal length.

Working to Grade C

8 1.36

9

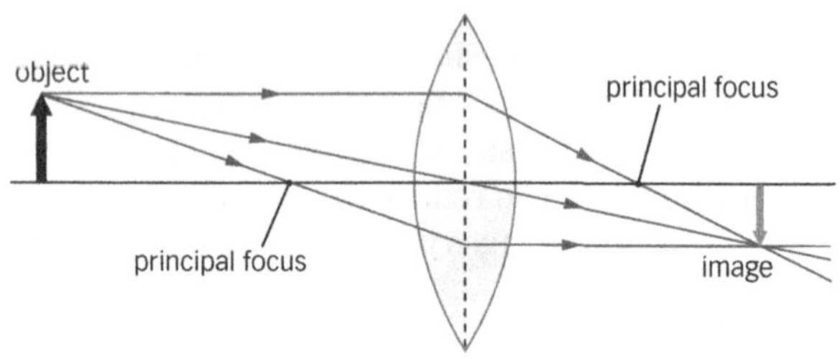

10

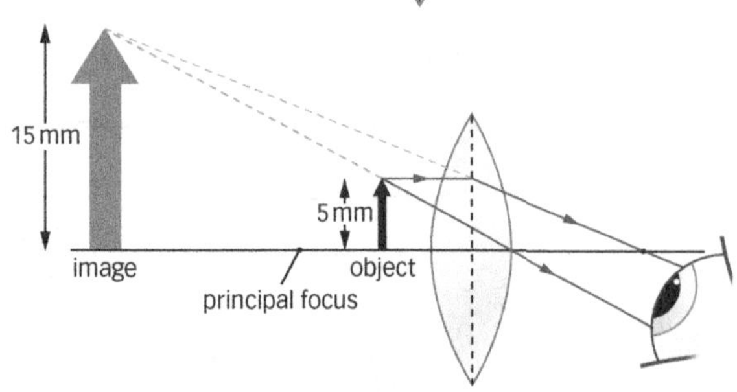

11 The image moves closer to the lens as the object moves away, so the lens must be moved towards the CCD to keep the image focussed on it.

12 10mm

13 It protects the retina from damage by too much light. It does this by reducing the size of the pupil as the light intensity increases.

14

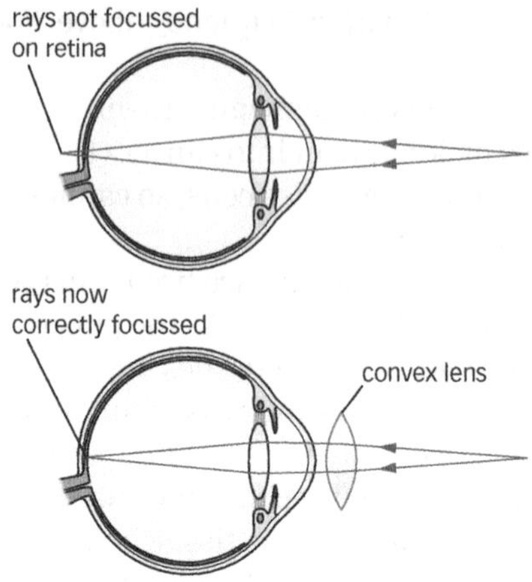

The convex lens increases the power of the eye, allowing the image to be focussed on the retina instead of behind it.

15 +6.7D

16

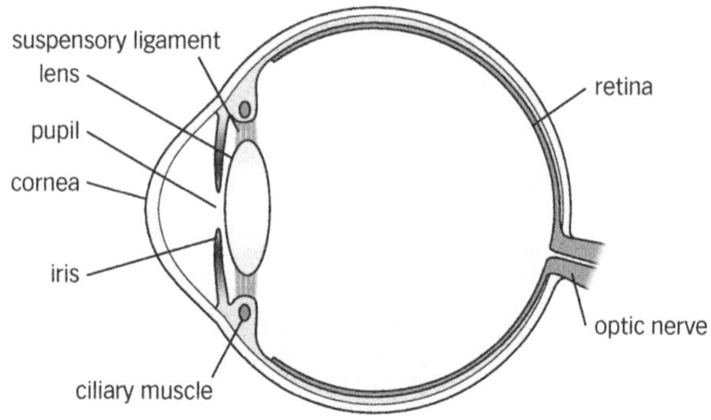

Working to Grade A*

17 +2.0

18 The eye lens is made fatter by the ciliary muscles, increasing the power of the lens so that the image is still in focus on the retina. The camera lens is moved away from the CCD to keep the image in focus on it.

P3 3–8 Examination questions: The power of lenses

1 a inverted (1), magnified (1), real (1)

b i

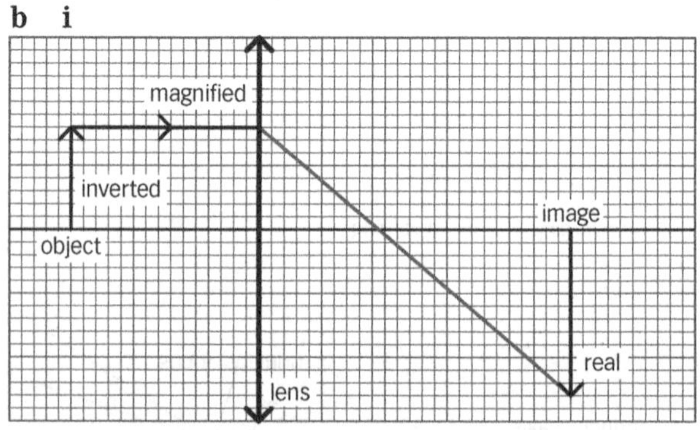

Straight line (1) between lens and image as shown (1).

ii power $= \dfrac{1}{\text{focal length}}$ (1)

focal length = 9.5 squares or 28.5mm (1)

power $= \dfrac{1}{0.0285} = +35\text{D}$ (1)

c

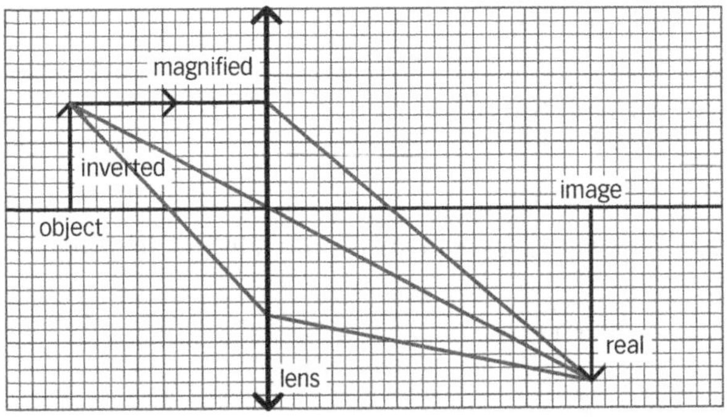

Any ray from top of object to lens and then to top of image (1 mark each)

2 a A is iris (1), B is CCD (1) and C is lens (1).

b The shape of the lens can be altered (1).

c

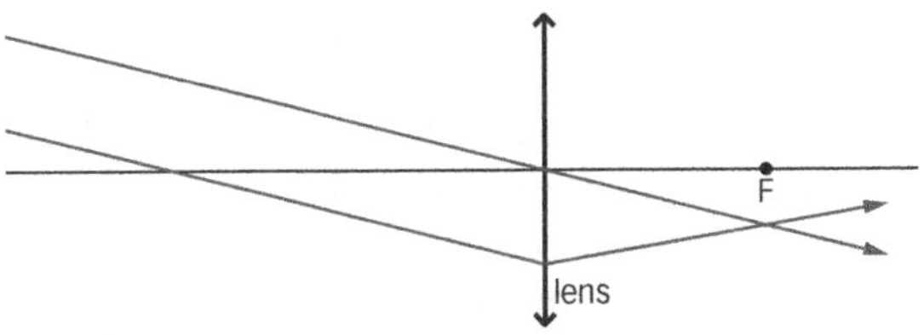

Rays to the left of the lens parallel (1).
Rays on the right cross at a focus (1).
Focus same distance from lens as F (1).

3 a The light slows down (1). Its frequency remains the same (1), so its wavelength must decrease (1), so it has to change direction.

b refractive index $= \dfrac{\sin i}{\sin r}$ (1)

$= \dfrac{\sin 45}{\sin 30} = \dfrac{0.707}{0.500} = 1.41$ (1)

c

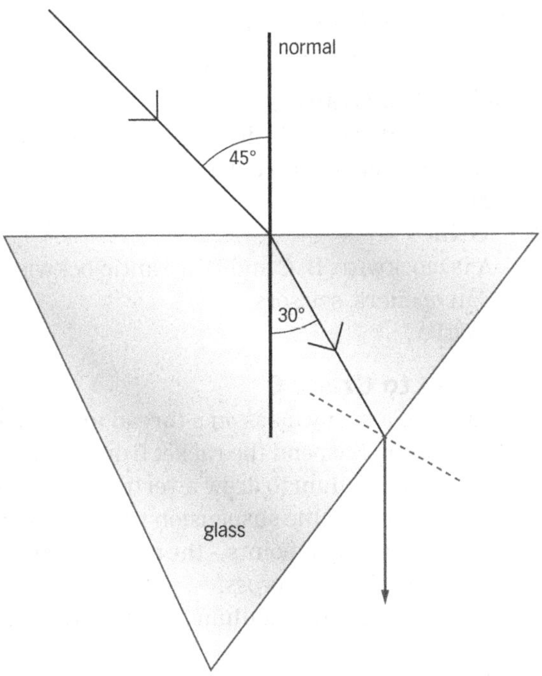

Straight line with arrow from correct place on glass (1).
At 45 degrees to surface (by eye) (1).

4 a power $= \dfrac{1}{\text{focal length}}$ (1)

focal length = 37.5 mm (1)

power $= \dfrac{1}{0.0375} = -27\text{D}$ (1)

b

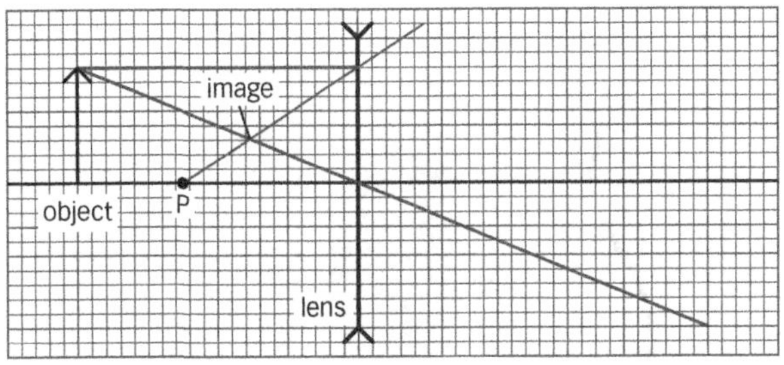

Ray from top of object through centre of lens (1).
Ray parallel to axis to the lens, then away from P (1).
Correct point labelled image as shown (1).

c magnification $= \dfrac{\text{size of image}}{\text{size of object}}$ (1)

$= \dfrac{3 \text{ squares}}{8 \text{ squares}} = -0.38$ (1)

P3 9: Total internal reflection

1 To look inside people with endoscopes, to carry information in optical fibres.

2 The light must already be in the slower of the two mediums, hitting the bondary at more than the critical angle.

3 46°

P3 9 Levelled questions: Total internal reflection, optical fibres, and lasers

Working to Grade E

1 For optical fibre communications, light shows at concerts.

2 A thin, long rod of very transparent glass that can carry cable TV signals.

Working to Grade C

3

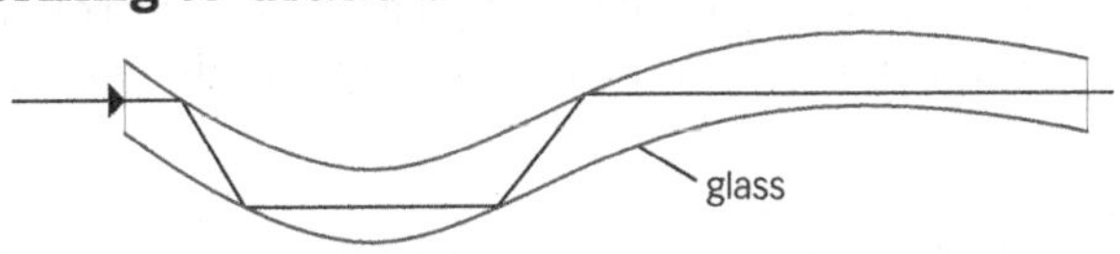

4 It doesn't spread out as it travels, so the signal strength doesn't fall rapidly as it travels, allowing a greater distance before the information gets lost.

5 1.49

6 The light must already be in the slower of the two mediums, hitting the bondary at more than the critical angle.

7 To seal blood vessels by heating them up with pulses of laser light.

Working to Grade A*

8 50°

P3 9 Examination questions: Total internal reflection, optical fibres, and lasers

1 a refractive index = $\frac{1}{\sin c}$ (1) $\sin c = \frac{1}{1.6} = 0.625$,
$c = \sin^{-1} 0.625 = 38.7°$ (1)

b 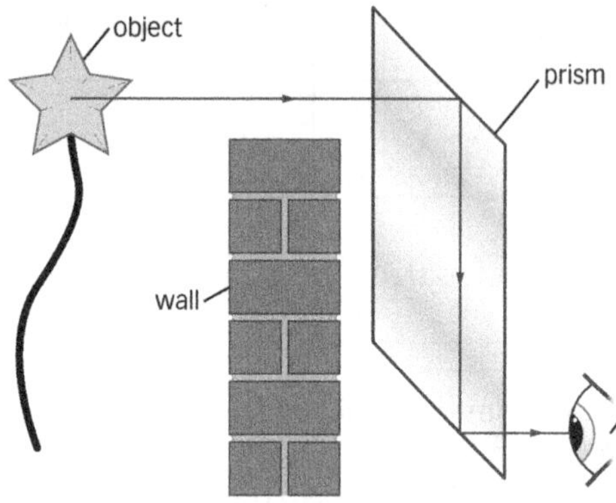

ray continues straight to angled edge of glass (1)
reflects to go vertically down glass (1)
reflects at bottom edge of glass to enter the eye (1)

c upright (1), virtual (1).

How science works: Lens magnification

1 The height of the image and distance from the screen from the lens are the dependent variables. The height of the object and the distance from the tracing paper to the lens are the independent variables.
2 The power of the lens.
3 She should calculate the magnification from the heights of the object and image before drawing a scatter-graph of magnification against distance of screen from lens. If she gets a straight line, then her hypothesis is correct.
4 Nina should check the data by doing the experiment again, perhaps by getting a wider range of variables.
5 There will be random errors because she cannot place the equipment exactly as it was last time, zero-errors from measuring from the wrong place (e.g. the edge of the lens instead of the centre), the limited resolution of her ruler (probably 1 mm).

P3 10: Falling over

1 Halfway down a line drawn from one corner to the opposite corner.
2 Lower the centre of mass, increase the width of the base.
3 No matter how little it tilts, its centre of mass will not be above the surface in contact with the table, so there will be a moment turning it until it hits the table.

P3 11: Swinging masses

1 The time taken for one complete swing.
2 length
3 0.25 Hz

P3 12: Moments

1 Anticlockwise
2 8 Nm
3 1.8 m on the right.

P3 13: Levers

1 Where the lever rests on the triangle of the ground.
2 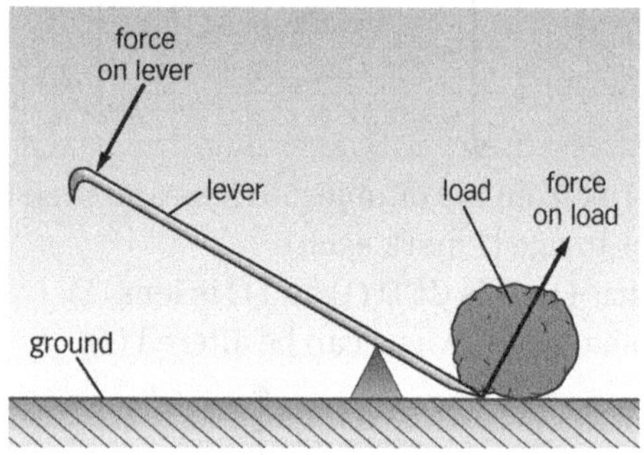

3 For the same applied force, increasing the length of the lever increases the anticlockwise moment on it. When the lever is not moving, the clockwise and anticlockwise moments are the same. An increased clockwise moment means a bigger reaction force from the load if its distance from the pivot does not change.

P3 14: Hydraulics

1 2000 Pa
2 Air compresses too easily when the pressure increases, whereas oil compresses very little.
3 2400 N

P3 10–14 Levelled questions: Moments, masses, hydraulics, and levers

Working to Grade E

1 Halfway down a line drawn from one corner to its opposite across the centre.
2 20 s
3 36 Nm
4 A is clockwise, B, C and D are anticlockwise.
5 Can openers, scissors
6 2000 Pa

Working to Grade C

7 Suspend a heavy mass on a thread to make a pendulum. Suspend the racket from any point and use the pendulum to draw a vertical line on the racket through the suspension point. Repeat for other suspension points – the centre of mass is where all the lines cross.
8 The mass of the pendulum and the size of its swing.
9 The clockwise moment ($20 \times 1.8 = 36$ Nm) is the same as the anticlockwise moment ($72 \times 0.5 = 36$ Nm).
10 Lower the centre of mass, increase the width of the base.
11 The liquid is incompressible.

Working to Grade A*

12 60N

13 1.6m

14 The nutcrackers are a pair of levers joined at their pivots. You squeeze the long handles together, applying moments to the levers. For each lever to be balanced, the clockwise and anticlockwise moments must be the same, so the moment from your hand is the same size as the moment from the reaction force on the nut. Since the nut is much closer to the pivot than your hand, the force on it must be larger for the moment to be the same.

P3 10–14 Examination questions: Moments, masses, hydraulics, and levers

1 a

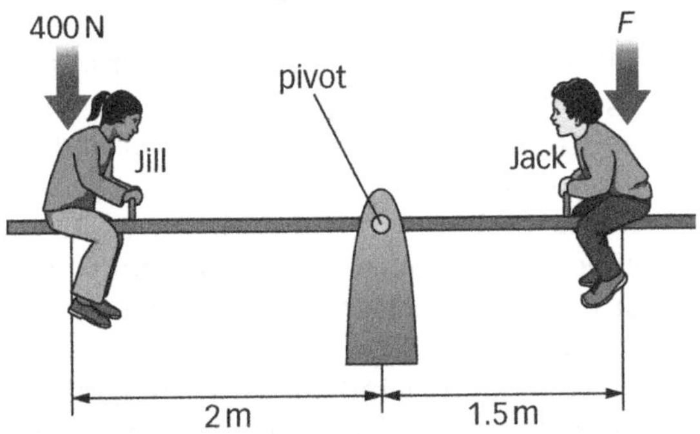

labelling the centre of the see saw (1)

b moment = force × distance (1)
$= 400 \times 2$ (1) = 800 (1) Nm (1)

c anticlockwise (1), the same as (1)

d clockwise moment = anticlockwise moment (1)
$F \times 1.5 = 800$ (1)
$F = 800/1.5 = 533$ N (1)

e Hang a weight from a string to make a pendulum (1).
Suspend the bat from a point on its edge (1).
Use the pendulum to draw a vertical line through the point of suspension onto the bat (1).
Repeat for other points of suspension, the centre of mass is where the lines cross (1).

P3 15: Circular motion

1 Towards the centre of the circle upon which that piece of track lies.

2 The centripetal force changes the direction of motion of the object, so that it can follow a circular path.

3 In the absence of any force to the right, you keep on moving forwards as the car turns to the right. As you collide with the left-hand part of the car, it pushes on you, providing the centripetal force which makes you have the same motion as the rest of the car.

P3 16: Electric motors

1 The field lines are circles in a plane at right angles to the wire, and centred on it.

2 A solenoid only has a magnetic field while there is a current in it. So when the current is turned off, it stops being a magnet.

3 Increase the turrning force on the coil by:
- increasing the current in the coil
- increasing the number of turns of wire in the coil
- increasing the strength of the magnet
- increasing the number of coils.

P3 17: Transformers

1 Two coils of insulated copper wire wound around a single loop of iron.

2 –0.05 V if the magnet is pulled out at the same speed.

3 230 V

P3 18: Power supply

1 Reduces the voltage of an a.c. supply and converts it to d.c. supply by using a high frequency transformer.

2 A step-up transformer increases the voltage of a supply, a step-down transformer decreases it.

3 0.33A

P3 15–18 Levelled questions: Circular motion and power

Working to Grade E

1 C

2 Reverse the direction of the current, reverse the direction of the magnetic field.

3 Electric motors, moving-coil meters and loudspeakers.

4 Changes the voltage of an alternating current supply.

5 Step-up.

6 The field lines are circles in a plane at right angles to the wire, and centred on it.

Working to Grade C

7 a increased
b decreased

8 Towards you.

9 To change the direction of the current in the coil every half turn, so that the forces on it always push it round in the same direction.

10 A coil of wire suspended over one end of a bar magnet from the centre of a cone of cardboard which is loosely held in place at its outer edges.

11 5.0V

12 0.10A

13 A switch mode transformer is much smaller and lighter, so can be fitted into small power conversion units connected to the mains supply.

Working to Grade A*

14 An alternating current in a transformer primary coil gives a continually changing magnetic field in the iron core and secondary coil. As the field in the secondary changes, there is a p.d. induced in it. A direct current would not result in any change of magnetic field in the secondary, so there would be no p.d. across it.

15 The p.d. across the secondary coil is less than the p.d. across the primary, yet the power in both coils is the same for an efficient transformer. Since power is p.d. × current, the current in the secondary will be larger than in the primary coil, so the resistance of the secondary needs to be less so that it doesn't get hotter. Increasing the diameter of the wire decreases its resistance.

16 The brushes allow current to enter and leave the coil as it spins round, via the commutator. The commutator switches the current direction in the coil each time that it does half of a turn, so that the moment acting on the coil always has the same direction.

P3 15–18 Examination questions: Circular motion and power

1 a centripetal (1)
 b S (1)
 c friction (1)

2 a T R S U Q
 all correct (3)
 one or two mistakes (2)
 three mistakes (1)
 b $\frac{\text{primary turns}}{\text{secondary turns}} = \frac{\text{primary voltage}}{\text{secondary voltage}}$ (1)
 $\frac{\text{primary turns}}{90} = \frac{230}{3}$ (1)
 primary turns $= \frac{230}{3} \times 90 = 6900$ turns (1)
 c primary current × primary voltage = secondary current × secondary voltage (1)
 $I \times 230 = 0.5 \times 3$ (1)
 $I \times \frac{0.5 \times 3}{230} = 0.0065\,\text{A}$(1)
 d It is much more efficient than a normal transformer (1), so waste less energy from the mains supply as heat (1). It is also much lighter (1) and smaller (1) than a normal transformer.

3 A is commutator (1), B is coil (1), C is magnet (1) and D is brush (1).

How science works: Electromagnets

1 The current and the coil turns.
2 The tightness of the coils, their place on the nail, the diameter and length of the nail, the material of the nail, the weight and shape of each paperclip.
3 Draw a scatter-graph of the number of paper clips against the current multiplied by the turns of wire and look for a straight line through the origin.
4 Doing more experiments helps to get around the effects of random errors and the finite resolution of her measurements (she can't get less than 1 paper clip).
5 It is difficult to wind the wire around the nail exactly the same each time. The ammeter will have a finite resolution, probably to only 0.1 A and different ammeters may give different readings for the same current. She may not be using the same nail or paper clips.
6 She would need to do an experiment to find out how her results depend on the size of the nail, so that she can extrapolate to a piece of iron the size of the electromagnet she is considering.

Appendices

Equations	
$a = \frac{F}{m}$ or $F = M \times a$	F is the resultant force in newtons, N m is the mass in kilograms, kg a is the acceleration in metres per second squared, m/s^2
$a = \frac{v - u}{t}$	a is the acceleration in metres per second squared, m/s^2 v is the final velocity in metres per second, m/s u is the initial velocity in metres per second, m/s t is the time taken in seconds, s
$W = m \times g$	W is the weight in newtons, N m is the mass in kilograms, kg g is the gravitational field strength in newtons per kilogram, N/kg
$F = k \times e$	F is the force in newtons, N k is the spring constant in newtons per metre, N/m e is the extension in metres, m
$W = F \times d$	W is the work done in joules, J F is the force applied in newtons, N d is the distance moved in the direction of the force in metres, m
$P = \frac{E}{t}$	P is the power in watts, W E is the energy transferred in joules, J t is the time taken in seconds, s
$E_p = m \times g \times h$	E_p is the change in gravitational potential energy in joules, J m is the mass in kilograms, kg g is the gravitational field strength in newtons per kilogram, N/kg h is the change in height in metres, m
$E_K = \frac{1}{2} \times m \times v^2$	E_K is the kinetic energy in joules, J m is the mass in kilograms, kg v is the speed in metres per second, m/s
$p = m \times v$	p is the momentum in kilograms metres per second, kg m/s m is the mass in kilograms, kg v is the velocity in metres per second, m/s
$I = \frac{Q}{t}$	I is the current in amperes (amps), A Q is the charge in coulombs, C t is the time in seconds, s
$V = \frac{W}{Q}$	V is the potential difference in volts, V W is the work done in joules, J Q is the charge in coulombs, C
$V = I \times R$	V is the potential difference in volts, V I is the current in amperes (amps), A R is the resistance in ohms, Ω
$p = \frac{E}{t}$	P is power in watts, W E is the energy in joules, J t is the time in seconds, s
$P = I \times V$	P is power in watts, W I is the current in amperes (amps), A V is the potential difference in volts, V
$E = V \times Q$	E is the energy in joules, J V is the potential difference in volts, V Q is the charge in coulombs, C

Fundamental physical quantities	
Physical quantity	**Unit(s)**
length	metre (m) kilometre (km) centimetre (cm) millimetre (mm)
mass	kilogram (kg) gram (g) milligram (mg)
time	second (s) millisecond (ms)
temperature	degree Celsius (°C) kelvin (K)
current	ampere (A) milliampere (mA)
voltage	volt (V) millivolt (mV)

Derived quantities and units	
Physical quantity	**Unit(s)**
area	cm^2; m^2
volume	cm^3; dm^3; m^3; litre (l); millilitre (ml)
density	kg/m^3; g/cm^3
force	newton (N)
speed	m/s; km/h
energy	joule (J); kilojoule (kJ); megajoule (MJ)
power	watt (W); kilowatt (kW); megawatt (MW)
frequency	hertz (Hz); kilohertz (kHz)
gravitational field strength	N/kg
radioactivity	becquerel (Bq)
acceleration	m/s^2; km/h^2
specific heat capacity	J/kg°C
specific latent heat	J/kg

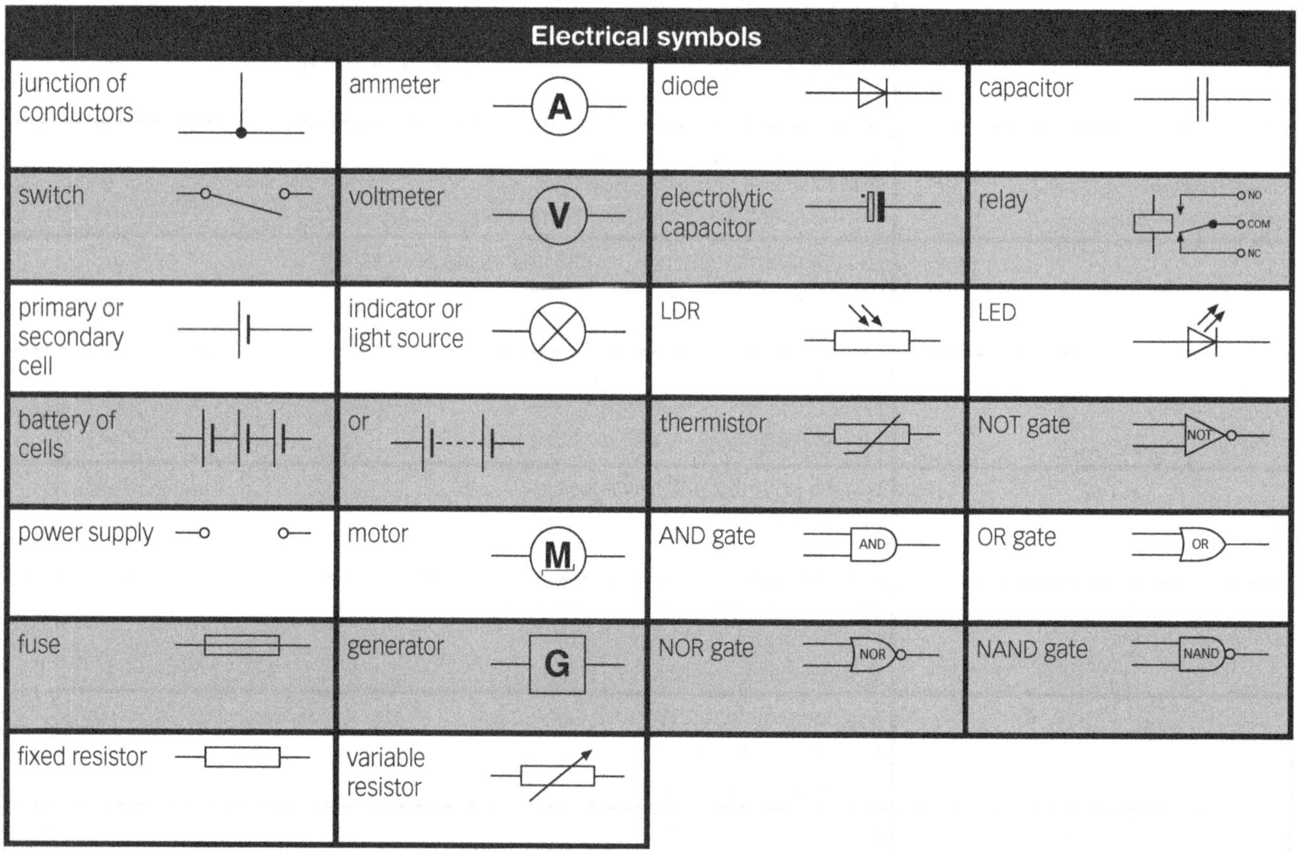

Index

OXFORD
UNIVERSITY PRESS

Great Clarendon Street, Oxford OX2 6DP

Oxford University Press is a department of the University of Oxford. It furthers the University's objective of excellence in research, scholarship, and education by publishing worldwide in

Oxford New York

Auckland Cape Town Dar es Salaam Hong Kong Karachi Kuala Lumpur Madrid Melbourne Mexico City Nairobi New Delhi Shanghai Taipei Toronto

With offices in
Argentina Austria Brazil Chile Czech Republic France Greece Guatemala Hungary Italy Japan Poland Portugal Singapore South Korea Switzerland Thailand Turkey Ukraine Vietnam

First published 2012

British Library Cataloguing in Publication Data

Data available

ISBN 978-0-19-913609-4

10 9 8 7 6 5 4 3

Printed in Great Britain by Bell and Bain Ltd, Glasgow

Paper used in the production of this book is a natural, recyclable product made from wood grown in sustainable forests. The manufacturing process conforms to the environmental regulations of the country of origin.

FSC www.fsc.org MIX Paper from responsible sources FSC® C007785